Teaching For

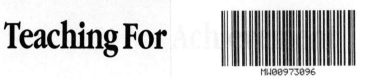

MW00973096

TEACHING FOR ACHIEVEMENT
IN URBAN MIDDLE SCHOOLS

BEVERLY BIMES-MICHALAK

Clark Publishing, Inc.

The author and publishers wish to extend our warmest thanks to all of the teachers and students who contributed materials to this book. We are also grateful to all of the authors and educators who have granted permission to reprint copyrighted materials.

Cover and interior design
Todd R. Kinney

Cover photo
Judy Brock

1 2 3 4 5 6 7 8 9 10 RRDC 02 01 00 99 98
ISBN 0-913054-49-4

Table of Contents

Chapter One
It all Begins with Motivation 1

Unlock patterns of failure and turn reluctant learners into willing and engaged students. An array of active learning strategies illustrates how to hook students on learning and create a student-centered classroom.

Chapter Two
Writing as a Tool for Learning 61

This chapter shows content teachers how to use writing to link prior knowledge to new knowledge, to get students to process and monitor their learning, and to reformulate and extend knowledge. Each use of writing is richly illustrated with classroom assignments and examples.

Chapter Three
Raising Achievement 117

Specific, research-based strategies to raise students' achievement are presented in this chapter. Each strategy is illustrated with classroom examples.

Chapter Four
Taking the Pain out of Assessment 169

How to create a balanced assessment program by: embedding assessment in instruction; assessing both the processes and the products of learning; using various kinds of alternative and authentic assessments—including classroom and school-wide portfolios; and creating scoring guides and rubrics.

Chapter Five
Putting it Together: Reform, Standards, and Other Stuff

Presents the "big picture" of how the strategies presented in chapters 1-4 fit into a standards-based, instructional framework. In addition, the issue of reform—its hindrances and promising practices—is discussed. Finally, a framework of professional teaching standards is presented.

Appendix
Unit Design:
Template and Example Units

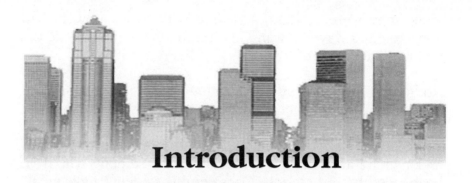

Introduction

During my first visit to the neurologist, I anxiously awaited his prognosis. Trying to build rapport and to ease my anxiety, he slipped into casual conversation, asking my vocation. When I responded that I worked in urban schools, he seemed surprised. Lowering his voice, he said, "Well, that certainly is a challenge." He then went on to explain that, as a researcher at the Hershey Medical Center, he had worked with the Hershey School for Boys. However, he exclaimed, "*These* were nice kids." I wondered what nightmarish visions he had conjured up of urban students; clearly, he had a definite, terminal prognosis for them. I quickly added, "It may surprise you, but I work with nice kids, too." What I should have said is that I work with many amazing, resilient kids who are capable of withstanding the liabilities of growing up in danger-filled and high-risk environments. Just as many others do, my doctor had stereotyped urban students, totally unaware of their mind-boggling talents and abilities.

In *Amazing Grace,* Jonathan Kozol tells how he is continually touched by the resiliency of children growing up in high-risk environments. He speaks about their "life force" which "keeps pressing against the dismal barriers in which it is contained." Those of us, who teach and work in urban schools, are, likewise, touched by our students' unusual strength.

Unfortunately, not all of our students have this resiliency. Many come to us downtrodden by overwhelming, bigger-than-life problems—problems that we, ourselves, will never have to face. Unable to protect students from the harsh reality of encroaching dangers and life-draining problems, urban teachers truly understand the wish-filled words of Jonathan Kozol, "... that while they were in class, someone with magic powers had appeared and waved a wand and turned the world outside the building into fields of flowers."

Not having magic wands, we face the challenge of making our classrooms places of hope, where students who come to us cloaked in years of failure can discover their unique abilities and talents—places where they begin to believe in themselves and in their futures. This is a difficult task for students who have been failed by our schools. Consider this student's indictment:

> When I was in kindergarten, a lot of things happened. I broke the connect four game and my teacher threw me outside. In third grade, I can't remember that well. I can remember when I had to go to the bathroom and so I ran to the bathroom. Mrs. S. said Steve on the fence. I said why. She said because you are running. I said I need to go. She said go where? I said to the bathroom. She said to bad get on the fence. I said Ahhh. She said double time so I sat down on the fence waiting for the bell to ring. The bell rang. I ran as fast as I could but no use. All of a sudden my leg got really warm. I looked down at my pants. My pants looked like Lake Titikakka All over my pants. All the kids laughed at me so I started to flick them off.
>
> In sixth grade I had Mrs. F. She was mean. She always put me in the corner and gave me lunch detention.
>
> When I was a youngster, I always dreamed of becoming a pilot in the Air Force. After a while I set my goals on being a famous detective on the east side of Tiawana but my dreams are again crumpled to the ground. Now I will be a bartender.

As an eighth grade student, he laments his lost youth and shattered dreams. He is not alone. In any class, there are students who have lost their hope.

No one teacher can possibly have all of the answers for the challenging task of restoring hope and awakening these defeated students to the possibilities of a fulfilled life. Research shows that in successful schools faculties spend time collaborating on instruction and having meaningful conversations about learning and students. Yet, many teachers never have the opportunity to collaborate with other teachers about instruction, increasing their sense of isolation and hopelessness.

During the past ten years, I have been part of a national network to reform urban schools through Writing to Learn (WTL), a staff development program sponsored by the Council for Basic Education. When the Edna McConnell Clark Foundation funded some of our projects, I joined their efforts to bring about reform and to raise achievement in urban middle schools, offering Writing to Learn in their other project schools and developing an Integrated Language Arts Program in Louisville, Kentucky. However, Writing to Learn has also been implemented in the intermediate grades of four through eight and at the high school level of grades ten through twelve.

Teachers, in this WTL network of thirteen urban districts and in the Integrated Language Arts Program, have taught together, shared their successes, reflected on teaching, worked through failures, encouraged each other, and even cried together. As a result, we have emerged as stronger teachers with the heart-held conviction that all of our students can learn. However, we have more than convictions. Through our combined learning, we have discovered strategies that really work in our classrooms. These strategies are placed within the framework of high expectations, high support, and high content. Driven by our convictions and fueled by our successes, we are helping our students make the journey from underachieving, reluctant learners to motivated achievers.

However, we've discovered that there is no "quick trip tik" for this journey, nor is there only one route. As teachers and travelers on this journey, we continually reflect on our approaches, strive to make our classrooms places of thoughts, and search for promising practices to make us better. Therefore, we are restless travelers, continually looking at our maps for better, alternative routes. We no longer see our role as reconnecting the jagged pieces of our students' lives. Rather we help students to discover their own capable selves and enable them to take control of their learning and their lives.

When I talk about teaching being a journey, I realize that this book, too, has been a journey for me—a journey that I have put off for years. When encouraging colleagues asked about a book, I always responded, "I'm much too busy." Little did they know that I was filled with self-doubts: How could I possibly capture in words the classrooms, teachers, and students that I have worked with over the years? Could I report the challenges, disappointments, accomplishments, and hope of these students and teachers in such a way that readers would really understand? Did I have enough courage to write about the wrong turns which led our reform efforts into dead-end streets, forcing us to swallow our pride and return to square one?

I reluctantly agreed to do the book . At the time, I didn't realize how much the book would eventually mean to me and what a sustaining force it would be in my life. Just as I signed the contract, I developed all sorts of unexpected health problems.

During this two-year period, I probably would have been nonfunctional and very focused on myself without the responsibilities of the book. However with it, I had a new purpose to my life. As I wrote about all of those who have contributed so richly to my knowledge about teaching as well as to my life, forward-looking thoughts began to emerge. I also had time to stop and reflect on my learning, and, in the process of writing, I made a lot of discoveries and new connections. The book was more of an odyssey than I had ever expected.

I want to thank my publishers Dana Hensley and Diana Carlin for their encouragement, faith, and patience. The odyssey of a book would never have occurred without the constant prodding of my college professor husband, Stanley, who made me aware of the fact that it's easier to talk about a topic than to write about it. His watchful eye kept me focused and on task.

Not surprisingly, many of my new connections came in what is the last chapter. The last chapter, "Putting it All Together: Reform, Standards, and Other Stuff," is an attempt to make sense of my odyssey as a reformer and as a teacher. During this two-year-book-writing adventure, I have experienced a dramatic change.

Two years ago, I didn't know where I stood on standards-based reform. For what other reason would I have placed the topic of standards in the last chapter? In retrospect, it was a perfect placement, for now, more than ever, I realize that through writing we gain understanding. As I wrote the book, I came to understand how essential standards are to making urban schools places of achievement. I'm glad to report that not only have I recovered from my health problems, but I have also recovered from my tunnel vision regarding standards, realizing their importance in ensuring urban students an equitable education.

Chapters One through Four show teachers how to translate research into instruction—instruction that will make classrooms more successful. These chapters include lots of strategies and classroom examples. Chapter Five explains how, as a teacher, I placed these rich instructional practices into a standards-based approach to learning and why standards are so important to urban schools.

I want to thank Patte Barth, Helene Hodges, and Chris Stewart for reading the manuscript and offering powerful suggestions. What would I do without colleagues who care enough to make me think?

Most of all, I will always be indebted to my dedicated teacher colleagues who understand that the greatest use of life is to spend it on something that outlasts it—our students. When I work with these talented teachers, I realize how much I have to learn.

Without them, there could be no book. From their students, I have learned many valuable lessons about learning and life. I admire their courage and their unconquerable souls. These students and teachers are my heroes, and to them, I dedicate this book. Because of them, I have led a fascinating, challenging, meaningful, and fulfilled life.

— Beverly Bimes-Michalak

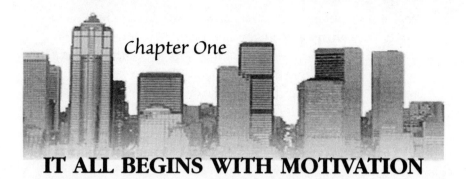

Chapter One

IT ALL BEGINS WITH MOTIVATION

In any classroom, the varying levels of motivation are staggering. Some students come to class with pencils poised, armed with notebooks and filled with a burning desire to know—brimming over with questions to be answered and problems to be solved. Some saunter into class, looking for opportunities to create chaos and cause teacher frenzy. Others come with open hostility, determined to avoid work at all costs while still others slip into another world far beyond the classroom walls. At the end of the year, the saddest reality of all is the realization that some students are leaving the classroom seemingly untouched—having gained little or nothing from the year's experience.

Yet, teachers are expected to reach and teach all of their students. Good teachers take this charge seriously; however, urban teachers often feel the task is beyond them, particularly since many of their students come from high risk environments. One teacher painted this disturbing portrait of her students:

> Our students are loving and lost. Most have lost their self-esteem, self-respect, love of learning, chances for success and dreams for the future. In spite of the many hardships in their lives, however, most are still warm, affectionate human beings. What they have not lost is their need to be loved.

In attempting to sort through the problem of motivation, another teacher described his students in this way:

> My students are an interesting set of contradictions. They want to be loved and praised badly, but they can never act like they want that. They want to learn, but that's not cool. And they want to be

cool. They have immense potential, but they don't know how to tap it. They often aspire to be parents despite lacking their own. They are needy, but they have so much to give. They are quick with an electrifying smile or a right hook. They know education is important, but they don't take advantage of it. They can drive you to unheard of frustration or make you as proud as a beaming parent. They can sink to depths you never thought possible, but they can achieve miracles.

Clearly, these teachers are confounded by the untapped potential and passivity of many of their students—as we all are. As urban teachers, we want our students to experience success both in our classrooms and beyond. Therefore, we fervently search for ways to help our students to believe in themselves once again, caring enough to invest in their learning. The stakes are high each year, for we realize that this may be the last chance for this group of students to make discoveries about themselves as learners, to take control of their lives, and to renew their hope in the future.

In order to develop a resilience, which makes them capable of overcoming the most negative outcomes of living in a risk-filled environment, students need to possess a deep sense of competence—a competence that assures them that they have, and will continue to have, an impact on a changing world and society. In *A Portrait of Young Adolescents in the 1990s,* Peter Scales (1991) stated that this sense of competence is made possible "by having at least one warm relationship with a caring adult and by having positive experiences with the wider community and its institutions outside the immediate home" (15). In many cases, the teacher is this caring adult. When students sense that a teacher genuinely cares about them, they are more willing to invest in the present and in the future. Without the caring, motivation is, literally, impossible. Thus, as teachers reach out and touch students' lives, they are in no way ordinary teachers, for they replace hopelessness with hope.

Nevertheless, students' competence is not solely built upon our caring about them. If students are going to be competent enough to be full participants in life, they must have a command of the subjects we teach. And, herein, lies the problem. When students come to us under-prepared, we are frustrated and often overwhelmed. Our students' deficiencies become bigger-than-life, and we become consumed by their inadequacies. Thus, we suddenly feel the compelling need to stuff all sorts of information into them at a rapid-firing pace—never taking time to look to the left, to the right, or to pursue an intriguing question. We just don't have the time! The "geraniums may die on the windowsill," but we go right on teaching.

Nancie Atwell (1987) addressed the challenges and the rewards of teaching middle schoolers:

> Surviving adolescence is no small matter; neither is surviving adolescents. It's a hard age to be and teach. The worst things that ever happened to anybody happen every day. But some of the best things can happen, too, and they're more likely to happen when junior high teachers understand the nature of junior high kids and teach in ways that help students grow (25).

In order for us to "teach in ways that help students grow," we need to move beyond the paralyzing, over-used idea that adolescence is a time of raging hormones and realize that this is a time where students have clearly defined needs. The Center for Early Adolescence has defined seven key developmental needs of this age (Scales 1991, 13-14). Understanding these needs can help us restructure our classrooms for success, particularly if we place these needs at the core of our instruction.

❶ POSITIVE SOCIAL INTERACTION WITH PEERS AND ADULTS. Young adolescents identify with their peers and want to be accepted; thus, they need opportunities to interact with each other. In the most successful classrooms, the teacher creates an atmosphere of respect, honors the voices of students, and establishes a mentor-type relationship with them.

Instructional Implications—A variety of instructional approaches is employed instead of relying exclusively on lecture or whole class discussion; students do not work alone on all tasks. Since adolescence is an age where students are very social and concerned with peers more than with adults, collaborative and cooperative learning strategies, including peer evaluation, are employed. Some assignments and assessments are collaborative endeavors, assignments where students get to hear the voices and thoughts of their peers. As they work cooperatively and collaboratively, they meet their need for social interaction and figure out their own identity.

In addition, opportunities are provided for students to draw upon their rich knowledge to increase their own and their peers' understanding and learning. The teacher respects and responds to students in sincere and honest ways, inviting them to give feedback that will help structure the learning. The classroom is, in reality, a community of learners, where rich conversation abounds. Such classrooms may have frequent classroom meetings in which students assess and redirect the learning.

Time is set aside for conferences with peers and with the teacher. These conversations provide students with an important audience to rehearse their learning and an opportunity to receive feedback and to set goals for their learning.

Knowing teachers seek adult responses, beyond their own, to students' work. Parents are often asked to work through drafts of their children's work using a scoring guide or rubric; professionals are invited into the classroom to give students feedback on their performances and work. The teacher designs assignments centered around authentic audiences and purposes.

❷ **STRUCTURE AND CLEAR LIMITS.** Young adolescents often lack confidence in themselves, seeing only their shortcomings and failures. As a result, many find it hard to cope with the responsibilities of unstructured situations. Feeling overwhelmed and wanting to be independent, they often act out with inappropriate behavior. However, given a structure and clearly defined expectations, they can be successful. As they become successful, they are more willing to become independent.

Often students become disruptive because the structure of the learning invites it. Not many of us function well in an environment which is completely free, particularly if we have not been successful or if we don't have any confidence in ourselves. Not knowing what is expected leads to uncertainty which soon escalates to chaos. It's hard to stay on task when the task is not clearly defined and when a person lacks a sense of direction.

Instructional Implications—Teachers use content standards to direct students' learning. Students and parents should know and understand the content standards—what students should know and be able to do—by the end of the course. This creates an agenda for learning and can be presented to students the first day of class in the form of a syllabus or a written description of the class. This document clearly defines the expectations for students, describes the learning experiences, and explains how their work will be evaluated. Some teachers elect to write a letter to students and parents describing their agenda for learning. Whatever the format, the standards guide the learning in the class, keeping the students and the teacher focused.

Design and present learning activities and assignments carefully so that students understand the purpose and the expected outcomes. Students are given much feedback by the teacher and peers so that they can improve their work, becoming more efficient and competent learners.

Underachieving students function best when the classroom is informally organized, but, at the same time, there is a definite structured environment. In other words, students have time to work and to converse with other students and freedom to move and make decisions. In this kind of environment, there is freedom within a structure. Sound impossible? It isn't; it just takes careful planning. For instance, in a math class, a teacher might set up six learning stations. At the beginning of the hour, the teacher explains that students will be working in teams and that they will have to: *complete* at least three learning stations within the next three days; *conference* with their teams—identifying remaining questions and problem areas; *schedule* a team conference with the teacher; and *complete* a learning log entry.

Teachers soon discover the role pacing plays in effective instruction. With block scheduling, good pacing has become even more critical. Keeping students actively engaged in meaningful learning for this extended period takes a lot of planning. Lingering too long on an activity or asking students to do menial and insignificant work are sure ways of inviting inattentiveness and chaos into a classroom. Good questions to ask are: Why are we doing this? Does it matter? Is there an alignment between the task and the time allotted for it? Are my students involved in the activity, or is there time for them to get off task? What is the classroom feeling as students do this activity or assignment? How are my students reacting—frustrated, bored, rushed, calm? Is the assignment demanding enough? Have I included challenging tasks that force them to employ problem-solving and higher-order thinking skills?

Assignments, where students have the opportunity to choose from many options, help to meet the specific learning/reading style needs and interests of individual students. These assignments also build students' independence and autonomy, creating an excitement for learning. When students are presented with an array of authentic, open-ended problems and questions, the distance between the classroom and the outside world grows shorter, and students feel more compelled to learn and to remain in school.

Students must have many chances to problem-solve, make decisions, and take responsibility for their decisions. They should also be given the opportunity to take responsibility for their learning and their behavior and understand the consequences for neglecting either. Furthermore, the class is structured so that students understand they will not be allowed to be passive spectators. Students, the teacher, and parents share the accountability for students' attendance, completion of homework and assignments, class participation, and performance. Students understand that passiveness will not be tolerated or accepted. Students' progress is monitored by implementing a goal-setting program and involving parents in it.

❸ **PHYSICAL ACTIVITY.** Middle school students are in the process of rapid physical development. Therefore, they have a lot of energy, requiring physical activity and time for relaxation and fun.

Instructional Implication—Plan activities that involve movement such as role-playing, simulations, manipulatives, games requiring movement. As mentioned previously, consider the pacing in a class, making sure that students are actively involved in the learning rather than sitting passively the entire period. Break up periods of direct instruction and discussion with group or paired tasks. Plan field trips and opportunities for students to work beyond the classroom such as interviewing activities, working with students in other classrooms, and making presentations to elementary students. Have areas in the room where students can move to do specific tasks. For instance, in a language arts class, there can a reading corner, a publishing corner, and a conferencing area. In other classrooms, there can be learning stations and simulations. Of course, not all assignments can be designed around learning stations, but it is one way to get more movement in the classroom.

❹ **CREATIVE EXPRESSION.** Middle school students need opportunities to express their feelings in writing, art, music, sports, etc. In a study of middle-school students, Oldfather and McLaughlin (1993) observed the connection between motivation and students' self-expression, noting, "through authentic self-expression, they (students) experience a direct connection to who they are, what they know and care about, and how they think. Learning becomes personal, integrated, meaningful, and empowering" (8).

Instructional Implication—Weave a variety of expressive activities into the content being taught. By providing in-class time for students to express themselves, students are more likely to take ownership of the material and to gain keen insights. (Examples—interactive journals, where teachers have informal dialogues with students, learning logs, reflective pieces, class meetings, literature circles, discussion groups—where students have the opportunity to discuss issues that are important to them, and study partners.

Teach in an integrated way, taking into account the different intelligences. Use music, art, skits, role playing, and writing as a way to generate fresh responses from students.

❺ COMPETENCE AND ACHIEVEMENT. Plagued by self-doubts, young adolescents are very vulnerable. Their lack of self-esteem can actually paralyze them. Therefore, they require multiple opportunities to discover that, with effort, they can achieve more challenging and complex tasks. Their accomplishments should be recognized by others.

Instructional Implications—Break challenging work down into a series of approachable steps so that all students are guaranteed a measure of success. This scaffolding of instruction works, for it increases the rehearsal time for learning.

Provide multiple opportunities for students to receive feedback from peers, parents, and teachers. As students work with others and hear conversations about the process of learning, they gauge their work against the work of others gaining keen insight.

Host class celebrations, where adults, friends, and relatives are invited into the class to witness exhibitions of achievement.

Publish students' work. If you run out of creative ways to publish this work, ask your students to brainstorm. (One class identified thirty-five ways to publish their work!)

Engage students in authentic learning experiences involving authentic audiences and purposes so that they know they can be participants in the world beyond the classroom.

Use portfolios for students to assess and reflect on their work; to document their growing competence and achievement in reaching the standards; and to inform others.

Create a goal-setting program, where students are required to reflect on their achievement, to assess their strengths and weaknesses, and to set goals. Share with parents.

Conference with students.

❻ MEANINGFUL PARTICIPATION IN FAMILIES, SCHOOLS, AND COMMUNITIES. Young adolescents are curious about the world in which they live. They want what they learn in school to reflect life beyond the classroom. "Real-world" assignments make this vital connection for students. These kinds of assignments produce products that serve a genuine need, or purpose, in our society. In making these assignments, teachers often draw upon the work that professionals do in their workplaces or upon activities that adults need to know how to do to lead competent lives.

Instructional Implications—Bridge the gap between the classroom and the real world. Engage students in authentic, performance-based activities with real audiences and purposes. Invite professionals into the classroom to work with students and to provide feedback. In a science class, students can design a plan to measure the pollution in their community and conduct the experiments. Before reporting their findings to an appropriate city official, they can ask a scientist to review their work and to give them feedback.

Develop thematic and issue-based units. Allow students to select some of the issues and problems that they want to investigate. In a unit entitled, "Surviving the Money Crunch," Michele Whitney, a math teacher in Long Beach, has students consider the issue of needs vs. wants, affordability, employment, and the good life. In assignments addressing these issues, students use scatter plots; stem and leaf plots; logical reasoning; the terms mean, median, and mode; representative sample and survey; histograms; spreadsheets, and statistics as a tool for persuasion.

In a language arts/social studies class, Caroline Baughman, a humanities core teacher at Newcomb Academy in Long Beach, selected the theme of "The Power of Perseverance" for a unit on ancient Egypt. Within this theme of perseverance, her students focused on the issues of stability, power, and tolerance then and now, bridging the gap between ancient Egypt and the problems of living in 20th century America.

❼ OPPORTUNITIES FOR SELF-DEFINITION. Due to their vulnerability, young adolescents require opportunities to build a consistent self-image—not an easy task when they are seeing themselves in many new, emerging roles and from varied perspectives. They need many opportunities to reflect on their actions and their work. In turn, they realize that self-reflection encourages growth.

Instructional Implications—Structure an array of instructional activities which allow students to see themselves interacting in a variety of settings and groupings. In these activities, include group work, partner assignments, teacher-student conferences, individual work, inter-age learning experiences where students have the chance to work with younger children or older students, and interviewing of adults outside of the classroom so that students can see how they respond and are responded to in each of these situations.

Use an array of strategies to develop students' metacognitive skills. Metacognition refers to the ability to think about thought. Students with highly developed metacognitive skills, have the power to: look within and analyze their work and themselves; gain the ability to have an inner dialogue about these strengths and weaknesses; and plan strategies for problem solving. A portion of every class period is spent in some type of reflective activity. Metacognitive responses are modeled by the teacher, and class time is allotted for conversations about thinking. Students grow by hearing the thinking processes of others. Reflections are recorded in response journals, learning logs, portfolio reflections, goals, and letters to parents

A common denominator of each of these critical needs is the student's extreme vulnerability. When we're on the other side of the desk, it's easy to forget the vulnerability of the learner, particularly when it wears many facades of protective layering. Key to removing the protective, and often objectionable, layering is to structure our classes in humane and meaningful ways, where students have multiple opportunities to discover their unique capabilities.

Caroline Baughman understands the importance of considering the needs of early adolescents by planning lessons that engage them as learners. As the culminating activity for a unit on Egypt, her students plan an Egyptian Banquet to *celebrate* their studies. Caroline describes the planning of the banquet in Fig. 1.1.

At the banquet, students revealed their newly acquired knowledge of ancient Egypt by making grape-juice toasts. Dominic Faridani wrote these powerful phrases in Fig. 1.2.

Students enthusiastically responded to their teacher's charge to "make history come alive" by designing the costumes in Fig. 1.3.

Ms. Baughman's imaginative culminating activity integrates the knowledge students gained during the unit into the festivities, allowing them to celebrate their learning. By letting her students make costumes, prepare skits, and even write dinner toasts, she acknowledged her students' different learning styles and preferences. Many underachieving students are kinesthetic/tactile learners so that having activities such as these levels the playing field for achievement.

Culminating Activity

"EGYPTIAN BANQUET"

This culminating project or activity challenges students to synthesize and apply their historical knowledge encompassing both *Mara, Daughter of the Nile* and the studies from the textbook, *A Message of Ancient Days*. It is so interesting to hear the students build toward this "banquet" during the whole unit which runs about six weeks. They are informed from the first day that they will need to research, read, and creatively put together an Egyptian outfit to wear to the banquet which is a celebration of our studies. This memorable event is truly evidence of minds turning on and "history coming alive!"

Planning for this banquet actually triggers and maintains student interest, participation, and ultimately, **academic achievement**. History tells us that communities through time have come from diversity. If we just tap into who and what we are, we can use our literacy to better understand each other and our world by reenacting earlier lifestyles.

I have briefly bulleted the following points to think about when putting together a banquet such as this:

- A scoring guide has been shared with the class before the banquet for expectations of the day (see Fig 1.1a).
- Students come in costume for the core time. Nonparticipants are assigned to another class if needed.
- Each student must have written out at least twenty "toasts" for the banquet (see Fig. 1.2).
- A food sign-up chart is posted two weeks before the banquet.
- Give notice to staff who will be enduring any disruption during time of changing into costumes. This is a simple courtesy, and students are exempt from the tardy sweep.
- Today is the day skits will be performed so that groups have been practicing. They dramatize such events as mummification, the Hall of Judgment, daily life, parts from the *Mara, Daughter of the Nile* book, etc.
- Musical entertainment is performed from stick balancing, to belly dancing for the pharaoh, and, of course, the infamous "Walk Like An Egyptian." They love this!!

Fig. 1.1. Caroline Baughman's planning guide for the "Egyptian Banquet"

NAME

_____

CORE_____

"EGYPTIAN BANQUET SCORING GUIDE"

____ OVERALL EXCELLENT JOB!!
- You looked terrific and prepared yourself well for the banquet.
- The pharaoh is very proud of you!!

<u>CHECKED ITEMS DESIGNATE AREA OF DEFICIENCY WHICH LOWERED
YOUR GRADE:</u>

____ Inadequate number of written banquet toasts
____ Toasts lacking evidence of Egyptian facts from studies
____ More effort needed on costume design
____ Attitude not appropriate for banquet
____ Neglected to contribute to banquet food
____ Participation not satisfactory

**MS. BAUGHMAN
HUMANITIES CORE**

Fig. 1.1a. To make the banquet a quality celebration, students were given these guidelines

Dominic Faridani
Newcomb Academy
History C2
March 25, 1997

20 Egyptian Toasts
"I propose a toast to ..."

- Thutmose, for being the greatest military leader ever.
- Menes, for contributing to us the double crown.
- Imhotep, for building the first pyramid of Egypt and the largest structure anywhere.
- Hieroglyphs, the writing which binds us all, letting records be made of discoveries and great pharaohs.
- Hatshepsut, for beautifying Egypt with her monuments.
- The Nile, for making our Egyptian life possible and providing us with food, paper, sandals, and much more.
- Anubis, for weighing all hearts and being the fair judge he is. ...

Fig. 1.2. Dominic Faridani's toasts reveal his knowledge of ancient Egyptian beliefs

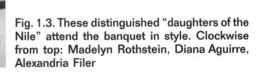

Fig. 1.3. These distinguished "daughters of the Nile" attend the banquet in style. Clockwise from top: Madelyn Rothstein, Diana Aguirre, Alexandria Filer

This thoughtful teacher spends a great amount of time in structuring her classroom for success. Her Egyptian unit began with her developing a thematic, issue-based unit that would bridge the distance in time between this historical period and her students' lives, and, at the same time, address the district standards of:

> historical perspective,
> cultural anthropology,
> geography and human activity,
> listening,
> presenting ideas,
> responding to text,
> independent reading,
> and writing for a variety of purposed and audiences.

By the time students finished the unit, they had a reason to celebrate, for they had spent six weeks participating in purposeful learning. When learning is purposeful, students are more likely to be motivated.

MOTIVATION GETS IN GEAR WHEN TEACHERS BELIEVE IN THEIR OWN EFFICACY

Frustrated by unmotivated students, a group of Writing to Learn teachers in Reading, Pennsylvania decided to keep year-long case studies of successful and unsuccessful students. At the year's end, they were amazed at how much they had learned from focusing on their unsuccessful students. In looking at their students' failures, many discovered alternative routes that they might have taken, and they rediscovered some fundamental principles of learning and motivation that could lead other students to success. By consistently keeping annotated notes about their students and reflecting on these notes with colleagues, they felt that they had grown increasingly wiser, resulting in a new confidence. A teacher wrote, "I feel wiser now having learned from Danny. The next time someone like Danny walks into my room ... I'll know better what to do."

These teachers experienced the power of reflective teaching. In an article on reflective practice, Bud Wellington (1991) compared the reflective teacher to a defiant wildflower, stating that, "Reflective practice, like a tenacious wildflower in the city, vibrates with vitality, raising our awareness, and calling us from passivity to action" (4). The answer, for these teachers, came from within, commanding them to action. Reflective teaching increased their efficacy—the belief that they could have an impact on students' learning and motivation. Thus, they lost their feeling of helplessness.

Teachers with a strong sense of efficacy see motivation as a solvable problem rather than a disheartening representation of their inability to teach or their students to learn. Hence, they see low-achieving students as being teachable and are willing to expend a great amount of energy and time to reach them (Ashton and Webb, 1986).

McDaniel (1984) reports that teachers, who lack efficacy, respond to low achieving, unmotivated students by:

> seating them farther away from themselves, calling on them less frequently, paying less attention to them, giving them less time and fewer clues for answering questions, criticizing wrong answers from them more frequently, praising their correct responses less often, and interrupting their performance more often (46).

Low-achieving students very quickly perceive a teacher's disdain, lack of tolerance, and low expectations for them. They respond by becoming even more passive or more disruptive. Thus, the low expectations become self-fulfilling prophesies.

Develop a Working Understanding of Motivation

The good news is that there is a wealth of helpful research on middle-level motivation, which Oldfather and McLaughlin (1993) have succinctly summarized:

a. develop task-involved rather than ability-involved classroom goal orientations.

b. use intrinsic rather than extrinsic rewards.

c. require complex and challenging work rather than fact-focused, low-level thinking.

d. build classroom experiences around interactions and tasks that enhance perceived self-competence.

e. provide opportunities that promote perceived self-determination rather than perceived control.

f. create an interactive, personal, and informal rather than individualistic, competitive and formal learning setting (2).

In their investigation of middle-school motivation, Oldfather and McLaughlin conducted a longitudinal study of what happens to students' motivation as they make the transition from elementary to middle school. They found that students were less motivated in middle schools and felt less involved and connected to their learning. The study affirms that students are more motivated when their ability to construct meaning is honored in the classroom:

> Our efforts in the classroom should be directed toward developing classrooms in which students find their passions, discover what they care about, create their own learning agendas, and most importantly experience meaningful connections between who they are and what they do in school (Oldfather and McLaughlin 1993, 3).

When students are taught in this way, they want to learn, for their teachers firmly believe that each of them possesses:

▶ Passions to be awakened
▶ Knowledge to be activated and connected
▶ Curiosity to be aroused and unleashed
▶ Understanding to be cultivated
▶ Commitment and perseverance to be charged
▶ Unique abilities to be unveiled

As teachers, we help students to make vital discoveries about their passions, knowledge, curiosity, understanding, commitment and perseverance, and abilities. When students discover that they possess these precious treasures, they are never the same; they become willing participants in life and in school.

MOTIVATION INVOLVES
MOVING FROM CENTER STAGE TO THE WINGS

Students will never make these important discoveries about themselves unless we are willing to restructure our classrooms so that students have freedom to learn. Anita Graham (1994), a teacher in San Diego, uses these words to describe her transition in moving from a teacher-centered classroom to a more student-centered one:

> I see my role now as active, but strictly behind-the scenes. It is my job to set the stage and create the environment for successful learning. But it is the students themselves who are in charge of their learning. They should be on center stage (10).

Anita came to a Writing to Learn Project viewing herself as an especially good expository writing teacher. She thought her participation in the Project would allow her to pick up a few points and to refine her eighth grade language arts class, for she was quite satisfied with it. According to her, she, " Didn't anticipate any earth-shattering changes."

In her teaching, Anita stressed writing as a process, and gave literature-based writing assignments, making sure that students had practice in all of California's required expository formats. She described these essays as end products, where students showed her what they had learned during the literature units. Although she, admittedly, felt a bit guilty over the fact that students had very little time to write on self-selected topics or for self-expression, she rationalized by thinking it was a necessary sacrifice in that, "You cannot do everything." She controlled the production pace of these literary pieces by doing the editing herself, attacking each student's paper with "missionary zeal." Students simply had to recopy their drafts into final, polished copies.

During the Institute, Anita felt the need to restructure her class. Instead of listening to lectures, students found themselves working through challenging tasks in cooperative learning groups. Instead of relying on Ms. Graham's copious comments to revise their papers, they became self-editors by having time to work with peers and by hearing lots of conversations about the work a writer does—all in a workshop setting. Instead of prescribed assignments used for the sole purpose of assessment, students were given choices, based on their structural needs and the freedom to write on self-selected topics. Instead of evaluation being teacher-centered, students grappled with the criteria of evaluation, using them as a guide to develop and refine their work.

As she restructured her class and gave her students more control over their learning and writing, the change in her class was much more than just cosmetic; they were "inside out" changes:

> I find my students more willing to write and more willing to take risks. As a result, they are making discoveries about their writing selves; they are more creative; they can write for a variety of audiences and purposes; they see writing as a process rather than a product; they write much more often; and they are learning how to become self-editors. But, more importantly, writing has become an actual learning experience (Graham 1994, 7).

Sharon Major, a dynamic science teacher in Louisville, Kentucky, had a similar experience when she decided to make her class more task-oriented and student-centered. In teaching science, she wanted to share her informed passion for science with her students so that they might, in turn, develop a passion of their own. She realized that one of the best ways to do this was to place the teaching of specific science skills into a problem-solving context so that students could discover that science was a very useful subject to learn.

However, she had a real concern: Would her students really learn the scientific skills outlined by the Kentucky Educational Reform Act? These performance-based skills included: making hypotheses, testing a hypothesis, understanding variables, recording data, drawing conclusions, reporting data, measuring accurately, and using equipment properly.

She gave the problem to her students. Together, they decided to create a consumers' lab where they would test products and report on them. The students decided on the products to test and designed the experiments. To report their findings, they published a consumers' newsletter and sent it to faculty and parents. In addition, they hosted a consumers' fair, where students set up lab stations and gave demonstrations. Thrilled with her students' performance, she said that they were using lab techniques that she had learned in college.

On their next project, these same students became forensic scientists. They invited forensic scientists into the classroom to work side-by-side with them. During their project, they learned an array of sophisticated lab techniques as well as problem-solving strategies. They were not intimidated by professionals in the field, for they had been treated as respected colleagues. Furthermore, their experiments showed that they could learn.

As Sharon watched her students conduct experiments and listened to their conversations, her initial concerns about her students learning scientific skills were alleviated. Her students had a working knowledge of science. And better yet, they were truly motivated.

The "Consumer Reports" paper in Fig. 1.4, prepared by Ms. Major's student Tiffany Woolfolh, demonstrates an enthusiastic response to science and an understanding of the scientific method.

In these classes, students were highly motivated, for they had taken charge of their learning. Their teachers had successfully created *communities of learners*. Hence, their students no longer viewed these teachers as the ultimate authorities who programmed and "legislated" their learning.

In a community of learners, students feel free to express themselves because they know their contributions are valued by teachers and peers. As a result, they are active participants

Tiffany Woolfolh

Consumer Reports
Lip Balm Information

I work at consumer reports and we're the company who tests products to make sure you buy what's best for your money. For the past two weeks we tested four lip balms. Chapped lips are caused because unlike the rest of your body, your lips don't have pores. Therefore they do not get any natural oils so the lip balms supply the moisture barrier so it won't get chapped.

We tested four lip balms. They were Blixtex Medicated™, Blixtex Regular™, Chapstix™ and Vaseline™ Lip Therapy. We did four tests. They were: Stay-on test to see how will the lip balms stay on; Moisture Barrier test; All temperature test to see if it stays the same in hot or cold weather because you don't want a melted lip balm in hot weather, or the lip balm will freeze in cold weather; and the Waxy-Oily test. My overall ranking of the lip balms were - Chapstix the best, Vaseline Lip Therapy, Blistex Medicated, and Blistex Regular.

On the Waxy Oily test, we decided to use our arms

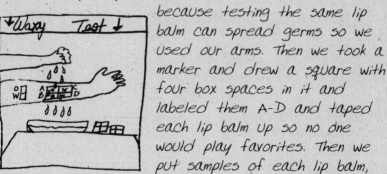

because testing the same lip balm can spread germs so we used our arms. Then we took a marker and drew a square with four box spaces in it and labeled them A-D and taped each lip balm up so no one would play favorites. Then we put samples of each lip balm,

Fig. 1.4a. Tiffany Woolfolh's lip balm report

one in each box and then we drew two other boxes that were separate from the others. One drop had oil in it. The other box had wax. We got the oil from cooking oil, the wax by rubbing a candle on the box. And we recorded how each lip balm felt. Then we rubbed petroleum jelly on top of the four boxes and then took sponges and dipped it in water and dripped over the boxes. We then patted the boxes once with a paper towel to see how well it stayed because you lick your lips all the time. The Moisture Barrier test was to see if the lip balms block water. When you drink water, you don't want it to come off. On my test, Blistex Medicated was the best, then Chapstix, Vaseline, and Blistex Regular.

On All Temperature Test we heated the lip balms and recorded how they felt. Then we froze it and recorded how it felt. We used our arm to test this.

I think Chapstix was the best. It only cost .82¢, and did well in all tests.

Fig. 1.4b

in their learning. Students come to realize that learning does not occur through a teacher-directed monologue, but, in fact, it occurs through a continuing dialogue, resulting in rich collaborative learning experiences designed by both teacher and students.

BUILDING COMMUNITY IN CLASSROOMS

However, these rich collaborative learning experiences, in themselves, will not create and sustain a community of learners. From the very first day of class until the last day, teachers must plan and devote in-class time to activities that will build and extend the community.

At the beginning of the year, this means creating a warm, non-threatening atmosphere, where students accept individuals' differences, support each other, work together, and feel free to take the risks of being active learners. Carla Watson, a teacher in Long Beach, California, begins the important act of community building with an exceptional oral history project.

She begins by explaining that America is like a quilt with different colors, hues, and ideas that are patched or sewn together as a nation, adding that the class, too, is very much like a quilt. To provide a setting, she brings in her grandmother's patchwork quilt and other quilts and reads poetry to them. In addition, she reads aloud a picture book, entitled *The Patchwork Quilt* by Valerie Flourney, a heart-warming story about how a grandmother builds a special relationship with her granddaughter and shares many family traditions through the making of a patchwork quilt. This leads to a discussion about values: What are they? How are they identified and clarified? How do they develop? Then she gives these directions to her students:

ORAL HISTORY/QUILT PROJECT

Each of us has a unique family background. Who we are, what we are—our talents and our weaknesses—all come from our families. Most importantly, we gain our values from our family.

Think about your own family and its unique qualities. What values does your family hold most dear? Interview your parents, aunts, uncles, and grandparents.

Your assignment has three parts:

1. Construct a 12-inch square quilt piece which symbolizes you and your family—its history and its values.

2. Compose a description of your quilt piece. Tell the story behind your symbols. Please type and try to complete your story on one typed page.

3. Tell the story of a family member who taught you "Words of Wisdom" What did they teach you? Why is this important to you? (The stories are videotaped.)

Each quilt piece is mounted on a contrasting color of paper before putting them together to form a patchwork quilt.

Knotted with love... the quilts sing on...

Sample Quilt from Cubberly Middle School

Involving students in important classroom decisions is another way of building community. This involvement can take the format of class meetings. In class meetings, students make decisions about publications, projects, deadlines, strategies for learning, and celebrations of achievements. They may even spend this time in: designing rubrics and scoring guides—documents which tell how assignments will be evaluated; monitoring the progress of the class; and handling disturbing classroom interruptions.

When a class has been so disruptive that neither teacher nor students want to return, it is time for a class meeting. Too often, teachers try to solve the problem alone when, in reality, it is not entirely their problem. Students, not only need to recognize the problem, but they also need to be part of the solution. During the class meeting, the class identifies disruptive behaviors, generates alternative responses, and devises a plan of action. Students respect being treated in a mature way and take the task very seriously. The class meeting clears the air and restores a productive working environment without emotions escalating—emotions that can create anxiety, stifle motivation, and shut down learning.

BUILDING CLASSROOM TASKS
AROUND REAL WORLD LEARNING

A key to keeping students motivated is to build the classroom tasks around real world learning experiences. During the past several years in WTL, I have witnessed the motivating power of the following showcase of real world learning experiences planned and executed by creative teachers and students:

Milwaukee—A home economics class formed a professional catering company. To begin, they checked the competition to gain information about product and pricing. This included talking to the managers at Burger King and McDonalds and focusing on salads. Then they offered a price-competitive salad luncheon to teachers at their school. Following this success, they expanded to catering special functions—preparing the food, presenting the food, and serving it. As servers, they donned white shirts and black ties. After a function, they held a formal evaluation of the event, including the food, the costs, the presentation, and the service, making notes if there were deficiencies. In effect, they gave themselves a report card and set an agenda for improved services.

Milwaukee—A team of talented teachers were tired of their special education students being treated as second-class citizens, isolated from the rest of the school. Therefore, they decided to make their class a television newsroom. Their students produced a weekly newscast, viewed by the entire school. This newscast also included the weather taken from the weather station that they set up outside of their room. This same group of special students began writing grant proposals for additional funding to support their efforts.

Cleveland—A special education class produced a guidebook to the school, which was printed commercially and sold as a fund-raiser for the school. The art work from this book was used as a bookmark to promote the Ohio Young Authors' Conference.

Cleveland—A music class wrote reviews and promotionals for a former student whose group cut a recording. (The student musician wrote many of the lyrics in his language arts and music classes.)

San Diego—Eighth-grade physical education students wrote a code of ethics for future generations of physical education students at the school. The printed code was signed by all students, framed, and hung in the school.

San Diego—An eighth-grade class organized a trial around a controversial local monument—a cross. They invited local lawyers and officials to participate with them in the trial.

Wichita—A group of students, disatisfied with their math book, wrote a textbook of their own to be used by the next year's students. They called it *K.I.S.S: KEEP IT SHORT AND SIMPLE.*

Louisville—A language arts class designed a school-wide literacy project. Their first project was having the whole school listen to a book being read aloud. The reading was broadcast over the televisions in each classroom following the morning announcement.

Various people participated in the reading, including janitors, cafeteria workers, students, administrators. An eighth grade class created a story hour where they read stories to elementary students.

Chattanooga—Students investigated the long-term effects of pollution in the Tennessee River. In this interdisciplinary, thematic unit, they conducted water studies, compiled data, surveyed residents, and reported their findings to a real audience of city commissioners and other officials. As a result of their initial study, they received a $300,000 grant to extend their study over a three-year period. Their teacher, Mattie Shoulders, and many of her students became activists and joined various environmental groups. Mattie exclaims, "At age 54, I have become an activist by becoming involved in local and state environmental issues. I am now giving back something to my community after spending many years of not being involved, and it is exciting." She attributed this involvement to a change in her instruction. According to Shoulders, when you base your instruction on issues, it is impossible to keep real world learning out of your classroom and your life. The instruction had a life-changing effect on her students and her.

Each of these projects reflects the essential elements of honoring students' voices, collaborative learning, and a shared sense of knowledge. When students are engaged in real-world projects, they feel their learning is worthwhile, and they have a continuing desire to learn. These tasks allow students to see themselves as competent individuals; thus, their self-competence begins to emerge (Oldfather and McLaughlin 1993).

However, not all assignments in the classroom can be real-world tasks, for these kind of projects take considerable time to design, implement, and complete. Thus, these extended projects usually take the form of culminating activities for a unit of study. Then, a question lingers: What can a teacher do on a daily basis to keep students motivated and involved in their learning?

MOTIVATION INCREASES AS STUDENTS DISCOVER THEIR POTENTIAL AND WORTH

Even confident teachers, who are convinced that they can engage the most reluctant learner, experience problems when their students do not believe in themselves. Many students, cloaked in years of failure and defeated by life's problems, are positive that they are, indeed, stupid, and many perceive themselves as helpless victims whose lives are out of control. Loretta Hawkins, a Chicago teacher, combats these destructive beliefs by sharing these words with her students at the beginning of each year:

> Do not allow anyone to convince you that you are not intelligent, not good and not valuable. If you cannot read, then it means one thing: you cannot read. If you cannot write, it means that you cannot write, and if you cannot count, it means you cannot count. If you cannot do these things, then that is why you are here. If you cannot do these things, then that is why I am here . . . I am convinced that if I can convince them that is true, then I can teach them anything (1989, 4).

Still, it's hard for students to believe in themselves when they are faced with failure. Discouraged with the results of her first algebra test, a teacher in Washington, DC, abandoned her lesson plan for the day and decided to deal with the reality of failure. As she walked hesitantly into the room carrying their test papers, she noticed that her students looked as if they were waiting their "sentence."

Wanting to dispel the deadly atmosphere, she asked her students to write about how they feel when they fail a test. As students shared their writing and spoke honestly of their feelings, the atmosphere of the classroom changed. One student said, "I don't ever want to come to the class again." Another student's quivering voice announced that he felt like jumping off a cliff, while another blurted out that she rips up the test so that she never has to look at it again.

Others went beyond their feelings and made excuses for their failure: teachers don't like me; I don't really try on tests; I can't do math, so I always fail; teachers always make tests too hard and try to trick you; and my "luck runs out" on tests. One student shrugged his shoulders and said, "What's new?" The teacher used the discovery of their feelings to restructure her class, asking her students an important question, "If we spent another week learning this material and then took another test, what could we do to this week to help you learn it?" This question led to a wonderful discussion about learning, giving the teacher some concrete ideas for restructuring the classroom for success, including the formation of study groups.

MOTIVATION INVOLVES HELPING STUDENTS TO UNLOCK PATTERNS OF FAILURE

The students' responses to their failure are better understood when placed within the context of the reasons students give for succeeding or failing. Weiner (1979) found that students attributed their success or failure to task difficulty, effort, luck, and ability. In looking at students' perceptions of why they succeed or fail, it's also helpful to search for patterns. Researchers have categorized these patterns into stable-unstable and internal-external. The stable-unstable categorization refers to whether or not a student has a pattern of failure, and the internal-external refers to where the blame is placed for this failure—within the student or some external force. (Alderman 1990).

For instance, students who say such things as "teachers try to trick you" and "teachers don't like me" are attributing an outside force—the teacher. On the other hand, the student who says she failed because she can't do math blames her own lack of ability for all of her failures in math. She is convinced that no matter how hard she tries she will always fail.

This is also true of the student who says, "What's new?" He has a consistent pattern of failing tests so that it becomes the expectation and the outcome. When he fails, he responds by putting even less time and effort into the task. Thus, he does nothing, for it is better to not have tried and failed than to try and still experience a devastating failure. In contrast, achieving students, after failing, spend more time and effort, analyzing their learning strategies and searching for more effective strategies (Dweck and Goetz 1978).

Students who hold internal/stable attributions, view themselves as helpless victims who cannot experience success. Even if they do experience a success, they dismiss it as being a stroke of luck, or a fluke, not taking credit for it. Motivating students, who see themselves as victims of inability, is extremely difficult, for they are paralyzed by their poor self-esteem.

In an attempt to build students' self-esteem, teachers often respond inappropriately by creating undemanding and rote assignments so that students can achieve success quickly. In addition, they add a splattering of empty and meaningless esteem-building activities.

For instance, I once observed a teacher, who with cheerleader enthusiasm, bounced to the front of her classroom and bellowed out to her students "How many of you feel good about yourselves?" Immediately, every hand shot into the air. Then she asked them to write about one achievement of which they were exceptionally proud. Most of the students did not even respond. Those who did were lost in generalities: I'm nice; I'm a fun person; I care a lot, etc. The teacher concluded by congratulating the students, giving them the false impression that everything was fine. Although she didn't realize it, she was setting up her students for a crueler kind of failure in the future. It is impossible to build students' self-esteem without their expending genuine effort.

James Beane (1991), in writing about the self-esteem controversy, states that increasing self-esteem is not the simple work that many conceive it to be. In fact, he warns, "It is not enough that young people like themselves. They must also have a sense that what they say, and think, and do counts for something" (26). According to Beane, this personal efficacy must be connected to a collective one, where students see themselves as belonging to groups and where they have power to bring about change. In this collaborative, non-threatening atmosphere, students work on solving challenging, real-life problems.

Self-esteem is not built through isolated activities or undemanding and meaningless assignments. Self-esteem emerges when a student devotes an enduring amount of effort and time to perform challenging and meaningful tasks. As students begin to have success with difficult tasks, they start believing in themselves.

Therefore, instruction needs to be restructured so that students will have the experience of explicitly linking their successes to their own efforts and abilities. When students discover that they are in control of their successes and failures, they become more willing learners.

Peter Scales (1991) suggests that there is a difference between self-worth and self-efficacy: "Self-worth might be increased by chanting 'I am somebody,' but no chant will raise self-efficacy, the sense that one's actions can have an impact in the real world" (44). As teachers, we should provide students with learning experiences that allow them to discover that they can succeed in real world tasks and have an impact on society through the expenditure of genuine effort and dedication to tasks.

Kelly Kellar, a teacher in Long Beach, teaches in an alternative education program sponsored by the Los Angeles County Office of Education. Alternative Schools with Purpose, A.S.W.P., challenges students to take responsibility for their achievement.

At the beginning of the school year, she sent a A.S.W.P. letter/contract to parents and students (see Fig. 1.5).

On the first day of school, she has them look at their cumulative folders and to take notes on their GPA, absences, and conduct record. In a log entry, they reflect on their record and describe what they could do differently to change it. They end the log entry by setting goals. At the end of the trimester, they are given this assignment:

Write a short essay evaluating Mrs. Kellar, A.S.W.P. classmates, classwork, and your performance. Are you reaching your goals? Has this class helped? How? Should you stay in A.S.W.P.? Why or Why not? Finally, What is your goal for the second trimester?

To report their progress, Kelly's students prepared the newsgram in Fig. 1.6.

LONG BEACH UNIFIED SCHOOL DISTRICT
Walter B. Hill Middle School
"An Accelerated School" September 5, 1996
1100 Iroquois Avenue
Long Beach, California 90815
(310) 598-7611

Welcome to the ASWP class:

I hope everyone had a restful and fun summer. My family and I were very busy. We spent part of the summer traveling and doing projects around the house. I was also able to become a student for a week. I attended a class called **WRITING to LEARN** where I learned many new ways to improve the learning in our class. Some of these ways you will be using during this coming school year, and I hope you will enjoy them as much as I enjoyed learning them.

As you can see in the attached newsletter from last years ASWP class, our class was very proud of the goals they achieved. I plan on this being another exciting year for us and expect all of you to live up to the commitment you made upon entering this class to improve your attendance, grades, and/or conduct. While you are mostly responsible for yourself, you will have support from your parents, teachers and administrators through-out this year.

As **STUDENTS** in ASWP, I expect you to treat yourself and others with the respect deserved. I expect you to work to the best of your ability and follow our classroom rules.

As the **TEACHER** in ASWP, I will treat you with the respect you deserve. I will follow our classroom rules, and I will be open to your input and ideas to improve our classroom. I will also keep you and your parents informed about the progress you make in our class.

As **PARENTS** of ASWP students, you will be expected to support your child's accomplishments and be willing to come in for conferences as needed. The home/school connection is extremely important in helping your students reach their own personal best.

Classroom management is not meant to discipline or punish but rather to establish a safe and positive classroom, where the teacher can teach and the students can learn in a peaceful, enjoyable setting. I encourage all assistance and/or suggestions.

After reading this contract with your student, please sign to indicate your commit-ment to his/her success.

I look forward to this year with your student.

Sincerely,

Kelly Kellar

Kelly Kellar
ASWP Teacher

I HAVE READ AND AGREE TO ENTERING THE ASWP CLASS.

PARENT SIGNATURE _____DATE_____

STUDENT SIGNATURE_____DATE_____

TEACHER SIGNATURE_____DATE_____

Fig. 1.5

WHAT IS A.S.W.P.

Mrs. Kellar's students have designated **ASWP** as **ACCOMPLISHED STUDENTS WITH POTENTIAL AND PRIDE.** What is it really? Alternative Schools with Purpose.

The purpose is to work with students in an alternative way so as to motivate them to have a desire to achieve. Students entering ASWP must demonstrate a willingness to improve by agreeing to come into the class. They may not be forced (this isn't a punishment). Students only enter the program after an interview, giving their consent and gaining parent permission.

In ASWP the class size is limited. This enables students to develop a support group and therefore improve attendance, academic performance and conduct.

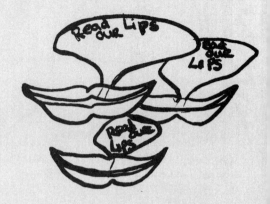

READ OUR LIPS

As students of ASWP we have taken our average GPA of .81 in June 95 and turned it to a 1.7 as of Feb. 96. To beat that our April report cards showed a 2.13 average. Some ASWP students had this to say...
-"ever since I have been in ASWP my grades have improved a little."
-"first semester .53 now 3.0"
-"before .87 now a 2.0...used to be F's now I have B's and C's"
-"I was here almost two years and I never got good grades until I went in ASWP."

We also would like you to know our average attendance for each month has been above 80%. Some of us rarely saw a classroom last year, but now we are here all the time.
"I was absent sixty nine days first semester...in ASWP I have been absent seven days." At least seventeen of us were absent more than sixty days last year. At this time only five of us have been absent more than twenty days with truant absences.

We want you to know that while some teachers and students think this is the "stupid" class it's not. If you would at least be in our class for five minutes you'll know what's going on- the same as any other class!

Fig. 1.6a

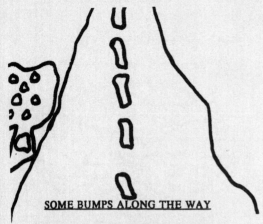

SOME BUMPS ALONG THE WAY

Aside from all the criticism ASWP has taken we have had a few lows this year. Out of the thirty-six students enrolled we have lost ten to DT's and RIA's. Three have moved and one has run away. We have also had to SARB three students for excessive truancy.

A FEW GOOD STUDENTS

We are looking for a list of candidates that may fit the following description. Please submit the names of any student you feel may qualify by Monday, June 10.

ASWP is for students who

-have failed three or more classes per semester.
-consistently miss school {20 or more days}.
-are extremely shy and would benefit a smaller class size.
-have extenuating circumstances {i.e. home problems, poor self-image} and may need extra support.
-need to visit administration regularly for minor infractions such as disruptions, constant tardies or truancies.

ASWP is NOT for

-overtly defiant students.
-students unwilling to commit.
-students who don't want to improve or don't care.
-a place to deposit behavior problems.

A BIG P.S.

I want to thank everyone for that little (sometimes a lot) extra that has been given to help myself and my students accomplish what we have this year.

Thank you sincerely,

Kelly Kellar and the ASWP students

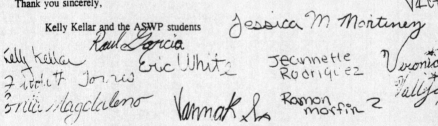

Fig. 1.6b

GOAL SETTING LINKS STUDENTS'
SUCCESSES TO THEIR OWN EFFORTS

Involving students in goal setting is an excellent way to help students monitor their progress and to link their successes to their own efforts. Those students, who set goals for themselves and evaluate their progress in reaching these goals, develop concrete ways for looking at their learning. As they look at their progress, they move beyond their "learned helplessness" condition and are willing to invest more effort in finding better ways to learn.

Research suggests that when students set goals for themselves rather than following teachers' goals, they are more motivated. They perceive that the classroom tasks have more value because they are more closely aligned to their personal goals and interests (Schunk 1990). When students set goals, they are actually taking ownership of their learning. Rather than viewing classroom tasks as "being boring" or "having nothing to do with anything," they see their learning as being significant, for they have become of the architects of their own learning. For instance, one student wrote:

> I'm not real happy with my math grade. I am going to try not to make a lot of mistakes. This trimester I will get prepared for tests early, do things the first time they are given, and listen to the teacher real good. I'm not going to be afraid to raise my hand when I don't understand. I may even ask Mr. _____ to go a little bit slower.

Another student declared:

> I can do better in English this trimester by proof reading my work more carefully and doing my work more slowly. I can also do my homework right when I get home. I probably need to read at least one hour a day, write four pages a day, and learn to pace myself.

It's obvious that these students take their goals seriously. Thus, they are more likely to become proficient learners—learners who place value in their tasks, understand what the tasks require, and can identify the resources they need to complete them. In this student-centered approach, negative attitudes become more positive as students' perceptions about classroom work change (Marzano 1992).

BEGINNING WITH GOALS

Arlana Bedard, a teacher in Long Beach, California, introduces her students to goal setting by sharing her own personal and professional goals with them. Using an overhead projector, she records her inner dialogue—the conversation that she is having with herself about setting these goals. Speaking her thoughts aloud, she explains that her goal to be better organized is both professional and personal, saying that she creates a lot of extra work and stress by not being organized. (As an aside, she shares a few of these horror stories.) At school, she will work on filing things, keeping her desk orderly, and keeping up with the paperwork. At home, she will organize her house—her cabinets, drawers, bills, etc. In formulating another goal, she confides that she has always wanted to write poetry and that this year in their writers' workshop she is going to focus on poetry. In talking about professional goals, she tells her students that she is not satisfied with the class portfolios, and she wants to refine them with their help.

She explains that these goals, and the resulting tasks, are ones that really interest her and that spending time on developing a plan for achieving them is very exciting for her. As part of the process, she divides her goals into short-term and long-range, brainstorms what she will do to achieve them, and devises a plan for monitoring them. Throughout the year, she continues to monitor her goals and sets new goals. Much class time is spent in holding conversations about goal setting with teachers and students talking about their goals. In doing so, she creates a community of learners, where teacher and students share their learning, and, at the same time, models that goal setting is something that they will use throughout life.

To help her students get started in goal setting, Arlana has developed the handouts in Fig 1.7.

Arlana Bedard
Hughes Middle School
Long Beach, CA

Name:

GOAL SETTING

1. Let's begin by looking at what we've done in school so far ...

      a. What have you done well?

      b. How can you do even better?

      c. What are you not real happy about?

      d. How can you work on improving yourself in that area?

2. Ok, now let's set some goals for ourselves. Write three goals you plan to achieve by the end of this trimester. Decide how you are going to reach them and how you will know you have reached them. Consider some of the areas listed in the box below.

    1.

    2.

    3.

> writing, reading, working with groups, study habits, organization, speaking with the teacher, asking for help, prepared for class—materials & attitude, etc...

Fig. 1.7a. Ms. Beddard's goal setting handout helps students get started in goal setting and provides sample objectives

---

Arlana Bedard
Hughes Middle School
Long Beach, CA

GOAL-SETTING LETTER

DATE _____

DEAR _____,

PARAGRAPH ONE—How do you feel about what you have done in school so far this year?

PARAGRAPH TWO—What you want to do better in and why you need to.

PARAGRAPH THREE—How you plan to accomplish your goals and how your parents can help.

                                 LOVE,

                              _____

Fig. 1.7b. Student goal-setting letter template

As students begin to set goals, it's important for them to learn how to set short-term, proximal goals. Usually, students begin by setting long-range goals, and they become overwhelmed when they can't see a logical way in which to proceed. They try to tackle all of their deficiencies at once instead of breaking their goals down into a series of approachable steps. One teacher describes this as students' attempt "to swallow an entire elephant at once—an impossible task." However, she explains that "bite by bite, it becomes a do-able task." When students try the whole elephant approach, they do not see progress, and they abandon their goals. To help students in the "bite-by-bite" approach to goal setting, consider the following:

❶ **Select one or two goals at a time**—Focus on only a few goals at a time. These goals should be short-term and specific. Usually, goals are too general to serve as guiding statements for learning. Examples of poorly written goals are: "I want to do better in math," or "I want to write better." A better goal for math would be: "I have never understood how to multiply and divide fractions. During the next two weeks, I am going to learn how to do this." Another goal might involve word problems. In language arts, a more specific goal would be: "I know I should have learned this before, but I never know when to start a new paragraph. I just keep on writing and writing, filling pages without stopping. During the next month, I am going to work on paragraphing." Another language arts goal might be, "When I read I love the way authors create leads that just seem to draw me in. I can't wait to keep on reading. I'm going to work on writing leads in my writing. I'm going to spend this quarter looking at good leads and trying to write them." A goal in social studies might be to read a map and be stated in this way, "My dad was so angry with me. We were on the way home from taking my sister to college, and he asked me how many miles it was to the Interstate. I couldn't tell, and we missed the turn off. I'm going to learn how to read a map. What do all of those numbers mean anyway? I probably can learn how to do this during the next week."

These goals are more specific, and they mention a time-frame. The time-frame keeps students on task, helping them to focus their efforts and attention. It also sends the message that this is only one of many goals that they will be setting during the year.

❷ **Devise a plan for reaching the goal(s)**—Just setting goals is not enough. Students need to commit, in writing, to an action plan. Based on their knowledge of how they learn, they devise a specific plan, including what they will do to learn the skill, what help they will need from others, and what resources are available.

❸ **Inform parents/guardians**—Parents/guardians should be shown the goals and involved in monitoring them. Many teachers have students write letters home, telling parents of their goals, plan of action, and progress. They, then, ask parents to write a response to their child.

❹ **Evaluate progress on a regular basis**—Having students reflect on their goals builds their metacognitive skills. As students begin to "think about thought," they gain the ability to: have an inner dialogue about the problem; develop alternative problem-solving strategies; and devise a plan of action and evaluate it. Questions to guide this reflection might include:

- ◆ What contributed to my success in reaching this goal?
- ◆ What obstacles did I have to overcome? What did I learn from overcoming these obstacles?
- ◆ What did I learn about myself as a learner in the process of reaching this goal?
- ◆ In looking back, what would I have done differently?
- ◆ While working on this goal, I discovered that I also would like to learn...

Students then record their reflections in a learning log. On a quarterly basis, they can revisit their reflections and write a summative assessment. In writing this reflective piece, students are forced to confront the tangible evidence of their learning and their ability to set and reach goals.

When students set goals consistently throughout the year, they are less likely to attribute their successes to luck, lack of effort, task difficulty, or ability. Realizing that their successes are directly linked to their own efforts, they are more willing to invest in their learning rather than looking for excuses not to learn.

Goal setting is also an effective and meaningful way of involving parents in their children's work. Too often, middle school parents do not have any idea of what their children are learning in school. After working with her child on goals, one parent responded, "For the first time in years, I know what my child is learning."

As students set goals and find ways to attain them, they are learning a life-long skill which will contribute to future successes beyond the classroom walls. They also learn the intrinsic reward of persistence in achieving difficult tasks.

In 1991, I worked with a special education class in Cleveland, Ohio. Their teacher, Madeleine Macklin, expressed some concern as she returned to her classroom after the summer training, "I can feel tension building inside of me. I keep convincing myself that I can do it. We will support as well as challenge each other to succeed in this class."

Over the year, I watched her students undergo a dramatic change. At first her students were shocked at the expectations and the goal setting, and they rebelled. One student wrote, "She expects us to write every day. This is abuse." Later, this same student wrote, "Writing is good because you are expressing yourself. Sometimes you are alone, and you want to talk to yourself. So you write."

Many struggled to become autonomous learners. For years, they had relied on teachers to give them the answers and to tell them what to learn, rescuing them from the harder work of learning. A frustrated student said, "Listening to the teacher was easy; writing it down was the hard part." Another student complained, "The teacher kept a pencil in my hand; I couldn't get out of it."

But their teacher's dedication and their own hard work paid off. At the end of the year, the class published an anthology of their writings entitled, "What a Collection!" They invited relatives, friends, central office administrators, the principal, and other staff members to attend a tea where they presented their anthology. Parents and grandparents, themselves frustrated by years of low expectations for their children, cried proud tears. Finally, they had tangible evidence that their children could be successful learners. No wonder they applauded with writing such as this:

from "Whistle of the Train" by Nick Lefkowski

I was six years old at the time my grandfather took me on top of the bridge on 55th Street. We watched the long trains go by. There were about twenty cars that passed, and the last car was the caboose. The man in the caboose waved good-bye to me.

Then grandfather and I walked down the hill to pick herbal tea by the tracks. Grandfather's teas are good enough for anyone to drink. We gathered leaves from plants with clusters of white flowers and placed them in large black trash bags. Grandfather had enough tea for the whole neighborhood.

As I grew older, I wanted to go the tracks without grandpa. I wanted to climb down the hill and experience the tracks in a new way. Lony, my friend, lived next to the tracks so he was willing to go along.

I thought I knew the tracks, but we went much further than the tea plants where grandpa and I had been. Soon we found ourselves under a freeway bridge going up to the Broadway exit. I never even knew this existed.

This was an entirely new world. The grass was so tall that it was practically over my head. We cleared our way by hitting it with sticks, making a pathway. The grass was filled with snakes ready to attack, possums, raccoons, and sewer rats. I wished that I would have had my bb gun with me.

Suddenly, we heard a car in the distance. Our hearts started pounding, and we felt dizzy. We didn't know who it was. Just then a security guard pulled over and yelled, "Get out of here." Lon bravely said, "No" and threw a rock at the car. We both decided that we should get home right away. We ran faster than a flash. (from "A Writing to Learn Sampler." *Basic Education.* October 1992.)

As Nick, a tall, lanky boy, read this piece, I remembered the day he produced it. We had talked about his grandpa and him and how they had done everything together. Then he said things began to change; he didn't want to do anything with his grandpa. As a result of this conversation, Nick began to write feverishly. When the period ended, he didn't want to stop. He left reluctantly. Throughout the day, he kept reappearing in the room, cutting his other classes because he felt compelled to write. Spurred on by his success with this piece, he planned to do a series of short stories about his grandfather and him. Prior to this experience, Nick had never written anything more than a paragraph, for he thought that he hated to write. Imagine his own celebration when he found there was a writer within—just waiting to be published!

At their publishing celebration, each student was given a certificate of achievement. One student proudly proclaimed, "I've never worked this hard to earn anything. I'm going to hang it on my wall. Whenever I think something is too hard for me, I'll look at it, and it will remind me that I can do anything if I keep on trying" (Bimes-Michalak 1992, 4).

In order for goals to be a valuable instructional approach, there must be a strong teacher commitment to them. Students should perceive goals as being a point of departure for all learning in the class. Therefore, goal setting must become an integral part of all instruction. With goal setting, students are motivated because the desire to learn comes from within and is not teacher-manufactured.

HELPING STUDENTS BY
NOT LETTING THEM OFF THE HOOK

Finding the balance between being a demanding and nurturing teacher is always difficult. Most of us went into teaching because we care about students deeply. However, our caring can create problems for our students, locking them into a life-long pattern of dependency.

Out of compassion for students, who come to them lacking the essential skills that will allow them to be participants in society, teachers sometimes fail to set high standards and to challenge them. In a study of minority, at-risk students, Spencer and Dornbush observed that some concerned teachers substituted "warmth and affability" for challenge and high expectations, resulting in a kind of "racism without racists" (Spencer and Dornbush 1992, 142-43).

Evidence of this destructive and inappropriate affability is found in urban classrooms. When students are faced with problems, teachers find themselves wanting to rescue them—to make life more bearable. Thus, instead of seeing students as capable individuals, they tend to see them as defeated victims. Not wanting to add to their problems, or to create additional stress and confrontations, they "help" them by extending deadlines, accepting excuses for incomplete homework and tardiness, giving high grades for minimal or mediocre work, and tolerating inappropriate behavior. Since most of us really don't like confrontations in the classroom, it is, sometimes, easier to go on rather than to hold students responsible for the consequences of their choices and behavior.

Ironically, this "care-free" existence of never having to deal with the consequences of their behavior really destroys students' self-esteem. We, unintentionally, send them this destructive message: there is no bottom line. Absences, incomplete work, and inappropriate behavior will always be accepted by those you work with. And they learn our lesson well, for they will always look to others to either tolerate their problems or to solve them.

I will never forget a group of angry and disillusioned students in Washington, DC. They had been part of a cooperative program to bridge the gap between school and work. As part of the program, they attended school part of the day and then trained at the workplace in the afternoon. If they were successful, they would be hired after graduation as full-time employees. Most of them had not been hired by the companies. In listening to them talk about the experience, a common theme emerged: Why weren't you more demanding of us? Why did you tolerate our being late to class and not completing assignments? Why didn't you tell us we wouldn't be able to hang out? Why did you make excuses for us?

These students were set up for failure by well-meaning teachers. They were robbed of the joy of becoming autonomous, responsible persons. When we make excuses for students, we rob them of the esteem that comes from knowing that others can count on them. Furthermore, when we rescue students, we create a hostile dependency, and they unwillingly cling to us, lacking the self reliance to become independent. When faced with an array of complex problems and responsibilities, they become nonfunctional.

Steven E. Landried (1989) calls this rescuing of students educational enabling. He defines enablers as, "people who allow students (or colleagues) to be lazy or irresponsible without feeling appropriate consequences for their behaviors," and states that we must continually, "assess the degree to which we inadvertently encourage and reinforce irresponsible behaviors that essentially undermine students' self-esteem" (79). Landried concluded that adults in the school can break this pattern of enabling by "modeling first-rate standards of performance and reinforcing the idea that significant learning and personal growth come only from hard work and persistence" (82).

As teachers, it's difficult to admit that many of our actions may actually let students off the hook, dramatically escalating the problems in our classrooms. In attempting to help students, we may be assuming their responsibilities and setting them up for future failures beyond our classrooms. Furthermore, in allowing students to escape the responsibility for their behavior and the consequences, we have let them fall into irresponsible patterns of responses.

NOT ACCEPTING "I Can't"

One way to stop rescuing students is to not let them off the hook when they say, "I can't." Instead, ask students to take out their learning logs and to write down exactly why they feel they can't do the task and what they need to be able to complete it. Then hold a quick conference with the student, devising a plan of action to turn the can't into a can. Many times, this "can't" will be adopted by the student as a goal.

When students are held accountable for their "I can'ts," they utter this statement much less frequently and with much more sincerity. More importantly, as they turn their shortcomings into genuine successes, they experience the ego-building triumph of being able to overcome obstacles and adversity with hard work and persistence. They learn the value of challenging themselves and working rather than making excuses for themselves.

HOLDING STUDENTS RESPONSIBLE FOR HOMEWORK

The benefits of homework are indisputable; however, some students feel as if they are exempt from it and avoid it all cost, causing a great amount of frustration for teachers and for faithful students who complete it. In handling the homework dilemma, it's important to ask ourselves a series of questions:

◆ Does the homework genuinely contribute to the quality of learning in our classes, or is it just busy work?

◆ What happens with the homework? Is something done with it, or does it exist in isolation from the instruction? What are the consequences for students not having their homework completed?

◆ Are our demands reasonable?

◆ Do students understand the reasons for the homework?

The results of this rethinking should be shared with students, making sure that they understand the role of homework in the class . The next step is to inform parents of your policy and to involve them in monitoring the assignments. Many teachers have found that the easiest way to inform parents is through the format of a friendly letter. Nancy Robinson and Kay Arnold, teachers at Southern Middle School in Louisville, Kentucky, send the letter in Fig. 1.8 home at the beginning of the school year.

Parents have responded well to the letter, feeling that they are a valued part of their children's instruction. In fact, many parents and children have begun to share books, having interesting conversations about their reading. One student recorded in her reading log, "I can't believe that mom went out and bought me the JFK book after we were talking about him. It wasn't my birthday or anything. I can't wait to read it." This is an urban parent responding to her child's thirst for knowledge. The sad reality is that, many times, we dismiss urban parents, thinking that they do not want to be involved in their children's schooling and never giving them a chance to respond to their children's work.

Sharon Cary Brown, a social studies teacher at Ooletewah Middle School in Chattanooga, Tennessee, has added a new requirement to her students' writing assignments. Recently, she sent the letter in Fig. 1.9 home to the parents of her students.

Parents' responses included:

I enjoyed participating in this assignment. Thank you for giving us the opportunity.

Excellent exercise but needs to be done on a weekly basis!

I had a blast!

Dear Southern Parent:

We wish to welcome your son or daughter to our language arts classroom. We started an exciting new program at Southern two years ago—Integrated Language Arts or ILA. ILA is a blend of writing, reading, listening, and speaking skill building. In order to facilitate the program, your child is in our class for approximately two hours each day.

Because reading and writing are fundamental, your child's homework is based on these skills. He or she is expected to read twenty minutes each night, Monday through Thursday, and respond in a reading-writing log. These written responses should be a minimum of one-half page each day, for a total of two pages each week. This folder should be kept at home during the week and brought to school on Fridays. Please ask to see your child's log each week, respond to his/her writing, and put your signature on the weekly work.

As an eighth grader this year, your student will be compiling a KERA required writing portfolio for state requirements. A completed writing portfolio is due in March, and we will notify you if your child is not on track on this project or is falling behind in class. Attendance is very important to meet all of these goals, so please see that your child comes to school regularly, and notify the school if he/she will be absent.

In order to create an environment that is rich in reading, we are building a classroom library, and we need your help. Please consider donating books for the project, including picture books, magazines, and paperbacks—new or used.

We look forward to learning and growing with your child. Feel free to stop by the classroom and learn with us. We always welcome parent input, and we hope to see you at Open House in September. Please tear off the form at the bottom and have your child return it. (You may want to hang this on the refrigerator to remind your student of Friday's weekly log!)

Sincerely,

Kay Arnold and Nancy Robison

I have read about the ILA program and am aware that my child will have required reading and writing each night for homework.

Signature Date

Fig. 1.8 Involving and informing parents

Dear Parents:

Throughout this school year, we are endeavoring to develop and polish your child's writing skills. During second semester all eighth grade students will take a state writing test. Therefore, writing skills are being incorporated in all classes.

Your child has already completed one major writing assignment in history class the first nine weeks. Tonight, the final draft to a second major writing assignment is to be completed.

Since I feel that your interest in your child's work is so important, I am including a new requirement for all writing assignments. This will take about ten minutes of your time. Please read the student's writing and complete the checksheet as well. I truly believe that this three-way approach will be successful and your child will develop better writing skills.

Thank you,

Mrs. Brown

Fig. 1.9 Parents as evaluators

I think this is a wonderful idea!

Melissa put a lot of effort into her story. I thought it was great!

Let me know how I did on my grading. It's been a while since I've had English class! (I won't say how long!) I really think this is a good idea. I think Casey will get a better grade as a result of this 3-way approach. Thanks!

Out of one hundred and fifty parent responses, only one was negative. Clearly, these parents wanted to be involved with their children's work, and, with most parents, this is the case. However, they don't always know how to help their children. This talented teacher took the time to share the evaluation criteria with parents and asked them to respond using the check list, giving their children valuable feedback. Her principal was so impressed with the idea that he made copies of all of the parents' responses and shared the idea at a district principals' meeting and with the rest of his staff.

Many times students don't do homework because they feel it really doesn't matter, particularly if they don't get any feedback. They view it as another paper to put in file X. When students fail to bring their homework to class, teachers need to show a genuine concern by saying, "Something must have happened last night that kept you from doing your homework. I don't want this to become a pattern for you. Just write a note about what happened and what you will do in the future to never let this happen again. If you need some help in making a plan, I'll be glad to help you." This learning log entry is then sent to parents, and they are asked to write a response to their child.

One math teacher has students keep an on-going list of homework and other assignments. Each quarter, she has them turn their recorded data into a graph and provide an explanation of the graph. The graphs and explanations are then given to parents for a response.

Figs. 1.10, 1.11, and 1.12 show examples of handouts used to help students keep track of their progress and to devise ways to improve their work.

STUDENTS ARE MORE MOTIVATED WHEN THEY FEEL THEY ARE MISSED

Absenteeism is a major problem in urban schools. It's almost impossible for students to remain motivated when they only make infrequent appearances in a class. To combat this nonchalant attitude toward attendance, students need to sense that they are missed when they are absent.

One teacher, as a way of bringing closure to a class, has her students write notes to students who are absent. In their notes, they tell the students that they missed them, explain what happened in class that particular day, give the assignment, and include any classroom gossip. She gives the notes to students who live by the absent ones, and they deliver them. The absent students receive four or five notes from classmates, telling them that they are missed in a very special way. Students thrive on this extra attention, and they know exactly what they have missed. For the students who are writing the notes, they have had a chance to review their learning for the day.

LOOKING AT YOUR GRADES

1. How do this week's grades compare with others that you have received in this class?

2. Why are your grades (lower, higher) this week?

3. What will you do to raise them next week?

4. List the things that we did in class this week that you really understand.

5. Is there anything that you didn't understand this week?

6. What will you do to learn these things?

Fig. 1.10 Creating self-regulated learners

```
┌─────────────────────────────────────────────────────────────┐
│                                                              │
│        THOUGHTS FOR THE WEEK                    ▦▦▦          │
│                BY                                            │
│                                                              │
│   _____                            │
│                                                              │
│   DATE:   _____                                │
│                                                              │
│                                                              │
│   1. My happiest moment this week was  _____   │
│   _____   │
│   _____   │
│                                                              │
│   2. I really understand  _____      │
│   _____   │
│   _____   │
│                                                              │
│   3. I need to  _____  │
│   _____   │
│   _____   │
│                                                              │
│   4. I don't understand  _____ │
│   _____   │
│   _____   │
│                                                              │
│   5. Could you please help me with  _____    │
│   _____   │
│   _____   │
│                                                              │
│   6. I'm frustrated because  _____     │
│   _____   │
│   _____   │
│                                                              │
│   7. I'd just like to say  _____    │
│   _____   │
│   _____   │
│                                                              │
└─────────────────────────────────────────────────────────────┘
```

Fig. 1.11 Feedback through self-regulation

LET'S SEE............

    THIS WEEK I LEARNED.................

DATE   SKILL

Fig. 1.12 Helping students chart their progress

Another way of personalizing education and improving classroom management at the same time is to have students keep a class log . This log is kept in a central place in the classroom, and students take turns being the class scribe throughout the year. However, each student has multiple opportunities to be a scribe.

The student scribe is an observer, recorder, and commentator for the day. During the period, the student records vital observations, explains the lesson for the day, provides examples, gathers copies of handouts for those who are absent, notes special announcements, offers suggestions for the teacher, and includes any free comments. The scribe always signs the classroom log.

When students return after an absence, they check the log to find out what they've missed. Here, they will also find the handouts they've missed and the assignments. If they have any questions, they go to the class scribe instead of the teacher. This allows the class scribe to be the "expert" for the day. Nothing invites success into a class as well as having students become the experts, for they are taking ownership of the material and the class. Of course, class scribes are excused from homework so that they can prepare the log entry.

Class logs are an excellent management strategy, for they free the teacher to concentrate on new learning for the day instead of frantically searching for handouts and trying to remember the work of past days. At the end of the year, there is a complete, living record of each day's learning experiences written from a very important perspective—students'.

To make this strategy more successful, develop a format and spend time modeling how to respond as a classroom scribe. The first modeling session can be done collaboratively as a class, with the teacher serving as a recorder and intervening at appropriate times. For the next session, have students work in groups to do one log entry collaboratively. Collect these entries, and select the best one. Place this on a transparency, and ask the class to discuss why this is a good entry. Return the log entries to each group, and ask them what they would do to make their entry better. After these sessions, students feel confident about being a scribe, and their entries are better. Fig. 1.13 below illustrates a class log format that Shirley McCall, a Washington, D.C. math teacher, developed:

CLASS LOG

The class log is a record of what happens in our class every day. You are required to keep the log at least three times during the advisory. You may volunteer to keep the log one additional time during the advisory if you would like extra credit. As log keeper you are acting as a reporter, observer, and commentator for the day. Be thorough and write clearly. Start each entry at the top of a new page. Record the following information:

_____ Date:

_____ Homework assignment: Please add a box around this information so that it is easy to see. It should appear at the beginning of the entry, immediately after the date.

_____ Announcements: Include any tests, quizzes, or projects that are announced or special announcements that are made about changes in schedules and so on.

_____ Objective: State the objective(s) for the lesson.

_____ Account of activities: Write a detailed account of what happened during the class. Tell what we did and HOW we did it. Write down examples of some of the problems and EXPLAIN the process used for their solutions.

_____ Handouts: Staple in any handouts that are distributed. Be sure you include enough for everyone who is absent.

_____ Comments: Write your comments about the day's lesson and give the teacher any suggestions you might have. Also write any personal comments, making the log lively and interesting.

_____ Signature: Be sure to sign your name at the end of your entry. If students, who are returning to class, have any questions, they will come to you, the Scribe.

Fig. 1.13 Class log format for a math class

This year-long record provides an excellent tool for assessing teaching. Reading and reflecting on students' perceptions provides excellent insights for revising one's teaching and for remembering the students who have touched our lives, contributing to our own learning.

When I was co-director and instructor of the Pennsylvania Writing Project at Penn State, JoAnn Smith, a participant, secretly kept a class log of the Summer Institute. On the last day of the Institute, she handed me a Penn State notebook. As I opened the notebook, I was greeted with the words of Flavia: "Some people come into our lives and quickly go. Some stay for a while and leave footprints on our hearts, and we are never, ever the same." In the pages of the log, she captured the wonderful experience of our time together, and I will be forever thankful. Even though that has been ten years ago, I can still pick up the notebook, read her log notes, and suddenly those ten years disappear. I have tangible evidence of the footprints that those teachers in the writing project left on my heart.

KEEPING THE DIALOGUE GOING

To successfully motivate students, we need to keep the dialogue going by responding to students in very personal ways. It is not enough for students to receive our written comments on assignments. Students must feel that they matter, and good teachers manage to find small ways, in the midst of their chaotic schedules, to communicate with individual students. This is not an easy task when you consider that many teachers work with as many as 180 students per day. To an outsider, these teacher strategies may seem simplistic; however, both teachers and students know that these small, personal touches make a tremendous difference in our lives.

A teacher in Long Beach keeps students motivated by encouraging positive behavior. During the course of the class, she jots down specific, positive behaviors on Post-its and hands them to students as they leave. This teacher loves to watch students' surprise as they receive a positive and genuine compliment in writing—compliments that they can hang on to.

Since she started the positive notes, she feels there is much less negative behavior in her classroom.

Another way to encourage a personalized dialogue in your classroom is to send classroom telegrams—urgent messages. These messages can be congratulatory or express concerns. However, since the cost of a telegram is determined by the number of words used, they are always brief. Students are invited to send telegrams to the teacher as well. A stack of telegram forms is kept in a central place in the classroom, allowing teachers and students to jot quick messages to each other. By the way, telegrams require speedy responses.

Have you ever noticed how students want to talk with you at the end of the hour, and there is never time since a new group of students is entering the room? As a result, students may leave without having the opportunity to chat, increasing their frustration. Shy students also are more willing to write a teacher a genuine concern rather than to say it face-to-face. Having the forms readily available gives everyone an equal chance to chat with you. It's a way of saying your thoughts are important to me; they count for something. Here is a sample telegram:

**TELEGRAM—URGENT MESSAGE
(WHAT'S ON YOUR MIND?)**

DATE: _____

MESSAGE:

_____
_____
_____
_____

RESPONSE:

_____
_____
_____
_____

DEVELOPING A PLAN OF ACTION

How many times have you been in the middle of an explanation, and the bell rings dismissing your students? Amidst all of the confusion of students leaving, you find yourself wondering, "Did they make sense of all of this?" When I don't have time to bring closure to a class, I feel as if I've failed. Right now, with this chapter, I find myself responding in the same way. "Has this been helpful? Will my colleagues be able to make sense of motivation?" The following is a summary of items to consider in developing a plan of action for motivation:

❶ **Classroom atmosphere**—The classroom atmosphere is interactive, personal, informal, and invitational. Students feel that what they say and do counts. As they search for understanding, they find a high support system of peers and teacher. In this atmosphere, the students' interests and curiosity contribute to a rich learning agenda. Thus, students feel that they are contributing members of a community of learners. Within this community of learners, students' voices are honored; there is a shared sense of knowing (Students feel that the teacher is not the only source of knowledge); and collaborative learning occurs. The teacher has a strong sense of efficacy, believing that all students can learn. As a result, students begin to see themselves as capable individuals, increasing their own self-efficacy.

❷ **Self-esteem**—To increase students' self-esteem link it to effort and to performance on challenging tasks. If students consistently fail, help them to unlock their patterns of failure by getting them to look objectively at their failures and to understand why they are actually failing. Then introduce them to a variety of learning strategies so that they enlarge their repertoire of ways to learn, selecting the ones that work best for them. Self-competence grows as students realize that the power to do well lies within themselves, and they assume the responsibility for poor performances rather than looking for excuses. This self-competence continues to grow as students assume the responsibility and consequences for their behavior, attendance, and other tasks such as homework. As teachers, we need to be aware of the crippling effect that our rescuing, enabling, or feeling sorry for our students has on them. We rob them of the opportunity of becoming independent and functioning individuals.

❸ Self-regulated learning—One of the habits of the mind that we want to develop in our students is the ability to regulate their learning. The self-regulated learner is a motivated learner who will have the continuing desire to learn for life. To make this a reality in the classroom, begin by implementing a goal-setting program. When students set goals, monitor them, and achieve them, they become competent and involved learners. As students look at their accumulated goals at the year's end, they have tangible evidence that they have learned, and they are astonished. Goal setting is also an effective and concrete way of involving parents/guardians in their children's learning.

❹ Real-world, challenging tasks—In order to be motivated, students need to feel that what they do and say in school will have an impact beyond the classroom walls. When school work is limited to busy work, where students fill in endless blanks and circle responses, students are lulled into a coma-like existence, failing to see the future in any such work. They need to have cognitively challenging tasks that allow them to make discoveries about their abilities. To awaken students to the joy of work, develop real-world tasks—tasks that involve genuine purposes and real audiences. When work goes beyond a teacher-audience and has a genuine purpose, students are more willing to devote more time and attention to it. Invite professionals and adults to give students feedback on their work and to celebrate their achievements. Time spent interacting with adults in meaningful ways will generate an excitement for learning. Although real-world tasks are rewarding, they are not always easy to generate. However, real-world tasks evolve more naturally when teachers organize their teaching around thematic, issue-based units. When issues are identified, authentic assignments and tasks seem to evolve naturally.

❺ Personalize the learning—Although personalizing the learning is an integral part of creating an atmosphere for learning, it's so important that it needs to be mentioned separately. Consider that some students won't even approach a subject unless they feel that the teacher genuinely cares for them. Middle-school students are so vulnerable that they need to be continually reminded that they, as individuals, are important. Little things that we do each day can have a life-changing impact on students. Letting students know they are missed when they are absent, tucking a positive comment into their hands as they leave, asking genuine questions about their lives and interests, and providing opportunities for genuine dialogues all communicate that you care about them.

❻ Intrinsic rather than extrinsic motivation—Although it is easy to fall into the trap of providing extrinsic rewards to motivate students, the best kind of motivation is intrinsic. When students are challenged and discover that they can do more than they ever thought possible, they become motivated. Extrinsic motivations such as pizza parties and candy bars pale in comparison to the discovery that I am, indeed, a capable person, who can deal with the problems that life gives me.

Linda Moore, principal of Rogers Academy in Long Beach, joyfully joins a community of learners

When students are truly motivated, there is no down time for teachers either. As students move into the directors' chairs of their learning, they create whirlwind paces for us as we try to keep up with their ravenous appetites to learn and do. But isn't this better than facing a room full of corpses—a room full of uninspired learners? In an article, addressing the challenges of teaching, Asa Hilliard III views teachers as " . . .the mediators who provide or fail to provide the essential experiences that permit students to release their awesome potential." (35).

When Jimmy Carter accepted the nomination to become the Democrat's candidate for the presidency, he stated that the President's power to build or to destroy is awesome. As I listened, I thought you don't have to be a President to have this power. Teachers have this same power every day of their lives as they interact with students. Within each of us is the power to help students become motivated and competent learners if we view our classrooms as places of growth—places where students make exciting discoveries about themselves and their potential.

Christi Howarth joins a literature circle in her class as they search a text for understanding

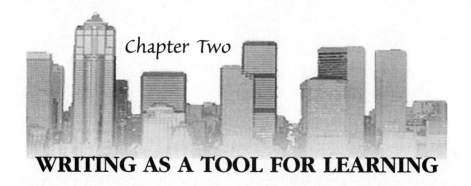

Chapter Two

WRITING AS A TOOL FOR LEARNING

During a recent staff development session, teachers were struggling to develop writing assignments to help students process their learning. A frustrated teacher blurted out, "What's wrong with having students read a chapter and answer the questions at the end? It has worked for years." A critical question is: "How well has it really worked?"

In thinking about this question, I was reminded of a classroom experience in a home economics class in Washington, DC. Throughout the training, the teacher had resisted using writing in her classroom, saying that home economics was a practical class—a class where students learned specific skills which did not allow time for writing. She reluctantly allowed me to visit her class.

The day's agenda was on the board: answer the questions at the end of a chapter on baking. Seeing students' unenthusiastic response to the assignment, I asked the teacher if I could do an alternative lesson.

Stepping to the front of the classroom, I stated, "I have a problem. Perhaps, you can help me." Immediately, I had everyone's attention. I explained that I was recently married for the second time, confiding that one of the reasons my husband married me was because I looked like Betty Crocker. One student said, "You know, you really do." I continued my saga, stating that as he walked down the aisle, visions of wonderful cakes and pies danced in his head. However, after experiencing a few of my culinary delights, he said, "You may look like Betty Crocker, but you're definitely not one of her kind of women." I hate to admit it, but it's true. Every time I try to bake a cake, it flops.

I gave this assignment: Based on your knowledge of the chapter you've just read on baking, write me a letter and tell me what I am doing wrong. The students responded with gusto. Not only did they give me excellent advice on baking, demonstrating their knowledge of the chapter, but they also gave me strong words of advice about what I could do with my husband! The room was charged with excitement as they listened to each other's responses with a critical eye. One student, who gave a wonderful, detailed explanation of how to bake an award-winning cake, ended with a P.S. that made us all howl. Her P.S. simply said, "If all else fails, get to know Sara Lee on a first-name basis."

As the class ended, students lingered. They wanted to know about the kinds of cakes that I had tried. One student even said that she was going to share her grandmother's favorite cake recipe with me, adding that it would be sure to win my husband's approval. Other students just wanted to know more about my husband, questioning, "Did he really say that stuff about Betty Crocker?" I replied, "Do you think that I could make up something that ridiculous?"

The point is: they were engaged and excited about the learning. That day, the teacher became a believer in the power of writing. She no longer saw writing as an intrusion but as a tool to increase her students' understanding of content.

This kind of meaningful engagement in learning cannot be generated by having students answer the questions at the end of the chapter. Most of the time, when we ask students to respond to textbook questions, we are simply asking them to recopy text. They can do this with very little thought, for they do not have to reformulate the information, making it distinctly theirs. The above assignment worked for students because it forced them to put their factual knowledge into a new, real-life context—one that they wouldn't soon forget.

When teachers assign worksheets and questions from textbooks, they lock their students into a passive and isolated approach to learning. How many times have we seen students not even bother to read the text, but thumb through the pages, finding the answers and dutifully copying whole portions of text without even grappling with the ideas presented in the text? Often, these robotic responses to learning are handed in and not even read by the teacher. Thus, it is not surprising that students feel writing is simply busy work, and they rebel by investing minimal time and effort in the assigned task.

Much of the writing in content areas does not increase understanding; it is simply a time-filler. Arthur Applebee (1981) who did a study of writing in the secondary schools, found that students do very little significant writing in their classes. Less than three percent of the time spent in writing responses to classwork or homework required students to write a paragraph or more. He noted that writing in the content areas consists mostly of copying short answer responses and circling answers— writing tasks that do not require students to think deeply enough.

These kinds of writing experiences do not prepare our students for the types of demanding writing and thinking that they will need in order to become productive and contributing members of society. An NAEP report addresses this problem:

> The results ... suggest that American schools have been successful at teaching students to formulate quick and short interpretations, but they have not yet developed in students the skills they need to explain and defend the judgments they make. The end result is an emphasis on shallow and superficial opinions at the expense of reasoned and disciplined thought ... A society in which the habits of disciplined reading, analysis, interpretation, and discussion are not sufficiently cultivated has much to fear (1981).

Despite our growing knowledge of writing, not much ground has been gained in the last decade. According to the latest NAEP Report, students' writing proficiency has not improved significantly; just about half of the students in grades 4, 8, and

11 value writing; students lack revision skills; and, as students age, they write less frequently on their own (1990).

As a society, we are paying the price for not producing literate students. A recent report on adult literacy indicated that nearly twenty-five percent of America's adults with an average of ten years of formal schooling had 4th-grade, or lower, literacy rates (Wagner 1995). One of the best ways to combat adult literacy is to show students that writing is an invaluable tool for learning. Students will only appreciate writing and become willing writers if we structure many opportunities for them to discover the power of writing and their writers' voices.

MAKING SENSE OF WRITING

Too often, writing is used only for the purpose of assessment—a way for students to show what they have learned. Therefore, writing appears only in finished products to be evaluated by the teacher. If unsuccessful students only experience this type of writing, then they will learn to hate writing and to avoid it.

It reminds me of when I took typing in school. During the warm-up periods, my hands, literally, flew over the keys. I could type, "Now is the time for all good men to come to the aid of their country," faster than anyone around me. Just when I was on my way to becoming a world-class typist, Miss Witherspoon would ruin it by saying, "Class, we are now going to do a three-minute timed typing." Immediately, my hands froze on the keys as I suffered an anxiety attack. Needless to say, I hated typing. When writing is used for the sole purpose of assessment in classrooms, students will experience this same kind of anxiety because all writing becomes a "timed-writing" experience.

When writing is limited to assessment, most students write only enough to convince themselves that they can't write and to convince their teachers that they can't teach writing. If we are going to produce willing writers, who can write for a variety of purposes and audiences, we need to extend our uses of writing in the classroom.

In the best classrooms, writing permeates all instruction and is not just used as an assessment tool. In my observations of hundreds of classrooms, I have noticed that these classrooms have one commonality: The teachers have moved away from traditional, teacher-centered models of learning. They do not see themselves as transmitters of knowledge. Instead, they view students as having the ability to be interpreters of knowledge and constructors of meaning. Consequently, they do not view their students as vessels to be filled with information but rather as candles to be lit so that they can burn on their own energies.

In these type of classrooms, writing exists in a more collaborative atmosphere, where teachers use writing to move students toward new learning, building on the resources that students have and leading them into more complex contexts (Applebee and Langer 1987).

Out of this collaboration comes the cherished belief that the process of knowing will lead to greater learning as teachers strive to find ways to give students ownership of their learning. In these classrooms, writing is used for a variety of meaningful purposes to enhance students' knowing. If a teacher is unwilling to move away from a traditional approach to instruction, writing will probably remain superficial and have very little impact on students' learning.

Keeping in mind this more collaborative approach to learning, Applebee's and Langer's (1987) framework for writing in content areas serves as an excellent tool for implementing writing in all classrooms:

1. To introduce a subject; to bridge the gap between prior knowledge and new knowledge.

2. To monitor learning; to process knowledge.

3. To extend or to reformulate knowledge.

BRIDGING THE GAP BETWEEN
PRIOR KNOWLEDGE AND NEW KNOWLEDGE

A science teacher, beginning a unit on bacteria, confided that he hadn't had much luck with this unit because students became frightened by the scientific names. As a result, he lost them immediately. Instead of starting his unit in the usual way, he decided to begin by asking students to jot down any thoughts they had when they heard the word bacteria. He also encouraged them to tell any family stories about bacteria. Students looked puzzled when he mentioned the word "stories," but they soon began to write. It seemed as if the mere thought of writing stories made it less threatening, and they wrote freely.

As they shared their thoughts, we heard stories about how someone had gotten food poisoning at a church picnic, how a relative had gotten blood poisoning, how a student's neglected leg injury had turned into a serious infection, and so on. Their bacteria "horror" stories were filled with an abundance of information about bacteria, and they seemed surprised that they really had so much knowledge about bacteria before they even studied the topic.

As the students told their stories, the teacher recorded a few words from each on an overhead transparency entitled "Fact or Fiction?" He announced that during the unit, they would be returning to these stories to see if bacteria really caused these illnesses and to find more information about the specific bacteria involved. Immediately, he had the students hooked because he had personalized the unit by linking new knowledge to prior knowledge and by using this prior knowledge as a wedge to keep students involved throughout the unit.

However, the learning didn't stop there. One student, looking exasperated, raised his hand and said, "Are all bacteria bad?" The writing and discussion had captured the student's curiosity, and his desire to learn had led to a surprising, teachable moment. As a result of his genuine question, the class was hurled into activity; they decided to investigate the positive uses of bacteria. They brainstormed about where they could get such information, whom they could interview, and even what kind of experts they could invite to class.

The excitement grew as another student asked, "How do bacteria grow? Can we grow some?" Something as simple as having students write to access their prior knowledge led to this class redefining the direction of the unit and designing meaningful tasks—tasks based on students' need to know. This class definitely had taken charge of its learning—learning that would take them beyond the classroom and into the real world. The unit had a new life of its own—an inquiry-based one—because of the students' desire to learn.

In talking with the teacher after class, he said that at one point he almost squelched the learning and caught himself just in time. As students were telling their stories, he felt obligated to tell them that some of their stories were based on inaccurate information about bacteria. However, thoughtfulness and creativity emerged, salvaging the learning. Instead, an idea germinated that would allow him to seize the opportunity to use their stories as a vehicle for further inquiry and investigation. Thus, he recorded their stories on the overhead under the title of "Fact or Fiction," announcing that they would be investigating their stories throughout the unit. Fortunately, this talented teacher understood that he should build on his students' knowledge. He could then place the new knowledge into a meaningful context. Although this teacher didn't realize it, he had exchanged places with his students, letting them take control of the learning. As a result of the day's lesson, the unit changed. With the able help of his students, instructional tasks were designed to help them to evaluate their prior knowledge about bacteria and to extend the new knowledge to practical applications.

The initial writing in this lesson had become much more than just a once-and-done activity to engage students. During the unit, their investigations led them to other kinds of writing, including lab reports, scientific notations kept in a science log, a professional journal article, analytical writing, hypothetical writing, and a script for an instructional video on bacteria, based on their investigations. Thus, writing served as a vehicle for learning throughout the entire unit.

The technique that this teacher used initially to access his students' knowledge is called structured freewriting. In structured freewriting, students are given a topic and are asked to write continuously for a short period of time, without thinking about correctness, grammar, spelling, or syntax. In putting their critical selves aside, students are free to write quickly, discovering what it is they know or don't know about a topic.

Although this kind of freewriting is a wonderful way to access knowledge, it is not always effective for all students, and it can be overused. Whenever a strategy is overused, it usually becomes ineffective. Peter Elbow (1981) suggests loop procedures— procedures to encourage divergent thinking about a topic (59-77). These include:

▶ First thoughts	▶ Prejudices
▶ Instant version	▶ Dialogues
▶ Narrative thinking	▶ Stories-Incidents
▶ Scenes	▶ Portraits
▶ Vary the audience	▶ Vary the writer
▶ Errors	▶ Lies

The science teacher extended the structured freewriting on the topic of bacteria to include one of Elbow's loop writing strategies—stories-incidents. In this particular class, very few students chose to freewrite about bacteria. Instead, they chose to write their bacteria stories. However, not all of these loop strategies work well in all content areas and for all assignments in generating information. For instance, in social studies classes prejudices, dialogues, stories, and scenes work particularly well.

When students have experienced years of failure, they need to feel that a subject is approachable, or they'll give up before even trying, putting their heads down on their desks and tuning out. Writing is a powerful way of edging these reluctant learners into learning by helping them remember that within each of them is an untapped fountain of knowledge. We often forget, what the science teacher discovered through writing: Students come to us with pockets of authority which will enrich the learning in our classes beyond our wildest expectations.

The mosaic is another strategy used to access prior knowledge. This activity, designed in a WTL project in Bakersfield, California, builds upon the concept that learning is very much like a mosaic—a unique and colorful design created by many different pieces. The learner never knows exactly how the pieces are going to fit together or what wonderful design will emerge.

For instance, to begin a unit on immigration, the mosaic technique would be used in this way:

❶ Place students into groups and distribute three sheets of the same colored construction paper to each group. Have one student tear the construction paper into small, irregular pieces. Tell the students that they will have five minutes to generate as much information as possible on the topic of immigration. So that all students are included, each student takes a turn placing a word or phrase, regarding immigration, on a piece of the torn construction paper. If a student can't think of anything, he or she passes, and the next student proceeds. (Some words and phrases that students generated on the topic of immigration were: courage, unknown, crossing over, separation, rejection, a better life, education, money, jobs, wetbacks, border patrol, hope, economic advantages, freedom, desperate, imprisoned, regrets, prejudices, stereotypes, fear, leaving family and property behind, Ellis Island, integration, acceptance, push-pull factor, adjustments, disappointments, danger, climbing, dreams, thinking of the future, escape, subsidized, welfare, and responsibilities.)

❷ At the end of the time, instruct students to use their words to create a symbolic or graphic representation of the topic. (For instance, for immigration a symbol might be a dollar sign to represent the economy of immigration, a stick figure between two lines to represent the push-pull factor, a boat to represent the crossing of borders.) These symbols are then glued onto a large piece of construction paper. After they finish their design, they write a brief statement about their topic. The group then tapes their design to a wall in the class and selects a person to share their symbol and five of their words with the class.

❸ Before the presentations begin, each group receives three more sheets of a different colored construction paper. Once again, students are instructed to tear this new construction paper into small, irregular pieces. As the groups present five of their words to the class, they listen carefully, adding any words that their group missed on the newly torn pieces of construction paper. After each group reports, the students enlarge or expand their symbolic representations by adding these new pieces to their mosaic design.

❹ Then the students are asked to look at their designs and to place the words or phrases into categories. *(For example, some categories for immigration might be the economy, the push-pull factor, acceptance, etc. In reality, these categories will eventually become the issues to be studied in the unit.)*

❺ After they find their categories, students generate at least one question for each category that they would like to investigate during the unit.

❻ As groups share their categories and questions, they are compiled into a class list of categories and questions. These then become the issues and the big questions that students will investigate during the unit.

❼ Students brainstorm on what kind of activities and classroom tasks they will need to do to guide the investigations of their issues and to find the answers to their questions

❽ Their mosaics and issues are placed on the walls in the room. Throughout the unit, they are asked to add new information in yet another color of construction paper and to enlarge their original designs. In addition, they add new categories and new questions. They may also replace some of their original questions with better questions.

By looking at their growing mosaics, categories, and questions, students can see how their learning has grown, forming a new and wonderful design. As their designs are enlarged, they, literally, become a fungus, taking over every inch of wall space.

It's not unusual to walk into a middle-school and see an array of posters and construction paper projects spilling from the classroom walls into the halls. However, upon closer examination, many times the work is simply decorative, requiring very little thought and representing unchallenging tasks. As I think about the endless hours of cutting and pasting spent to make the displays, I wonder: What happens next after the cut-and-paste period has ended? It's as if the display has become more important than the learning, and teachers are in this incredible race to fill the hallways—using the displays as evidence of their students' learning. Granted, students' work needs to be displayed, but such work should represent demanding assignments and significant learning.

Unlike these cut-and-paste projects, the mosaic designs represent in-depth learning as students begin to place factual information into broader, issue-based categories. Students have taken on the difficult task of defining the issues to be investigated in a unit—a task that can be mind-boggling even to teachers. This higher-level thinking emerges from a non-threatening activity which allows students to access, to share, and to build upon their prior knowledge. Students respond well to learning that is based on open-ended tasks such as these, for the learning is based on their need to know and not on prescribed and formulated tasks which a teacher creates in isolation from students.

Some teachers use logs as dispatches, to get students involved in the learning as they come into the classroom, or to present an anticipation set. DonnaJeanne Nemeth, a teacher in Cleveland, developed a series of assignments on weather (see Fig. 2.1), all stemming from the log entries that students did at the beginning of each period. These logs provided a sense of coherence for everything that was done in her class, for they led into the learning of the day.

For years, many content teachers have begun the year by having students write autobiographies of their experiences with the content area. In this autobiography, students trace their earliest memories of the discipline, continuing through the last year.

EARTH SCIENCE: WEATHER

INTRODUCTORY ACTIVITY: At the beginning of class every day (five minutes) students will look out the window at the thermometer and the clouds and fill in the following chart:

Date	Clouds (draw)	Temp.	Record (type)	Air feels

(This chart will be kept by the teacher and passed out daily for two weeks.)

LEARNING ACTIVITIES:

1. Look at your weather chart. Write five sentences that tell what kind of weather matches what shape of cloud. Write one sentence that describes the shape of a cloud that is seen the day before a rain or snowstorm. Share this information with your learning partner. Did your learning partner give some interesting details that your writing was missing? Add them to make yours more interesting.

2. With your learning partner, use the reference books and the charts in the room to make a cloud chart. Include a drawing of each type of cloud, its name, the type of weather it brings and the kind of weather it predicts. These will be posted in the room.

3. Pick your favorite cloud and draw its shape on your paper (1/2 sheet of paper). Put its name in the center. Fill the rest of the shape with words that describe your cloud and the weather it brings. Join with your learning partner and help each other form phrases with your words. (Ten minutes)

4. The teacher will now model with the class the writing of the shape poem using phrases from the class.

5. Join your learning partner and read your poems to each other. Praise and offer revisions by answering these three questions:

   - Does the poem describe the cloud?
   - Does the poem tell about the weather it brings?
   - Does the poem fill the outline of the cloud?

6. Rewrite the poem with the suggested revisions. It will be posted in the classroom.

EXTENDED LEARNING:

1. Read aloud to the class some myths about weather, almanac entries, and folklore. Explain that people have always described the weather with self-written myths, for example—rain is the angels crying. As a class think of five more examples of myths to describe weather phenomena.

2. Ask students to focus on the clouds, trying to make up their own myth of how the clouds cause weather phenomena. Then have them illustrate their myth. Example: Thunder is the Mario brothers bumping into each other.

Fig. 2.1 Donna Jeanne Nemeth constructed the activities in this weather assignment from student logs

This is very helpful for the teacher to identify when, where, and why students may have begun to encounter difficulties and to have problems with a subject or when students began to discover their talents for a subject. Then at the semester and at the end of the year, students add this year's chapter to the autobiography.

Often teachers write their own autobiography of the subject, along with the students, telling how they fell in love with what they are teaching. Nancie Atwell's (1987) philosophy is that teaching middle school students is really just "sharing our informed passions" (25). The best teachers are passionate teachers—those who care deeply about what they teach, feeling compelled to share their subject matter and this passion with others. Beth Ann Rolleston, a passionate language arts teacher at Tyner Middle School in Chattanooga, wrote this autobiography about how she became hooked on books and how she feels about writing to share with her students:

> My mother always bought me books. It was her one weakness in spending money on me. I could not ever convince her that GAP jeans at $20.00 a pair were worth the expense or that the mall would be a lot "cooler" than Sears Surplus or Lamonts as places to shop for clothes, but take mom with you to a bookstore, especially a Christian one, and she'd blow her whole budget on books. You didn't even need a winning smile or a convincing argument.
>
> Buying–owning–reading books was necessary to encourage, more necessary than clothes with the right brand names. I didn't always agree, but I treasured books and still do. My biggest "commodity" or asset going into my marriage was books, boxes and boxes of them shipped from Seattle.
>
> Each book was an experience I couldn't bear to give up—an experience that I wanted to pass on to my children as my mom passed books on to me.
>
> I'm not sure why writing became so important to me except that it was easy after having read so much. I always had a secret desire to be a writer, an author. It seemed so glamorous—publishing a book. Authors seemed to be people who had somehow

"transcended" real life, somehow gone beyond into another more holy realm since they had written a book. Their lives would no longer be ordinary ... even though they probably are. I never really wanted to meet an author because the mystery would be gone, the mystique, the "other-worldliness."

Students appreciate this kind of honest and real writing, where teachers share a very personal part of their lives with them.

Barbara VanOast, a science teacher at Newcomb Academy in Long Beach, changed the autobiographical assignment, making it distinctly hers (see Fig. 2.2).

In creating her assignment, VanOast explained, "My eighth grade students are at the age where they are beginning to make choices—which science courses they are going to take in high school, what careers they are going to consider, etc. I want them to see that these decisions can be informed ones, based on their talents and interests which they have displayed during their entire lives." However, the assignment provided her with many valuable insights into her students. After reading their autobiographies, she commented, "I feel as if I know them so much better, particularly the ones who are so quiet in my class."

From reading their responses, it's obvious that this assignment caused students to pause and reflect about their experiences with science, helping them to make vital discoveries about themselves and their interests. In the following piece, Katelyn Bowers describes her awakening interest in astronomy and her concern for the planet in Fig. 2.3.

Brian Fischer traced his burning desire to become a pilot through his autobiography. In his earliest memories, he talked about loving to climb trees, his love of friends, and hating to take naps. In his reflective moments, he confessed that, "I really wish I was little again because I could have fun and not be so stressed out by school." In recalling his favorite early experiences with science, he mentioned: a field trip to the aerospace museum; a report on the flight of the intruders; rock climbing because "I had to overcome my fears;" and flying his model airplanes.

AUTOBIOGRAPHY ASSIGNMENT

Part 1: Talk to your parents about how you spent your time in your **pre-school days—birth to 5 years.**

What were you curious about?
What kinds of questions did you ask?
What were your favorite toys?

Part 2: K-5th Grade—Write about your science experiences, field trips, assignments, science projects, science teachers, etc.

What do you remember?
What was fun?

Part 3: Middle School—6th & 7th Grades—Write about your science experiences in and out of school, museums, field trips, etc.

Part 4: Look for a thread that carries through these first three parts which shows an interest or skill from **pre-school to 7th Grade**. Think about your potential:

— Your future.
— How you want to spend your time in a career; perhaps, a science career?
— What are your dreams and goals?

Part 5—8th Grade science experiences not yet assigned.

Fig. 2.2 Barbara VanOast's modified autobiography assignment

Brian confided, "I love to fly because it relaxes me and lets me feel free and do whatever I want."

Continuing with his experiences in 6th and 7th grade, he said that he learned about airfoils and how to make them. His spare time was spent in studying flying and reading about famous pilots. According to him, "Flight is the most important science thing that is around me daily." In the next entry, he confided that he flies his models daily and offered to bring pictures to

Katelyn Bowers
Newcomb Academy
Science
January 10, 1996

my Interest in stars

A long time ago, about 8 years, I went to Big Bear to watch Haley's comet. I can still remember how we waited so long just to see a light go whizzing by in the sky. Now I realize how some people like astronomers waited almost their whole life just to see that comet. Also, I remember the lunar eclipse and how amazed I was. Ever since then I've had a strong interest in it.

I always go to summer camp in Big Bear (Camp Oaks). I always love going up there because every single night (unless it's clouded) you can see how wonderful the stars look. You would think after 13 years of seeing stars you would get bored with them, but every time I see them I'm still amazed. But since I live in a polluted environment the chance to see stars has been taken away from me and I don't want my children to not be able to see the stars in a clear black sky, so I've always thought of a way to clear air pollution.

In my head at night I will always think of a way to get rid of it. Like you know where there's an opening in the earth, maybe we could take a huge fan and blow it out. I think of weird stuff like that or for example, take a large vacuum cleaner and vacuum all the air into it. Sounds pretty unreachable, but like most people say, I'm going to shoot for the stars.

Fig. 2.3. Katelyn Bowers traces her growing interest in astronomy

share with his teacher. Finally, he ended with this powerful statement about his future:

> *Building it yourself I think is much more respectful. When you make something you have more respect for it and you can feel the enjoyment when it flies. My dreams may seem out of reach for a kid, but I'm not a kid, I'm a young man.*

These autobiographical pieces are so rich because they are written honestly in the students' own powerful voices. Donald Murray (1982) stated that:

> Voice gives writing the sense of an individual speaking to an individual. The reader wants to hear a voice. Voice carries the piece of writing forward; it glues the piece of writing together. Voice gives writing intensity and rhythm and humor and anger and sincerity and sadness. It is often the voice of a piece of writing that tells the writer what the writing means (46).

MONITORING LEARNING AND PROCESSING KNOWLEDGE

Teachers, in the various content areas, will be more likely to use writing if it is consistent with their classroom goals and is unobtrusive. The writing must be perceived as an instructional tool, helping teachers to achieve their instructional goals. Content teachers consistently worry about how they will find the time to create writing assignments and then to evaluate all of the extra writing. In addition, they wonder how they will find time to add writing to an already packed curriculum.

For these teachers, writing strategies to assist students in monitoring their learning and processing textual and new knowledge make sense. Since the purpose of this kind of writing is for self-knowledge, and the audience is the learner or self, this writing does not always need to be evaluated. Writing for self-knowledge most often takes the form of learning logs.

Learning logs should not to be confused with journals. Although both have their value, their purposes are quite different. In journal writing, teachers set aside a time each day, usually at the beginning of class, for students to write in their journals. Most of the writing is non-directed and very personal. Students are free to vent their feelings, to write on self-selected topics, and to reflect on events in their lives. Sometimes, the teacher may make the journal writing time more directed by giving the students a topic. However, the focus of a journal is to allow students to discover the joy of personal writing, to become more fluent writers by writing more frequently, and to provide a storehouse of ideas from which further writing can generate.

Although learning logs may share some of these same purposes, their main purpose is to facilitate learning. Therefore, the entries are much more structured, providing students with an array of strategies to engage them in texts, to aid them in reformulating knowledge, to increase their understanding, to allow them to monitor their learning, and to set goals. In addition, the writing in learning logs may appear at the beginning of a class, in the middle, or even at the end. There is not a specific time period, such as the beginning of each class, set aside for log writing.

When teachers first consider using learning logs, they often ask the question, "How frequently should I have students write in their learning logs?" This is an impossible question to answer. To say that students should write in their logs two or three times a week makes the use of logs too formulaic. Log writing appears whenever the learning demands it, and the more logs are used, the more uses teachers and students will find for them.

MANAGEMENT OF LOGS

First inquiries about learning logs and response always involve management: Do I keep the logs, or do students keep them? Where do I store them? How do I distribute them? Do I respond to them?

One teacher solved the problem by buying plastic crates—one for each period. As students enter the room, they pick up their learning logs from the crate. The teacher then takes attendance by simply observing which ones haven't been picked up.

Although the writing in learning logs doesn't have to be evaluated, students need responses to their learning, and learning logs provide an excellent opportunity for teachers to have a personalized dialogue with students and to see how each individual student's learning is progressing. It also provides teachers with a chance to probe students' responses, asking them to elaborate more and in-depth. When teachers take the time to write thoughtful responses in learning logs, students take the task more seriously. Teachers feel that the time is well spent, for the logs help them to reflect on their teaching and students' learning, and, in many cases, redirect instruction.

Various teachers handle the time management of writing responses in different ways. One teacher has her students organize their learning log entries every three weeks and create a table of contents for them. In the table of contents, she asks them to star the two learning logs that show the most learning for them and ones to which they would like her to respond. Another teacher staggers his responses, never collecting them all at once, but asking a few students at a time to submit their learning logs for responses. Other teachers use learning logs as points of departure for cooperative learning tasks, and students get feedback on their responses from peers as well.

USING LEARNING LOGS TO PROCESS TEXT

My husband is a college professor, and we were asked recently to talk to a group of freshmen students about how to study. It was a timely topic since the freshmen had just received their first college grades, and many were devastated. In talking with them, I asked, "How many of you actually read the assignments, but when you're finished you remember very little of what you read?" Almost every hand went up in the room. In response to their perceived lack of comprehension, I asked: What do you do when you read? Most students indicated that they underlined text with a highlighter. (My husband calls this painting.) It soon became obvious that most of these students had not been taught ways to process texts. As I shared with them strategies that middle school teachers were using with their students, they were both astonished and receptive.

Thus, one of the best uses of learning logs is to help students process text. When students write in response to text, they are forced to grapple with the information and to reformulate the text, making it their own. As the college students found out, highlighting will not achieve this.

As part of my presentation to the college students that night, I asked them to revisit a 7th grade social studies class with me, assuring them that this middle school teacher would give them some concrete strategies to help them understand what they read.

In this particular class, the teacher used three different learning log assignments to help students reformulate and transform text. She began by asking the students to take notes using the Cornell Study Method, which she dubbed "Big T Notes." In this method, students drew a Big T on their papers like the one shown below. On the right side of the page, students took actual notes from the text, numbering each note. After they finished, they returned to their notes, and read each numbered note carefully. On the left side of the page—next to the full note—they jotted down a few words, phrases, or even drew a picture or symbol to help them remember the full note:

BIG T NOTES	AMERICAN REVOLUTION
1. Loyalist + Fr. victory = rebels	1. In 13 years, the colonies went from being subjects of King George III, victors over rebels ready to overthrow England.
2. Stamp & Sugar Acts, riots	2. England's passing of The Sugar Act of boycotts/1764, and, particularly, The Stamp Act of 1765 caused Americans to protest with riots and boycotting the stamps and economic warfare.

After they were finished, they folded the paper in half, and, looking at the left side of the paper, checked to see if they could recall the full note. They then shared their "Big T notes" with a partner. These middle-school students had created their own study guide.

The second log activity was for students to take their "Big T notes" and turn them into a four-or-five sentence summary. Again, they shared their summaries with a partner. After this sharing, the teacher asked for students to nominate a summary that they thought was particularly good. These were then shared with the entire class, with the class commenting on why they were good. Students were given the opportunity to add or to delete information from their summaries.

The teacher ended the class by having students generate at least three good questions from the material. They then shared their questions. Unsurprisingly, their questions were extremely sophisticated, revealing an understanding of the text.

During this class, students had three different experiences with the same textual material. When students manipulate texts in a variety of ways, it increases their understanding, and they retain the information much longer. As a result, they find out that they no longer need to cram for tests, for they know and understand the information.

After I had finished sharing this 7th grade social studies class with the college freshmen, one blurted out, "I'm sure that it will work, but it will take a lot of time!" This must be the same reason that teachers elect to simply tell the students what is important in a text. By the time students even get to middle school, let alone college, they are conditioned. They want teachers to simply tell them what is important so that they can memorize the material, regurgitate it into the teacher's brown bag of learning, and quickly forget it—all with very little effort or thought. Understanding texts takes a time commitment from both teachers and students. However, the pay-off is big. Students leave a class having learned and with a sense of confidence that they can tackle difficult concepts and material in the future.

Teachers feel that they have succeeded by helping students discover that they are, indeed, capable learners and persons, by providing them with a variety of vehicles to decipher and to take ownership of difficult and challenging concepts and information.

BEGIN CLASS WITH LEARNING LOGS

My daughter came home from school one night and made the announcement that she had a huge physics assignment, but she wasn't going to do it. This surprised me because Terri was a good student. She then said, "I won't have to because Mr. Brown will tell us what's important so I'll just take good notes from him." Terri adopted this passive approach to learning for the entire year, never having to encounter the difficult physics text. She let Mr. Brown do all of the hard work of deciphering text and learning the material. Without realizing it, Mr. Brown encouraged his students to adopt a very passive approach to learning.

An alternative to this approach would have been to begin the class with a learning log entry. What three things do you remember from your reading last night? These learning log entries could be used as a point of departure for discussion or for a group activity. The tasks then would be centered around students' perception of text, forcing them to be more involved in the learning and allowing Mr. Brown time to focus on their needs, based on their interpretations of the text. Besides, students are more likely to read assignments if something is done with them in class. Other open-ended responses to text that could be used in beginning a class might include:

- ◆ What was learned from the reading?
- ◆ What was interesting?
- ◆ What was confusing?
- ◆ What questions do you have?

Carol Skinner, a math teacher in Louisville, Kentucky, uses reaction guides to help students process text. Students, working in pairs and using the text for support, respond to a series of agree/disagree statements. Fig. 2.4 shows her reaction guide for a chapter on data analysis.

REACTION GUIDE: CHAPTER 3—DATA ANALYSIS

DIRECTIONS: With your partner, take turns reading and discussing each of the statements below: Put a check if you agree or disagree with each statement. Be sure to support your answer with at least one example. Use pages 64-81 in your book for support.

1. The best way to compare the prices of five brands of shampoo would be a circle graph.

    ❏ Agree   ❏ Disagree

Because:_____

_____

2. The mean and the median for a set of numbers are always the same.

    ❏ Agree   ❏ Disagree

Because:_____

_____

3. A multiple line graph is a good way to compare two sets of data.

    ❏ Agree   ❏ Disagree

Because:_____

_____

4. You would have to complete a frequency table before making a scatter gram.

    ❏ Agree   ❏ Disagree

Because:_____

_____

5. All numbers in a set of data are greater than the mean.

    ❏ Agree   ❏ Disagree

Because:_____

_____

6. A multiple line graph is like a line graph except in a multiple line graph two or more lines are shown to compare data.

    ❏ Agree   ❏ Disagree

Because:_____

_____

Fig. 2.4. Carol Skinner's students use reaction guides to help them process their math text

The students' responses to this reaction guide then are used as a means of discussing the chapter. Reaction guides can be adapted and use in any content area.

DIALECTICAL ENTRIES

Another way to engage students in texts is by having them make double-entry and dialectical journals in their learning logs. In a double-entry journal, students divide their paper in half, recording their actual notes on the left side and then their personal responses on the right side. Personal responses might include a wide variety of responses: what they think the text means; a personal experience that the text reminds them of; questions, and statements of agreement and disagreement. However, this strategy works best if a teacher first models a double-entry journal.

The double-entry journal can be changed to fit the purpose of the content. Perhaps, in a science or social studies class, the students might list problems on the left side of the paper and solutions on the right side. In response to a piece of literature, students might write quotations on the left side and their personal responses on the right.

Several of the math teachers that I work with are using double entry log entries as homework assignments. On the left side students work the problems, and on the right side students explain the process, comment on any problems they had in solving the problem, and ask the teacher any remaining questions. Robert Alford, a teacher at Tyner Middle School in Chattanooga, received the response in Fig. 2.5 to homework.

The assignment turned out to be very informative to Mr. Alford. One student who had done all of the problems correctly confided in her note, "I kinda understand this, but I kinda don't understand it. I get mixed up on dividing and multiplying." Several other students said that they had forgotten how to change fractions to whole numbers. One student, even though he had two of the three problems correct, felt comfortable enough to confess, "I don't have a clue how to do this one." These students may

6

Gossett M.

① $\frac{-1}{3}x = 16$

-1 $\frac{-1}{3}x = 16 \cdot 3$

16
3
48

first you flip the $\frac{1}{3}$ over so it read $\frac{-3}{1}$ then you multiply 16 times 3 and your answer is 48 I'm not sure if it is posotive or negitive How would you find this out.

② $\frac{12y}{12} = \frac{-108}{12}$

$12\overline{)108}$
108

9

first try to cross out the 12y and get the verible by its self next you in divide 12 to each side then you divide 12 into 108 and your answer is 9 I'm not sure if it is negative or positive How would find this out.

③ $\frac{9x}{9} = \frac{3681}{9}$

$9\overline{)3681}$
36
081

409

409
× 9
3681

8

first you try to cross out the 9 and the xarible by its self next you divide 9 to each side. then you divide 9 into 3681 and your answer is 409.

Fig. 2.5. Through a double-entry journal, the student pinpoints his confusion

never have been so honest about their lack of understanding in front of a class, but the writing provided a safe place for a frank discussion with an understanding teacher. In reading their notes, the teacher decided that he needed to review several concepts before moving on. More importantly, he had this insight before he and his students painfully discovered their lack of understanding on a test. The double-entry journal became an invitation to learn.

In using dialectical journals, the teacher is modeling a way of looking at texts more critically. As students become accustomed to using a variety of dialectical journals, they will eventually be able to design their own.

INTERRUPT A CLASS WITH LOGS

Sustaining a whole class discussion and keeping everyone involved is almost impossible. Some students' hands seem to be on a permanent springboard. Before you've even asked a question, their hands spring into the air. Other students seem to think, "Why even bother?" Not only do these quick responses shut down the learning, but they are often disappointing, showing very little thought. Terribly shy students never find the courage to venture an answer. In a recent interview, a truant student (a student who missed twenty days a month) confided, "I was afraid to raise my hand and ask for help with math. Sometimes teachers would be sarcastic, make you feel bad. With a whole bunch of classmates around, you'd feel even smaller" (Patterson 1996, A-1). For a variety of reasons, a portion of any middle school population will never venture raising their hands to ask or answer a question.

Stopping the class and having students write is an excellent way to include all students in a discussion, to increase the time that students have to think about a question before answering, to give frightened students a chance to rehearse, or even to refocus. Try these variations:

> **Think-Pair-Write-Share**—Tell students that you want all of them to participate in the discussion and that this is such an important question that you just want them to

think about it for a minute before they say anything. After they think about it for a minute, they turn to a partner and share their answers orally. (This provides students with a period of rehearsal to try their answers out on a smaller audience and, at the same time, provides them with an opportunity to elaborate on their answer by piggy backing on their partner's response.) After this, you ask them to write their answers. Then students share these answers with the whole class.

Develop a question—Ask the students to develop a good question based on the discussion and present it to the class.

Reflect on the discussion—Pause in the discussion and ask students to write about what they understand from the discussion thus far, to ask refocusing questions, or to record any of their wonderings and thoughts.

Write a summary of the discussion—Ask students to turn to a neighbor and to write a four or five sentence summary of the discussion so far.

As a culminating task in their language arts class, Kay Arnold and Nancy Robinson, teachers at Southern Middle School in Louisville, asked students to write a critique of their class. One particularly shy student replied:

> ... I also liked how we had class discussions. Because I think it encourages everyone to talk and not just let only two people in the whole class talk. But out of everything we did this year. And if I had the opportunity to do something different. I'm shocked to say that I wouldn't do anything different.
>
> And I know that this year is probably just another year for you all, but for me this was a year I'll always remember.

This student's remarks reveal that students can and will engage in discussions if they are structured in ways in which they can be active participants.

END A CLASS WITH WRITING

To bring closure to a class, ask students to summarize what they have learned for the day. Take time to share their responses so that they can hear other students' learning. For richer responses, have the class collaboratively construct a summary together as a model before asking them to do it individually. An extension of the summary writing is to have students turn their summaries into possible newspaper banner headlines.

As was mentioned earlier, some teachers bring closure by having students write letters to students who are absent. Another interesting way to end a class is to ask students to respond to the question, "What else do you need to know?" or "What should we do next to help you understand this better?"

In a reading/writing workshop, a good way to bring closure to class is to have students write in their logs. They can answer such questions as: What have I accomplished today? How satisfied was I with today's work? What do I need to do accomplish more? What will I work on tomorrow? In these workshops, students almost always do an oral status of the class report. However, having students write individually in their logs makes it much more specific, tangible, and personal, and these comments can also serve as a vehicle for goal setting.

ADDITIONAL RESPONSES TO TEXT

In addition to having structured responses in their learning logs, students also need the opportunity to respond freely to texts without the teacher giving them a structure. In the following log responses from a language arts class, this student uses the log to record his maturing reading preferences, to make connections, and to plan future work:

October 2
Even though it goes against my beliefs and past experiences, I read a Goosebumps book. My reaction was to drop it and start another Tom Clancy book.

> I probably would have, but I commit myself to finishing every book I start... Maybe I was just bummed out from reading such a large book. I admit actually, that it depresses me to start a big novel. The feeling diminishes after I realize I'm about half through. Some books end too soon.
>
> October 5
> The last two weeks I criticized R. L. Stine, and here I am, finishing another Goosebumps story. I am the "Supreme Hypocrite." Well, they do say everybody's a critic. I'm a "critical critic." I miss nothing. I just looked back through my other reading logs. I make a lot of connections... My teacher in second grade once said, and I'll never forget, that you should always after you learn to read, read to learn.
>
> October 9
> I'm starting a personal narrative. I don't know the title, or the format. I could write in diary form, story form, or poem form. It'll be ready in almost a month.

In these unstructured responses, students have conversations with themselves, making vital discoveries about themselves as readers and learners.

DEVELOPING CHALLENGING AND ENGAGING WRITING ASSIGNMENTS

Many times, we get lousy writing because we have given assignments without really understanding what learning we want students to achieve. For example, my daughter, Terri, came home with this first writing assignment as a sixth grader: Write a mini-research paper on Egypt. Use two bibliographical references. She was groaning about the assignment to me, and , not wanting to be critical, I said, "The only way to get this assignment done is to start." Dutifully, she collected her papers and went downstairs.

About forty-five minutes later, she reappeared, making the grand announcement, "I'm finished." I couldn't believe it . This daughter of mine had clearly set a world record by finishing a mini-research paper in such a short time. As I read her paper, I was astonished to see that she wrote exactly like the esteemed authors of the *Encyclopaedia Britannia.*

Not knowing how to even begin to tackle the assignment, Terri decided to recopy someone else's thoughts on Egypt. Terri wasn't lazy or intentionally dishonest; she was a frustrated student who didn't know what to do with the assignment. Nor are our students always dishonest when they plagiarize; many times they simply are overwhelmed with the task.

Clearly, Terri's teacher hadn't given this assignment enough thought. When she collected the students' papers, she must have been terribly disappointed in their writing. Quite ironically, as her students, she probably didn't know what to do with the assignment, asking, "How in the world will I ever begin to evaluate these papers?"

If we spend time carefully framing our assignments and creating accompanying scoring guides, students will be unable to fulfill the assignment by simply recopying knowledge. A good assignment forces students to synthesize their knowledge and to place it into a new form, giving them ownership of the knowledge. Creating a good assignment takes time, but it is well worth the effort, for it saves both students and teachers a great deal of frustration.

In making more meaningful assignments these guidelines may be helpful:

❶ Make every assignment worthwhile—worth your students' while and worth yours.

❷ Make each assignment unmistakably clear. This takes time, patience, and trial and error to learn how to make assignments clear enough for students to proceed confidently; teachers have to know precisely what it is they expect their students to learn.

❸ Provide your students with the audience and purpose for the assignment. Most students assume that the teacher is the audience, and they try to psyche the teacher out by thinking, "What does the teacher really want?" A lot of energy is wasted, and the writing lacks honesty and voice. When students know the audience and purpose, they will remain more focused.

❹ Create assignments that allow your students to write for a variety of audiences and purposes. This will help your students to become flexible writers, fully understanding that the writer makes continuous choices, depending on the audience and purpose.

❺ Make your assignments realistic; don't cognitively overload them. Have you ever tried to do some of your own assignments? This will give you a good idea of how realistic they are.

❻ Have your students write frequently for authentic purposes and audiences. Design assignments that reflect real-world writing, writing for authentic purposes and for audiences beyond the classroom. Students take revision much more seriously when assignments are authentic.

❼ When you give your assignment, share your criteria for evaluation with students. Consider making an assignment sheet, where the assignment is given as well as the criteria for evaluation and any deadlines. Students then have a continuous guide to organize and to revise their work. There is no mystery in evaluation.

❽ Structure your class so that students have opportunities to revise their work through peer groups, conferences, and self-evaluation.

❾ Allow freedom within assignments for students to find out what counts for them—assignments where students are able to write honestly and in their own voices. This means that students need to be given choices within an assignment as well as having opportunities to select their own topics.

❿ Share your own writing with students. They need to see you as a struggling writer. As they give you suggestions for revision, they will grow as writers, and you will too.

Writing to Learn teachers incorporate these guidelines through a type of writing assignment called Think/Write. These assignments powerfully link the processes of reading, thinking, writing, and evaluating to increase students' understanding of difficult content material. Teachers have found, as researchers also have found, that it is impossible to teach critical thinking skills in isolation, but that the teaching of these skills works best within the context of the content they are teaching. However, forget the research, what is best about these assignments is that they engage students and produce thoughtful writing and meaningful learning by causing students to think about content in new and exciting ways.

In Think/Write assignments, the teacher develops a hypothetical situation evolving from the content being studied. The assignment is very specific in that it includes audience, purpose, and form, providing students with a point of departure for organizing their thoughts and for taking a rhetorical stance. In addition, the assignment includes a scoring guide so that students know exactly how they are going to be evaluated at the time the assignment is given. Many times, teachers elect to use Think/Write assignments at the end of a unit rather than giving a test.

Upon completing "The Crucible," Anita Graham, a teacher at Muirlands Middle School in San Diego, gave her eighth grade language arts students a choice of the assignments in Fig. 2.6.

THE CRUCIBLE
Directions: Select one.

1. Write the letter that John Proctor might have written to his sons if he had had time before being taken to the gallows. Elaborate on the thoughts he would share with the boys now that he is at peace with himself.

2. Imagine Abby as the adult she would have become. She is writing a short autobiographical account of this earlier time in her life. Write in the first person as Abigail—decide on, and maintain, the tone and attitude she would have in describing this incredible episode.

3. Write a sermon that Parris might deliver following the hangings of Rebecca Nurse and John Proctor. Establish and maintain an authentic tone.

4. Hale is a troubled man at the end of the play. A person facing similar conflict may try to express concern in poetry. Write a poem that Hale might write to explain and evaluate the questions with which he is struggling. Your poem might take the form of a list poem, or a diamonte poem. See the teacher if you are curious about these poetry forms.

(The above prompts were developed by B.G Davis in *Novel Ideas: The Crucible*, 1986. Anita extended the prompts by developing scoring guides for each one.)

SAMPLE SCORING GUIDES
FOR "THE CRUCIBLE" ASSIGNMENT

Choice #1: Proctor's letter to his sons

Each of the following is worth 2 points:

____ Writing contains at least three main thoughts that Proctor has chosen to share with his sons.

____ Writing is thoughtful—the main points selected for inclusion in the letter are appropriately selected and consistent with Proctor's character and events in the play.

____ Writing contains elaboration on each of the main thoughts.

____ Language and tone are appropriate and authentic.

____ Writing is well organized.

Fig. 2.6a. The scoring guides vary for each assignment for "The Crucible"

___ Writing is in correct letter format.

___ Spelling and punctuation are excellent.

___ Grammar and sentence structure are excellent

___ Writing includes name and date in upper right-hand corner; title centered on top line; it is in ink or typed/printed; it is double-spaced.

20-22 A
18-19 B
16-17 C
14-15 D

Choice #3: Parris' Sermon

Each of the following is worth 2 points:

___ Writing explains and defends the witchcraft trials and the hangings.

___ Writing explains and defends the convictions of both Rebecca Nurse and John Proctor.

___ Writing contains one or more lessons/morals the listeners are to learn from the trials and the death.

___ Writing seems convincingly real.

___ Writing is historically accurate.

___ Language and tone are appropriate and authentic for the speaker.

___ Writing is well organized.

___ Writing is in sermon form.

___ Grammar, spelling and punctuation are excellent.

___ Writing includes name and date in upper right-hand corner; title centered on top line; it is in ink or typed/printed; it is double-spaced.

20-22 A
18-19 B
16-17 C
15-14 D

Fig. 2.6b. Scoring guide for the sermon

This is a particularly good assignment, for it gives students a choice of different personas and discourse forms—speech, autobiographical segment, sermon, and poetry. Students feel more in control of their learning when they are free to choose. However, whenever a teacher offers a variety of options within one assignment, it is important to make the choices equally challenging so that each of the assignments is equitable.

Although this kind of assignment and accompanying scoring guides take a great deal of time to prepare, particularly in the beginning, they are well worth the effort, and they get easier with practice. For example, Anita Graham pointed out that the lower portion of every scoring guide is the same for every assignment—the portion dealing with writing, punctuation, grammar, and manuscript skills. Thus, she only changes the top portion to make the scoring guide assignment-specific. This veteran teacher adds that her students became hooked on scoring guides very quickly and rebelled if she failed to give them one. This is true of all students; they feel much more confident when they know how they are going to be evaluated.

Andy Remak, a social studies teacher at Kosciuszko Middle School in Milwaukee, created the Think/Write assignment in Fig. 2.7.

In Think/Write assignments, the focus is on content. The assignment is used as a way of helping students to increase their understanding of content material. Therefore, the scoring guide should reflect this by weighing the content portion more heavily. In addition, the prompt must clearly state the content that you expect to be included in the writing. The scoring guide cannot request anything that is not mentioned in the prompt. In the above sample prompt, the teacher included vocabulary words so that this skill does not exist in isolation but is woven into a meaningful context of writing. Mr. Remak set the scenario in the first portion of his assignment, a scenario that engaged students and brought about creativity. When reluctant writers assume another persona, it gives them a new freedom, for it is not intimidating or threatening. Many of them write better than

YOUNG PATRIOT PAPER

You are a young patriot preparing to fight your first battle. Sitting under a tree on top of Breed's Hill, you look over the valley and watch the redcoats gather. Not knowing whether you will live or die, you decide to write a letter to your family.

In your letter include:

1. Your preparation for the battle.
2. Your feelings and fears.
3. Two historical facts about the American Revolution.
4. Three vocabulary words from yesterday's list.

Paper requirement—25 point scale

3 points— Is written in letter form.

3 points— Clearly describes *preparation* for the battle

4 points— Includes at least *two historical* events or facts about the American Revolution.

3 points— Includes at least three of yesterday's *vocabulary words* used correctly.

5 points— Makes the reader experience the *feelings and fears* of the young patriot.

3 points— The historical events and facts are woven into the narrative and not just stuck at the beginning or end.— *organization*

2 points— There are very few spelling, punctuation or grammatical errors.

2 points— *First* drafts, *revision*, and *final* drafts are all handed in along with a note explaining changes you have made along the way.

Fig. 2.7. Andy Remak hooks his eighth grade history students with this think/write assignment

they ever believed they could, and they begin to trust their own voices in writing. In a discussion on how to get the power of voice in writing, Peter Elbow stated:

> It may be possible to get real voice by merging in your mind with another personality, pretending to be someone else. Shedding the self's concerns and point of view can be a good way to get real voice—thus writing fiction and playing roles are convincing tools (1981, 313).

When teachers create assignments, where students assume the personalities of others, they discover that they have found a wonderful and engaging way to teach.

The second portion of the assignment gives specific content expectations. If Mr. Remak revises this assignment, he might want to weigh the content portions of the assignment more heavily, and add another criteria to the evaluation, stating that the letter is convincingly written from the point of view of a young patriot.

Marshall Benson, a math teacher at Horace Mann Middle School in San Diego, developed the Think/Write assignment in Fig. 2.8, offering it as a alternative to a quiz on angles.

Mr. Benson's school had taken on the school-wide goal of raising students' literacy achievement. As part of California's testing program, students were expected to be able to write proficiently in a variety of modes, including the problem/solution mode. Thus, he designed this assignment—a first attempt to weave writing into his already strong math instruction. At the end of the unit, students could either take his conventional unit test or complete this assignment. The results surprised him. Some of his weakest students elected the writing assignment and succeeded. He came to our after-school meeting, literally, clutching these papers and wanting to share his students' successes. Based on his students' enthusiastic response, Marshall became and advocate of writing and math classes—he even volunteered to take on a leadership role in his district.

KNOW THE ANGLES

We all know that families can get along together and families can have problems. Write a short story about the ANGLE FAMILY. Include as family members acute, right, straight, obtuse and their two cousins—complementary and supplementary.

ASSIGNMENT:

a) Describe an angle family problem and give a solution.

b) Use all of the angle family members referred to above. Your description of the four main characters (acute, right, straight, and obtuse) must demonstrate a knowledge of their math definition, for example: "acute was smaller than the rest."

SCORING GUIDE: POINTS

PLOT
Was there a problem mentioned? .... (4) _____
Was there a solution? .... (4) _____

CHARACTERS
Acute mentioned in story? .... (2) _____
Math knowledge of acute demonstrated? .... (2) _____
Right mentioned in the story? .... (2) _____
Math knowledge of right demonstrated? .... (2) _____
Straight mentioned in story? .... (2) _____
Math knowledge of straight demonstrated? .... (2) _____
Complementary mentioned in the story? .... (2) _____
Obtuse mentioned in the story? .... (2) _____
Supplementary mentioned in the story? .... (2) _____

TITLE
Is there a title? .... (2) _____

Fig. 2.8. Sixth-grade math think/write assignment given as an alternative to a quiz

A few years later, Shirley Kroll, a math teacher at Rogers Academy in Long Beach, decided to use this same Think/Write assignment with her students. She, too, experienced great success with the assignment, sharing this student response at our after-school meeting:

> ### The Angle Family's Problem
>
> For 17 years obtuse and straight got along just perfectly. They had a little baby girl named acute, and a teenage boy named right. Right always complained about being in the middle and how some people treated him like a child, and some treat him like a grown-up.
>
> Then one day obtuse (the mother) replied to straight (the father), "I can't stand living with a fat old man like you anymore!" Obtuse walked out the door and never came back. Obtuse wasn't fat like her husband, but weighed just a little more than right, although she knew many other women named obtuse that were nearly as fat as her husband.
>
> Poor straight was left with the responsibility of two children. So the two cousins, complimentary, and supplementary, moved in.

The following Think/Write assignments represent a variety of content areas and some of the students' responses to these assignments.

To some teachers the assignment in Fig. 2.9 may seem too structured. However, Major's students were writing only brief responses without any paragraphs. Since it was a science class, they didn't bother with sentences, making their papers very difficult to read. Therefore, she structured this assignment so that students would have to respond in elaborated pieces with a definite type of organization. In a sense, she was modeling an appropriate way to respond to the prompt. When she read the responses of her students to this assignment, she was assured that her assignment had met her goals. Before responding to the Think/Write assignment, Ms. Major had her students create a cause and effect graphic illustrating the effects of light and temperature on leaves (see Fig. 2.10) so that they could refer to this during their writing.

LETTER TO A YOUNG TREE

Pretend you are an adult tree writing to a baby tree who has never experienced autumn before. Write a letter to this baby tree explaining the following items:

1. Tell what happens to the color of your leaves and why this happens.

2. Tell what happens to cause your leaves to fall off.

3. Tell the young tree what other changes he or she might experience as fall approaches. (Changes in weather, daylight, animal life, etc.)

4. If a tree could have feelings, tell the little tree what emotions it might have as it experiences all these changes.

SCORING GUIDE

You will receive up to 15 points for each of the following:

1. In the letter, you are an older and wiser tree talking to a frightened and confused young tree. Do your words offer any comfort to the little tree? Have you shared some of your feelings about the autumn changes since you have been through this many times?

2. In another paragraph, you need to explain to the young tree what makes your green leaves lose their color. Have you used good science terms such as chlorophyll and pigment?

3. In a third paragraph, you need to tell the little tree why its leaves will fall. Put your science book's reason in words that a young tree would understand. Did you mention hormone and dead cells?

DON'T FALL THROUGH THE CRACKS!

1. Have you indented each paragraph?

2. Have you started each sentence with a capital letter and ended with a period?

3. Is your spelling correct?

4. Did you begin your letter "Dear _____?"

5. Did you end your letter with something such as Sincerely, Yours truly, or Love?

Fig. 2.9. Sharon Major, a science teacher in Louisville, structured this assignment to get her students to write more elaborate responses

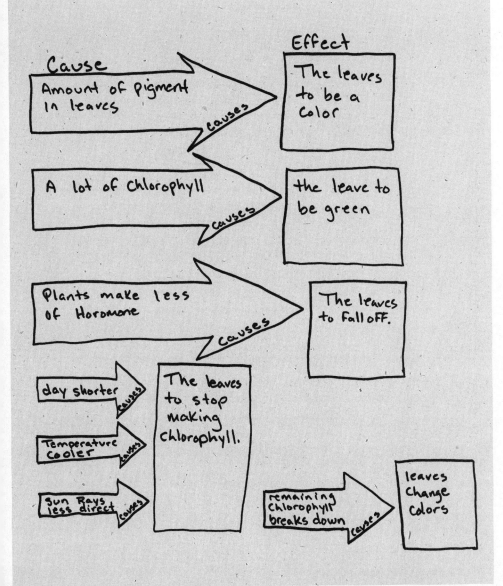

Anthony R.
Effects of Light and
Temperature on Leaves

Cause

Effect

Amount of pigment in leaves
causes
The leaves to be a color

A lot of Chlorophyll
causes
the leave to be green

Plants make less of Horomone
causes
The leaves to fall off.

day shorter *causes*
Temperature cooler *causes*
Sun Rays less direct *causes*
The leaves to stop making chlorophyll.

remaining Chlorophyll breaks down *causes*
leaves Change Colors

Fig. 2.10. A graphic organizer used as a pre-writing activity for the "tree" assignment

In reflecting on the scoring guide, Mrs. Major would probably want to state the science content she wants her students to master and weigh this more heavily than the other features. In Think/Write assignments, content always comes first.

The following elaborated response to the tree assignment was written by a student who had never written more than a paragraph previously:

Dear Young Oak Tree,

I know how you are feeling right now because of all the changes you are going through. When I was a young tree like you, I felt just like you. I felt lonely, bare and sad. I bet it is the way you feel. I am going to tell you a little about autumn.

In autumn, your leaves will fall off. When autumn comes with shorter days and cooler weather, leaves make less hormones. The leaves are controlled by a hormone made in the leaves. As a result, a layer of your dead cells forms where the leaves are attached to the trees. Then eventually your leaves will fall off.

Also in autumn your leaves will change colors. The period of daylight becomes shorter. The sun's rays become less direct. Daily temperatures are lower. These changes cause leaves to stop making chlorophyll. The chlorophyll remaining in the leaves breaks down and fades away. When the amount of chlorophyll decreases in your leaves, the chlorophyll no longer masks the other pigments. When most of the chlorophyll is gone, the leaf changes color. Your leaves will come back every year in early spring.

Also in the autumn the weather gets colder and the day gets shorter. When the weather gets colder the winds blow harder. You have some animals leaving you and some animals storing food in you. That is what happens in autumn.

> I hope you don't feel so lonely, bare and sad. I didn't have anyone to tell me what I have told you about autumn. I had to face the stuff that happens to all trees in autumn when I was a young tree like you.
>
> Well, got to go. Bye.
>
> Sincerely,
>
> Mrs. Oak Tree

When teachers begin creating Think/Write assignments, they often use the form of a letter, since the letter is non-threatening to students and represents a kind of real-world writing. As they begin to feel more comfortable with the format, they move beyond the letter and include a variety of discourse forms. The next three examples illustrate this concept.

Anita Graham's Huckleberry Finn assignment in Fig. 2.11 is a very challenging assignment for eighth graders, for they not only have to assume a persona, but they have to change an event in the story, predict what would have happened based on their knowledge of the text, and place all of this within the format of a speech. One word of caution, though: with younger, middle-school students, this detailed rubric may be overwhelming. Recent research shows that with younger students an elaborated one such as this may actually hinder writing. The study showed that, "Students utilized different kinds of rhetorical information at different stages" (Oliver 1995, 422).

School districts across America have written standards, or have adopted state or national ones, and are figuring out ways to weave these standards into the daily instruction of students. In almost every district where I've worked, two of the history standards are: the ability to interpret historical events and the ability to understand differing points of view. Virginia Hendon's

HUCKLEBERRY FINN

Your assignment: Imagine that Jim was not freed by Miss Watson, and Huck is brought to trial for his crime of helping a runaway slave to escape. "Become" Huck and write the speech you give at the trial defending and explaining your actions. Emphasize the main incident(s) that influenced your decisions, and why.

Each of the following is worth 3 points:

_____ 1. Writing provides background/context of the incident.

_____ 2. The significance of the event is implied in the beginning, but is not revealed until the end.

_____ 3. Writing narrates the scene vividly and memorably.

_____ 4. Writing contains pertinent dialogue, movement, gestures, names of people, objects, and sensory details.

_____ 5. Writing explains, in order, the main events of the incident. Writing sticks to relevant events.

_____ 6. Writing builds narration up to a climax.

_____ 7. Writing reveals the ultimate significance of the event—how it affected and changed "you" (Huck). It may be told as an insight at the time or from your present perspective.

_____ 8. Writing sounds authentic, and is told in the first person (I, me, etc.)

_____ 9. Spelling and punctuation are excellent.

_____ 10. Grammar and sentence structure are excellent.

27-30 A
24-26 B
21-23 C
18-20 D

Fig. 2.11. This think/write assignment for eighth grade language arts students presents and elaborated scoring guide

assignment in Fig. 2.12 is a beginning toward meeting these standards. However, it could be expanded to better meet the standard by including other points of view. This could be accomplished by giving the students several more choices such as:

▶ Write the speech that King George would give to his people, explaining why it is essential to keep America a colony.

▶ As a member of Parliament, write a position paper to be presented at a town meeting.

As students share their writing, they will come to understand the varying points of view of those involved in the American Revolution.

Sharon Cary Brown, a teacher in Chattanooga, extended the point of view on this assignment, having students take the position of a member of Parliament or a colonist, resulting in the lively, contrasting pieces in Figs. 2.13-14.

Hint: Although this is digressing from Think/Write assignments a bit, it seems appropriate to offer a hint at this point. If you are having students do opposing points of view papers, remember that position papers are always livelier if the writer has considered the other point of view and dismissed it in the writing with a counterpoint. Consider having students, during the drafting stage, exchange papers with someone who is taking the other point of view. For ten minutes, they continue the writing from this different point of view. Although, initially, it frustrates students. It helps them to frame more thoughtful arguments.

In a chemistry unit, Janet Underwood and Barbara VanOast, teachers in the Long Beach Writing to Learn Project, wanted to develop a culminating activity that would help their students to synthesize their learning from the unit and place it in a real-world context. She accomplished this with the assignment in Fig. 2.15.

Whenever teachers use a strategy repeatedly, they change it to better meet their needs. Anita Graham, who has been using

PRE-REVOLUTIONARY WAR

You are Samuel Adams. Your job is to convince colonists that they need to unite to gain freedom from England. Design a pamphlet that will attract the colonists' attention and say things that will convince them that they are not being treated fairly. You will need to include a specific incident such as the Stamp Act, Intolerable Acts, or the Boston Massacre that will "fire them up," convincing them of your point of view. Use at least three vocabulary words from the chapter. Use illustrations and color to help make your pamphlet attractive.

SCORING GUIDE

You will receive a possible forty points for your pamphlet:

10 points
Clear explanation of historical incident.

10 points
Compelling argument is given based on this incident.

10 points
In the form of a pamphlet; pamphlet is attractive.

5 points
Correct use of vocabulary words

5 points
Spelling and grammar errors have been eliminated, making it easy to read your pamphlet.

Fig. 2.12. Students enjoyed the creative discourse form of a pamphlet

Joanna Keyslan
10-13-95
4th period

Parliament Member Position Paper

As a distinguished member of Parliament, I feel I have much insight on the colonial crisis. My name is Jonathan Manuel Stewart III, and I pen this document in the year of the Lord, Seventeen-hundred and seventy-five. As a born Loyalist I have several comments on the issue of the taxation and other holds the British have on the colonists of new England. For one, England deserves the right and privilege to control each aspect of colonial life. Though it seems true that men deserve their own freedom, it is by the will of God for these colonists to become removed of those rights simply because they enjoy their freedom too much. What right have they to smother our reasonable rules and regulations?

Parliament has and is servicing New England in the most respectable way, control. Yet never before has any group of imbeciles refused to appreciate our regard to them. I do admit Parliament has appeared especially cruel to the colonies' needs, but seen from a different point of view, anyone would know we use the correct form of punishment for such misbehavior. New England colonists assume they know what seems best for them. This is obviously not true. What person in the right mind would refuse to quarter the troops that protect their families? Another thing I do not understand is how someone dump three ships cargo of perfectly fine tea into the Boston Harbor while dressed as Mohawk savages. Now that could not be the way they want us to perceive them!

These colonists have crazy ideas, such as attacking customs officials for the sole purpose of tar and feathering them! Brazen behavior such as this does not convince me that we should allow them more freedom. In fact, it makes me think officials should buckle down even harder.

One example of misconduct is the "Boston Massacre", as traitor-to-the-cause Sam Adams called it. I readily admit that a British officer began the shooting, but we would not have felt the need to fire, had the townspeople not attached us with snowballs and other miscellaneous items. I can only hope that activists such as the Sons of Liberty come to their senses and accept British rule indefinitely. Until

Fig. 2.13. Joanna Keyslan assumes the convincing voice of a member of Parliament

COLONIST POSITION PAPER

Tis such a horrible thing what the British are doing to us. Colonists. We work hard for every single shilling we earn. Tis no fair the British come and take it all away.

I feel there should be no taxation without representation. You see, We the colonists have no representatives in Parliament that we elected. Tis not right!

Just this week they passed the Townshend Acts. That means now the Redcoats are taxing the glass, paper, silk, lead and the very tea we drink! I have also seen British customs officials patrolling the dock. If we do not do something soon, they will be hovering over us like buzzards! As a result of this act, we have signed non-importation agreements and sent letters to the committee of correspondence.

I have joined a group called the Son's of Liberty. Paul Revere is the leader of our group. We have hung effigies in Liberty trees. The colonists have asked Parliament to repeal their taxes. They have repealed everything except for the tax on tea. Tis terrible! Just terrible!

The British become worse every day. I feel war is drawing near. Five people were killed the other day. We called it the Boston Massacre. Tis an awful thing what is going on.

They have also passed the Tea Act. There is no way on earth I am going to stand for this any longer. I am boycotting the tea. So are all the other colonists. Why should the British get any more of our money? We are all making homemade tea.

Last night some of the Son's of Liberty dressed as Indians and snuck on a British tea in the ocean. Tis a great thing they did, fighting for our colony.

Tis a horrible thing they have done, though. Those Lobsterbacks have shut down the port of Boston. I am afraid, afraid of what our town, our colony, our World is turning into. Things are all changing. Not for the better, but for the worse. Tis an incredibly scary thing. I feel a war is coming. All of us know some changes are going to take place soon. Some big changes.

Melissa Northey

Fig. 2.14. Melissa Northey presents an opposing point of view

Public Service Brochure

As a chemist for an environmental agency, you have been asked to develop a public service brochure that will alert the public about the dangers of common household cleaners and provide them with suggestions for alternative products. Since you want this brochure to be read, make it visually attractive and include valuable information.

In your brochure include at least ten household cleaners. For each cleaner, provide: the product name, ingredients, the chemical formula, the danger or hazard it presents, and a suggestion for an alternative product.

Scoring Guide

20 points ___ 10 common household products are analyzed.

10 points ___ Chemical compounds are correctly identified.

10 points ___ Correctness of chemical formulas.

10 points ___ Dangers or hazards are described.

20 points ___ Alternative Products are given.

10 points ___ Correct chemical terms are used; brochure shows a professional knowledge of chemistry.

20 points ___ Brochure is attractive and easy to read.

(When students finish their brochures, the class will vote on which ones should represent their class and be distributed to faculty members and parents.)

Fig. 2.15. Students synthesize their knowledge of chemistry in this real-life think/write assignment

think/write assignments for five years, felt the need to change her scoring guides, making them much more specific, after noticing that sometimes undistinguished writing received a top grade because the students had met the basic criteria of her scoring guide. As a result, she produced the assignment and scoring guide in Fig. 2.16.

The best way to end the discussion on Think/Write assignments is to end with characteristics of good Think/Write assignments:

CHARACTERISTICS OF GOOD
THINK-WRITING ASSIGNMENTS

Anita Graham, Muirlands Middle School, San Diego, CA.

▶ Give content top priority

▶ Build in stance and point of view and even provide an audience for writing

▶ Require imaginative thinking

▶ Get students personally involved in the subject matter

▶ Help students put their learning together and apply it to new situations

▶ Get students to think about what they already know, and build on the knowledge and experiences they already have

▶ Create situations so involving that students want to write and write well, using their knowledge in the process

▶ Are seen as purposeful by the writer

▶ Have clearly defined evaluation criteria

Name of Author _____ Graham/8 English
Name of Student Editor_____ Date_____

Essay Format: Evaluation—Judgment with Reasons

My Brother Sam is Dead

ASSIGNMENT: Imagine that 5 years have passed since the end of the Revolutionary War. The largest newspaper in the new United States of America has decided to publish a series of articles about the "The Worst Injustices that Happened During the War of Independence." Writing as if you were Tim Meeker, write a letter to the editor of the newspaper convincing him to include an article about the injustices that happened to your brother Sam and your father Eliphalet ("Life") Use the essay format "Evaluation—Judgment with Reasons" discussed in class.

1. (2pts)____In the **introduction**, you explain what you are writing about. You state your feeling that the suffering of your family during the Revolutionary War was so great that it needs to be written about. You BRIEFLY identify the injustices that happened to Sam and his father.
2. (4pts)____In one **body** paragraph you explain all about what happened to Sam.
3. (4pts)____In another **body** paragraph you explain all about what happened to his father.
4. (3pts)____**Body** paragraphs are well organized: each paragraph sticks to its own topic.
5. (4pts)____In each **body** paragraph, your reasons are well elaborated (marked by complexity and fullness of detail) and convincing.
6. (2pts)____Your **concluding paragraph** summarizes your argument and leaves the reader with a feeling that you have proved your point.
7. (2pts)____Writing is in correct **letter** format.
8. (4pts)____Your references to events from the book are accurate.
9. (2pts)____Your language and tone are appropriate: this sounds like a letter from Tim to a newspaper editor.
10. (2pts)____Spelling and punctuation are excellent.
11. (2pts)____Grammar and sentence structure are excellent.
12. (2pts)____Rough draft accompanies final draft; final draft is typed or computer-printed or written in ink (in cursive); name and date appear in upper right-hand corner, title is centered on top line.

YOUR SCORE/YOUR GRADE

Score	Grade
33	A+
31-32	A
29-30	B
26-28	C

Fig. 2.16. Anita Graham of Muirlands Middle School in San Diego, created this think/write assignment to help students master a distinct, required essay format

HANDLING THE INCREASED
PAPER LOAD AND EVALUATION

When teachers begin to think about weaving more writing into the curriculum, panic sets in. They wonder how they will find the time to evaluate all of it. After all, there are only so many hours in a day. To calm the hysteria, I remind them that much of the writing in Writing to Learn is for self-evaluation, for an audience of self or to help students decipher texts and to increase their understanding. Therefore, it does not require evaluation; however, it does need a response from teachers in the form of conversations from time to time. This takes much less time than formal evaluation and is helpful in informing teaching. The key is to *use writing for a variety of purposes.*

On the other hand, with more formal writing assignments such as Think/Write assignments, evaluation needs to occur. However, with a Think/Write assignment, you are designing an entire instructional component that includes different kinds of evaluation.

Too often, evaluation exists in isolation from the instruction, and the evaluation is left entirely to the teacher. When stacks of students' papers begin to line our desks, resentful feelings begin to brew , particularly if we feel that students have not put much effort into their written pieces:

Personally, I wish that I could regain all of the hours that I have spent writing copious comments all over students' papers, only to return them and have them take one look at them and throw them in the trash can. I now understand how futile my attempt was. George Hillocks (1986), in reviewing the research concerning teacher feedback, concludes that teachers' remarks, "regardless of frequency and thoroughness," have "little effect on enhancing the quality of student writing" (239) The reason it doesn't work is that students need continuous feedback during the writing process. When our comments are saved for the final product, they are too late to have a significant impact on the writer. In his review of the literature, Hillocks further found that:

Feedback has been characterized as negative or positive, intensive or partial, and even as marginal or termination. Except for positive and negative, these distinctions appear to make little or no difference. Given the time that teachers spend in making their marginal or terminal comments, this is discouraging (140).

However, students do need feedback, but it needs to be meaningful. And like it or not, this meaningful feedback does not always come from the teacher. In fact, peers are very important. In Think/Write assignments, the scoring guides can be used as peer evaluation guides so that students can give each other meaningful feedback on their written responses to the assignment. Responses to the scoring guide provide much better feedback to the writer than generic ones that many teachers use because they are assignment-specific. Also peer revision groups work better when they are given specific tasks, and the scoring guides provide this direction. The scoring guides can also be shared with parents so that parents can give students feedback. And finally, the guides can be used as a final self-evaluation guide in preparing final drafts.

By the time the papers are turned in, they have been more carefully crafted, having gone through revision. Students not only know the standards of evaluation, but they truly understand them, for they have been given multiple opportunities to work with them from the time the assignment was given to the time it was handed in. They also have received feedback throughout the process—all without much effort from the teacher.

Now, it's time to evaluate the papers. Scoring guides can save an enormous amount of time in the evaluation process and rescue teachers from awkward moments. Perhaps, you've experienced this scenario: Have you ever sentenced yourself to a marathon grading session, deciding that you will finally tackle a stack of papers—ones that have been haunting you for several days? Tired of feeling guilty, you roll up your sleeves and begin. About halfway through the process, you get confused. You mumble to yourself, "If this paper is a B, the one I graded an hour before couldn't possibly be." Then you frantically start changing the grades, reconsidering them all—adding precious hours to the process.

Despite the problems, you manage to finish the papers. The next day, you begin to return the papers, feeling so good about finally having them done. Just when you're feeling your best, a student raises her hand and says indignantly, "Why did I get this grade?" You desperately search for the answer, praying for divine intervention or, at least, a fire alarm. Lacking a graceful retrieve, you face the problem at hand, trying to reconstruct your late-night reasoning. The battle begins.

Scoring guides can virtually take the hassle out of evaluation and save you from these kinds of hassles. Grading is much more objective when it is based on a scoring guide. The 150th paper will have the same standards as the tenth paper. Thus, no confusion occurs, for you have identified your standards for evaluation.

When the papers are handed back, evaluation continues to be an integral part of the instruction. Instead of doing nothing with the evaluated papers, students are asked to get out their scoring guides and to look at a top paper, which has been copied and placed on an overhead projector. As they look at the paper, they have a discussion about its strengths, based on the scoring guide and their own observations. Then they look at their papers, and write a learning log entry. In this entry, they will analyze their grade, talk about what they will do to get a better grade, and set goals for the next piece of writing. No longer is the teacher put in the awkward and, often impossible, position of defending a grade. In addition, no paper exists in isolation in this process; each paper makes students better learners and writers. They see the progression.

Despite what the research cites, we, as teachers and learners, know that meaningful comments do have an impact on students' work. Do you remember the empty feeling and confusion you experienced when you were a student and you received a paper back with only a grade and no comments?

When making comments on students' work, we must make sure that they are thoughtful and essential ones; otherwise, we are wasting our time and effort. Many times, our comments are just too general to be very helpful. For instance, Hillocks (1986) gives this ironic example taken from a study of teacher comments, "Your first paragraph is too general. Be more specific." He points out that teachers need to be more focused and specific, giving this example, "Your first paragraph talks about the 'war effort.' Include a sentence or two that make up the 'war effort'" (240).

After struggling over responding to students' writing for thirty years, I've found these tips to be helpful:

❶ **Be honest**—Respond as a reader and not as a dogmatic judge proclaiming a sentence. Place the first person pronoun "I" in your comments. You'll be surprised how the "I" softens your comments, making you sound like a friendly reader rather than a critic. For example, consider: "I'm confused here. Could you add a few sentences to explain how this became such a big problem?"

❷ **Make your comments focused and specific**—Don't try to point out every problem that exists; this is very discouraging to developing writers. Focus on one or two items over several papers. Before students hand in their papers, I like them to do one last final evaluation by having them mark on their manuscripts. (Actually, this is a modification of Peter Elbow's technique of pointing.) I tell students that evaluation is not a monologue but just another chance for us to have a dialogue—a conversation—about their writing and I'll need their help for this to occur. I ask them to: mark smooth flowing lines over the parts that they are pleased with; place jagged lines under the parts that they are still struggling with and would like some help; and circle just right words. Then I have them write me a note telling me if they attempted something new and anything else they would like me to know or consider. When I evaluate their writing, my comments are focused on what they have marked. Thus, my comments are more focused and meaningful, for they have met the needs of the writer. When I hand back the papers, students pay attention to the notes. Their marking their papers also shortens the amount of time that I spend on individual papers, for it keeps me focused and guides my comments.

❸ **Make praise pertinent**—In order for praise to work, make sure that it is specific so that students can identify their strenghts and add them to their repertoire of successful writing strategies. "Good," or "Wow," may make a student feel better, but they do nothing to enhance writing skills. One student wrote in a journal once, "It's really frightening to do something well, and not understand what it is you've done." Instead, you may want to consider this type of comment, "You've really progressed in your use of details. You have selected vivid details to make your observation come alive for the reader."

❹ **Don't label**—Sometimes teachers don't want to really deal with a problem so they take an easy way out by labeling a passage. In reading a passage, a teacher may know that it doesn't read smoothly, but rather than analyze it, the teacher might simply place "Awk" in the margin. What does "Awk" mean to students anyway? Usually, they think that they and their writing are terminally awkward and just give up.

❺ **Suggest or ask questions**—Instead of correcting every mistake and fixing writing for students, ask questions or make suggestions, giving them the problem. When you ask a question, students understand that you expect a response, and the problem is theirs to consider. When teachers correct or fix writing, they take the ownership of the writing away from their students. This approach also denies students' voices, for it gives the impression that there is only one correct way to write—the teacher's way. Revising and editing are the job of the writer, and the best teachers of writing are friendly editors.

There have been a multitude of books and articles published on writing across the content areas and writing in general. However, whenever I go into classrooms, I am continually astonished at how much I still learn about writing. The talented and thoughtful teachers with whom I work, find exciting new ways to make writing a powerful tool for enhancing their students' learning.

Chapter Three

RAISING ACHIEVEMENT

Our local newspaper recently ran a series of articles on truancy, interviewing students who had spent most of their lives avoiding school. According to these AWOL students, they would rather "hang out" than attend school. However, when the reporter asked more probing questions, some disturbing answers surfaced:

> I was so far behind and so lost that I figured why bother."
>
> I thought the other students and the teacher thought I was dumb."
>
> Reading was so hard for me, and I was embarrassed to read aloud."
>
> I wouldn't participate. I felt that I was gonna mess up. They were like, 'Oh, you need the resource room (for extra help).' And I didn't want to accept that. I knew I didn't need that extra help. . . . They'd yell at me in front of other students. . . . Most of the days I didn't want to go to school because I knew there was going to be a test."

One student thought that teachers wrote her off too soon, saying, "I don't think you're gonna make it out of 7th grade" (Kopf 1996, A-1).

Rather than face their difficulties and confront their fears, they simply stayed away until a new alternative school drew them back. They praised the school for its small classes, flexible hours, and humane treatment. One student spoke about the struggle to support her two-year-old child, whose father was in jail, and her determination to stay in school. According to her, a high school diploma would automatically translate into a good job, securing both her and her child's future.

Schools should be places where students want to be as well as places where students' immense personal needs are met. However, nurturing is not enough. Schools must foremost be places where students grow—places where they can make vital discoveries about themselves as achievers. Students must leave our schools as accomplished learners, knowing that they can conquer the difficult and challenging tasks involved in becoming competent and productive individuals. In her book, *Believing in Ourselves: Progress and Struggle in Urban Middle School Reform,* Anne Lewis (1995) stated, "Schools that know how to put standards and substance into the phrase 'student-centered' also are more likely to produce higher student achievement (1)."

Consider the young mother who must rely on her own resources to support her baby. Will this school prepare her to enter an ever-more-competitive work force? If she were your student, could you confidently say to her, "Your achievement in my class will give you a stake in the future." Perhaps, the greatest charge to a teacher is to look in the mirror at the end of a day and to honestly be able to say, "I would have wanted my own (biological) children to have learned in this way." As parents, we want our children to be competent stakeholders in the future, and we should want no less for our students.

Our responsibility, as teachers, is to acquire a repertoire of powerful strategies which can turn the tide for unsuccessful learners. In being aware of the most promising practices and implementing them in our classes, we have a chance to turn chronic failers into achievers and prepare them to be participants in a fulfilling life.

However, this change cannot occur by blindly following a grocery list of strategies that someone hands you. Helping to change the destiny of underachievers takes an investment of time, energy, and a willingness to look at your work and teaching with a critical eye.

LOOKING FOR THE GENIUS WITHIN (ATTITUDE)

Without realizing it, we sometimes hold attitudes that inhibit achievement. Although we may eloquently state that all students can learn, many of us hold deeply rooted doubts about our students' and our own ability to make this a reality, particularly when reaching standards and raising standardized tests scores becomes an expectation. This achievement-killing uncertainty raises its ugly head when least expected. For instance, take these situations:

▶ Recently, voters elected to have a county district take over the city schools. To make the transition smoother, a committee consisting of business people, parents, city government, teachers and administrators from both districts was formed to devise a plan for merging the two districts, and its members spent over a year working on it. However, before the committee could present its plan, a copy was leaked. At a county principals' meeting, the principals rejected and criticized the plan. Newspaper headlines documented the principals' rejection. One of their major criticisms involved the statement that **all** students would be held to the same high standards. The principals, the instructional leaders and visionaries, went on record as saying that this was impossible. "... due to the varying levels of students." What they were implying was that the city's large minority population could never match their own students' achievement.

▶ At one school, higher tracked classes read more challenging assignments than those students placed in low-level classes. Teachers scampered to teach the advanced classes. Frequently, disparaging comments were made about the lower level classes as teachers marched grimly to their assignments. Unsurprisingly, being labeled and locked into low expectations, the students in the low-level classes scored lower on district and state tests and often became disruptive.

▶ Frequently, when I visit a teacher in a district for the first time, she will feel compelled to fill me in on the profile of her students as a reason for conducting the class in a mundane manner. Usually, the remarks are concluded by, "I'd like to do more, but with this class ..." or "You don't know my kids."

▶ One teacher said that she couldn't even begin to think about instructional strategies until after the state tests had been administered. Until then, she felt compelled to do test drills every day with her students. As she put it, "Instruction takes a back seat to the tests."

▶ Although research shows that students learn better in cooperative learning groups, many teachers never use them, explaining, "It would be utter chaos with these students."

▶ When I ask teachers if they send their students' portfolios home to be shared with parents, some dismiss the notion immediately, making such statements as: "I would never get them back;" "No one would want to read them in their homes;" and "How would they possibly respond?"

▶ Teachers call less on underachieving students, respond less positively to their comments and questions, and often sit them toward the back of the room, putting more distance between these students and themselves. Some teachers even breathe a sigh of relief when these students are absent, for it's one less problem they will have to deal with.

▶ Sometimes the sin is not one of commission but one of omission—failing to let underachieving students know that they are making important contributions to the class, letting them know they are missed when they are absent, and not following through on missed assignments.

▶ Teachers accept inferior work by rationalizing, "At least, it is something."

When students sense this rejection, they give up quickly, adopting the self-defeating attitude of, "Why even bother?" Such attitudes contribute to behaviors that deny the potentiality of students and create a dismal environment for learning.

When teachers and schools focus on the deficits that students bring with them, they usually make poor instructional choices. Knapp and Shields (1990) in their article, "Reconceiving Academic Instruction for the Children of Poverty," warned:

> ... by focusing first on what they perceive to be students' deficits, educators risk making inaccurate assessments of children's strengths and weaknesses ... In the worst case, educators have low expectations for disadvantaged and set standards that are not high enough to form the foundation for future academic success (753).

The parents of our students are entrusting their children to us— trusting us to provide a challenging and meaningful curriculum for their children. In one city, parents and grandparents spent an entire night in two-block long lines before a school's doors opened to ensure that their children would be enrolled in a magnet school for student achievement. Quite ironically, it is a school for achievement in name only. Under the guise of an emphasis on academics and achievement, students spend endless hours completing worksheets in isolation and moving at a snail-like pace.

One day, as I was leaving this school, the principal bragged, "We don't have time for innovation here; we're about the basics." Just about that time, a class of sixth graders passed us. The teacher sternly reminded her students, "No talking. Just make your list." She smiled proudly at her principal, announcing, "We're doing a noun walk!" The trusting parents and guardians don't understand the mediocre teaching methods and insignificant and meaningless tasks their children are being subjected to—all in the name of achievement.

When teachers concentrate on students' deficits, they fail to provide them with a foundation that will lead them to becoming achievers. In a recent report, the Commission on Chapter I (1992) firmly stated:

> There is ample evidence to show that under optimum teaching and learning conditions—those with high expectations and skilled instruction—children will learn at high levels. The proof is consistent: those encouraged to work with challenging content, to solve problems, and to seek meaning from what they study will make far greater academic progress than students limited to basic skills instruction (7).

In schools with high student achievement, administrators provide an informed and active instructional leadership, making a clear statement to teachers, students and parents: Academics are a priority. Since school is a place to learn, no one quibbles with the expectation that **all** of the stakeholders, parents, students, and teachers are expected to willingly assume the responsibility of doing everything in their power to produce engaged and successful learners.

REACHING FOR THE STARS (HIGH EXPECTATIONS)

Needless to say, all teachers want their students to achieve more. However, many find it difficult to even know where to begin when so many students come lacking the most basic skills. Feeling overwhelmed, the teachers and schools often look for quick fixes and, as a result, make poor instructional choices.

For instance, one middle school, after students scored dismally on a district reading test and other standardized tests, spent hundreds of thousands of dollars in adopting a school-wide language arts program that sentenced students to decoding sounds of letters for an entire year. The lessons consisted of students giving robotic responses as they pointed to letters while teachers read from a script, and snapped their fingers to move students onward, awarding points for correct responses and for "nice touching." (Can you imagine that students accepted this compliment without even so much as a snicker?)

With this kind of scripted instruction, students will never have the opportunity to interact freely with the teacher and with peers, nor will they read real books and materials. With no reading and writing experiences or meaningful discussions, they are being deprived of memorable literary experiences, experiences that will assure them that being literate is a way of taking control of their lives. Two hours of observations in this school left me numb and rebellious. Yet, the non-questioning students sat politely and obediently followed the directions, probably thinking that they were getting a "high tech, state-of-the art" education. Despite all of the staff development conducted in this reform district, this school remained uninformed about good instruction, continuing to blatantly, and even arrogantly, fail its students. I asked why the teachers didn't rebel. A cynical administrator replied, "It's easier this way. There is no preparation for classes required."

If not teachers, who will intervene on behalf of these students? It should come as no surprise that this school is located in one of the lowest social-economic and highest crime-ridden areas of a major city. As I travel from city to city, the neediest students seem to have the most inappropriate instruction—instruction that deadens the most inquiring young minds. No wonder the students vote with their feet, leaving the painful and boring memories of school behind. As teachers, we must demand that such senseless and demeaning instructional practices end.

When students come lacking skills, schools often respond by "dumbing" down the curriculum, forgetting the magical formula for achievement—the one of:

high expectations,
high content,
and high support for all students.

Low achieving students will never become achievers with a steady diet of drill and skill. However, it is always easier to give them a worksheet and forget about them. Worksheets and rote exercises always fail because students cannot and do not make the transfer of these skills to real-life experiences.

When I was coordinator of a gifted program, my staff and I worked hard on developing lessons that called upon:

> inquiry-based teaching,
> employed higher order thinking skills,
> developed divergent thinking skills,
> and encouraged students to do original research.

However, I always felt guilty, for I knew that **all** students would thrive on these kind of challenging, high content strategies. Why do we often reserve engaging and challenging activities for gifted populations? *Treating all students as if they were gifted, scrapping the rote drill activities, and exposing students to exciting and challenging work helps students to reap incredible gains.*

Knapp, Shields, and Turnbull (1995), researchers who have focused on learning in high-poverty classrooms referred to this kind of teaching as "Teaching for Meaning, " stating that diverse populations flourish with this type of instruction rather than rote and repetitive approaches. According to these researchers (1995), teaching with meaning includes instruction that:

1. allows students to see how discrete skills fit into the context of the application skills of communicating, comprehending, or reasoning.

2. gives students the tools to construct meaning.

3. is integrated to show the relationships among different content areas and between "what is learned in school and children's home lives" (771).

As part of the Edna McConnell Clark Foundation's initiative to reform urban middle schools, I have worked with schools and teachers who have had the fierce determination to raise their students' achievement by "teaching with meaning," resulting in some wonderful success stories:

▶ Mary Fipp, a teacher at Muirlands Middle School in San Diego, decided that she would not sentence her language-minority students to a drill-and-skill curriculum. As she looked at the records of her 24 students, she realized that the remedial programs of her school district had failed these students: Although many of these language-minority students had been in the district for several years, 18% were still reading at the second grade level, and none of her class was reading above the fourth grade level. Determined to offer her students a curriculum that would be more like the one offered gifted students in her school, Mary focused on a literature-based curriculum, using a modified reading/writing workshop approach.

She modeled reading by reading and thinking aloud with her students, and then allowed them to read the same passage to a reading buddy. While they were reading, they continuously recorded their thoughts in reading journals. Students also had the opportunity to participate in literature circles, where students working in teams, read the same book. In addition, they selected their own titles to read.

She allowed them to write from their own experiences and to write in response to literature. To show them her love of writing, she frequently shared her own writing with them. Soon they began to take ownership of their writing and wanted to revise. Their portfolios became proud displays of their work and achievement.

At the end of the school year, all of Mary's students had progressed:

14% gained five years in reading comprehension
15% gained from three to four years
33% gained two years

the rest gained at least one year (Lewis 1995, 62).

▶ A year after the Writing to Learn Project officially ended in Milwaukee, a group of dedicated teachers from Kosciuszko and Parkman Middle Schools continued the project, offering training and support for their fellow teachers. Their dedication paid off. On the 1995 district-wide writing assessment,

Kosciuszko improved from 39% of students receiving a passing score to 74%, putting it "ahead of the district norm of (70%) for the first time in the memory of most teachers."

Parkman's scores improved from 35% to 66%. These gains enabled both schools to move from the bottom category— that of schools needing improvement to the category of "improving schools " (Reported by Kathy Januchowski, Writing Lab Coordinator at Kociuszko Middle School and the impetus for Writing to Learn in Milwaukee.)

▶ Jardine Middle School in Wichita, Kansas dramatically increased school-wide writing assessment scores during a one-year period, raising the entire school's writing score at least one level.

AN INTEGRATED LANGUAGE ARTS PROGRAM

In Louisville, Kentucky, principals and teachers at Southern, Iroquois, and Western middle schools decided that they wanted to create a language arts program that would challenge their students, hook them on reading and writing, and, at the same time, be responsive to the research. Several teachers were discouraged. They had read Nancie Atwell's book *In the Middle* and Linda Rief's book *Seeking Diversity* on writers/readers workshops, and they wanted their students to experience the excitement of learning in this way. However, when they tried to implement readers/ writers workshops in their classes, they didn't get the results that Atwell and Rief described. They were at the point of abandoning the workshop approach, for the distance between Atwell's students in Boothbay, Maine and their urban students grew greater each day.

In response to all of these needs, we developed the Integrated Language Arts Program. This program kept many characteristics of the readers'/writers' workshop but modified the approach to be more responsive to the needs of our students and the research.

When I speak about the needs of our students, we found that much more modeling and scaffolding had to be provided in order for a workshop approach to work. Many of our students had never had the opportunity to take ownership of their writing and reading by writing from self-selected topics, by reading real books, or by growing up or learning in a literacy-rich environment. When Nancie Atwell talked about wanting to repeat the dinner conversations that her students had at home in her classroom, we realized that some of our students probably never had experienced casual conversation with adults over dinner. Also, many of our students had only experienced teacher-led discussions about literature.

Don't take me wrong: This is not an indictment of urban kids. It is an indictment of how we teach urban kids. It was not that our students were not capable of writing pieces filled with the excitement of their own voices, of discovering that they really loved being buried in piles of books, or of becoming excited about a piece of literature and finding that they possessed marvelous insights. They just hadn't had the chance to make these life-sustaining discoveries. They needed some guidance and an orderly approach to gradually transfer the learning from a teacher-directed approach to a student-centered one.

As we developed the program, we wanted, more than anything, to "teach with meaning." We wanted our students to see the connectedness among reading, writing, the conventions of language, listening, speaking, music, and art. We wanted students to see how being a literate person and having an appreciation of the arts could greatly enhance the quality of their lives. And lastly, we wanted our students to learn to respect each other.

In order to achieve this, we had to restructure the school day. Previously, reading and language arts had been taught as two separate courses. In this integrated approach, we created a two-hour language arts block. None of the schedules for the three schools looked the same, for teachers at each school devised a schedule that would fit into their school's instructional program. Also, we implemented a collaboration model where special education students were mainstreamed into middle school classrooms. Not only were the students mainstreamed, but the teachers were too. As a result, all students reaped the benefits of being taught by a special team of teachers.

The collaboration model was powerful. I'll never forget one student, Sterling. The year before the Integrated Language Arts Program he had been in a special education classroom. Sterling's attention span was non-existent; he always found creative ways to distract the class, causing chaos. While observing him in an Integrated Language Arts class a year later, I saw a different Sterling emerging. During class discussions, his hand always shot rapidly and energetically into the air. During independent reading time, he, curled up on a pillow with a book, forgetting about the rest of the world. (He had discovered Walter Dean Meyer and nothing could keep him from reading.) His writing filled pages of a journal, for he had found his writers' voice. Sterling discovered that he was a special student in every sense of the word.

When I interviewed him, he responded emotionally, in short sentences that hit like bullets, "I've changed. I love learning. I'm never leaving this class. I'm never going back." Another student chimed in with praise, "Two hours of language arts isn't enough—we need three."

Here is how we structured the program:

INTEGRATED LANGUAGE ARTS

❶ **Materials and organization**—We wanted to use a literature-based approach to learning using high-interest, adolescent literature. (Many of our students hated to read because of the instructional materials that had been used in the past.) To put the literature into a meaningful context, we decided to develop thematic and issue-based units. In this way we could also weave in art and music and real-world learning experiences.

Librarians, music, and art teachers became part of

our instructional team. Without one super librarian, Judy Mory, the program would never have gotten off the ground. She shared her expertise on adolescent literature, researched new books and materials, and spent marathon hours, as well as many of her own resources, to make the program successful. Her theory was that, "If I put the right book in a student's hands, the student will become a reader." Whenever Judy walked into a room, she came armed with books and ready to give a book talk.

❷ **Types of reading experiences**—Although we used adolescent literature as a basis, we also wove in a variety of other genres and non-fictional pieces. The thematic units helped students to see the connections between these different pieces of literature, making the learning very cohesive.

*In the program, students experienced **three** different kinds of reading experiences:*

① **Whole Class Reading Experiences**—Each unit began with the class reading a novel together. The teacher used this time to model making meaning and responding to literature. Time was spent in the following ways:

▶ *Reading aloud and thinking aloud.* The teacher showed how she made meaning by reading a passage and having a conversation with herself about the passage—asking questions, making personal connections, etc. The class engaged frequently in conversation about what readers do when they read. Often, a picture-book with the *same* theme was used to model this process. (Students love picture books; they are really universal in their appeal.)

▶ *Modeling strategies for comprehending.* Teachers devised several mini-lessons on reciprocal teaching, question-generating, discussions, selection of quotable quotes.

We frequently used the **GALLERY WALK STRATEGY** to generate student-centered discussions. In this strategy, a single, thought—provoking quote was placed on a piece of butcher paper. Several of these quotation pages were hung around the room. Students were invited to take a walk through the gallery of quotations and to read each quote. They, then, stood under the quotation that meant the most to them—one that they would like to talk about. Those, gathered under a quote, suddenly found peers who wanted to talk about the same thing. In these newly formed discussion groups, students discussed the quote and made personal connections and meanings. (This strategy can be used in any content area to help students process text; it's a good way to move away from teacher-led discussions, adding a new dimension to the classroom dynamics!)

▶ *Modeling discussions and conducting fishbowl demonstrations of small group discussions for when they work in literature circles.*

▶ *Responding to literature through writing*

② **Small group reading experiences (literature circles)**—For each thematic unit, we had eight sets of books—a set consisted of five books—to support the theme. Students were allowed to select which book they wanted to read with their peers. After book talks, the students would list their first three choices, and the students were grouped accordingly. Students usually received their first or second choice. Believe it or not, we started this approach before the term literature circles existed. We called them "group reads." Since then, there has been a wealth of materials written on literature circles. However, back then, we were pioneers and had to make our own discoveries.

In the literature circles, students applied the strategies for comprehending that had been modeled in the whole class reads and others of their own. The teacher spent her time scaffolding instruction by visiting each group and cueing when students needed help. During this time, she took notes on her observations and used them as a basis for mini-lessons and for topics as the class processed the group reading experience.

At the end of the class, the entire class came together and processed the group reading experience—describing what contributed to the discussion, what hindered it, the issues they discovered in their reading, etc. The teacher, in turn, gave them feedback about her observations.

Eventually, the teacher spent less time cueing as the students took on the leadership of the discussions. Then, once a week, each group scheduled the teacher to be an observer of the discussion. During these sessions, the teacher did not interact with the group, but simply acted as a recorder. At the end of the discussion, the teacher gave the group feedback from her notes. Students then assessed their strengths and weaknesses as a discussion group and developed a plan of action for improving. Their plans of actions were shared with the larger class. The teachers' observation notes were a wonderful tool for assessing the processes of learning and served as vehicles for discussion in our Project meetings. We spent a lot of time in processing our students' and our own learning, and we left our meetings feeling as if we were part of a great crusade.

A thematic unit entitled **Coming of Age** used these adolescent novels:

Whole class reading experience:

Roll of Thunder, Hear my Cry—Taylor
That was Then, This is Now—Hinton

Group reads/literature circles (5 copies of each):

The Friends—Guy
Let the Circle be Unbroken—Taylor
Dicey's Song—Voight
Tex—Hinton
Summer of the Swans—Byars
Maniac Magee—Spinelli
Leroy and the Old Man—Butterworth

③ **Independent reading**—In order for students to become lifelong readers and to develop reading preferences, they need time to read. Each classroom had a classroom library and time was set aside for independent reading. Students also kept reading response journals. In addition, students were expected to spend one-half hour each night in reading as a continual homework assignment. To support this, books could be checked out of the classroom library. We also borrowed carts of books from the local libraries.

To create an attractive atmosphere for reading, teachers searched garage sales for couches, chairs, rugs, lamps, etc. They also found good buys on books there!

❸ Types of writing experiences:

① **Whole class writing assignments**—In these assignments, students responded to the same prompt and scoring guide. Usually, they were literature-based or issue-based and represented a variety of audiences and discourse forms. Students would use the scoring guide to help each other in peer revision groups. In these groups, they saw how peers responded to the same rhetorical tasks and received advise on their writing. These small group discussions led to whole class discussions about criteria for evaluation and how students had or had not met them. Within each class, there were usually benchmark papers that evolved from this process, guiding the learning about writing. The whole class assignments also allowed teachers and students to work with and hold conversations about the KERA (Kentucky state assessment) writing evaluation rubric and portfolio assessment.

② **Collaborative writing assignments—** Students were allowed to write for a variety of audiences and purposes in collaborative writing assignments which usually grew out of the work done in the literature circles—scripts, editorials, video productions, panels, etc.

③ **Independent writing—**In the time set aside for writers' workshop, students were allowed to write frequently from self-selected topics in order to discover their writers' voices. (We found that, after having the other integrated language arts classroom experiences, they were much more willing to take on the responsibility of a workshop setting, producing much richer pieces and emerging as more competent and confident writers.)

I realize that this was a dream program in terms of financial support from the school district and not every teacher has the funds to have this many texts within a classroom. However, I have seen individual teachers recreate the same essential reading and writing experiences with the help of the school librarian, local libraries and fellow teachers. If the readers/writers approach is not working for you, you might want to try this adaptation.

Expecting students to do challenging work and then structuring your classroom so that students can accomplish these tasks is another way to say to students:

I believe in you.

When students work hard and develop the trait of perseverance, they *begin to believe in themselves*—the first step in achieving.

DEVELOPING
HIGH SUPPORT SYSTEMS IN THE CLASSROOM
(The Sociology of Learning)

High expectations need to be accompanied by a high support system—a system that helps students overcome the obstacles to achieving the high expectations set by teachers. As mentioned previously, high expectations are more readily reached in a classroom where there is a community of learners and where students receive support from several sources, including peers. In supportive classrooms, the teacher becomes less of a judge and more of a coach, providing students with lots of feedback throughout the learning process and structuring the class in such a way that students have lots of rehearsal time before they are asked to perform for evaluation.

By grouping students in a variety of ways, extra rehearsal time can be built into activities. Fig. 3.1 represents some of these groupings.

MAKING LEARNING EQUITABLE

Eliminate tracking

While students in high-track classes receive academically challenging work and are allowed more freedom to interact with peers, those placed in low tracks usually receive a second-class, remedial approach to learning—one without high expectations or support. This sorting and labeling of students places severe limitations on students and contributes to discrimination in our schools:

> ... research on tracking and ability-grouped class assignments has provided striking evidence that these practices have a negative impact on most children's school opportunities and outcomes. Moreover, the negative consequences of these practices disproportionately affect low-income, African-American, and Latino children (Oakes and Lipton 1992, 448).

However, just the thought of eliminating tracking can create a great amount of fear within the school and in the community. Some teachers fear that they will not be able to meet the curricular

Fig. 3.1. Grouping students in a variety of ways contributes to their growing

sense of self and competency; putting the "gears" of self into motion.

demands and teaching strategies required for diverse classes. More affluent parents fear that their children will be the losers when they are no longer placed in Gifted and Talented or advanced classes. Although these parents agree that the underachievers' scores will increase, they feel that it will be at the expense of their own children's scores.

Committed to untracking, a group of teachers at Muirlands Middle School in San Diego, vowed to teach all of their students as if they were "above average" in order to raise the achievement of all students in their school. Although the school is located in an affluent area, it has a diverse population, spanning a broad, socio-economic spectrum. This diversity is due to the district's Voluntary Ethnic Enrollment Program in which 32% of the school's population is bussed.

Some of the teachers and the principal, Cassandra Countryman, were haunted by the fact that the lowest classes were filled with their bussed minority students and that very few of the minorities were identified as gifted. Thus, there were two distinctively separate populations existing within Muirlands—each receiving different kinds of education and having very few opportunities to interact with each other.

It was troublesome to see the isolation of the bussed population. During one observation, a teacher asked a misbehaving student to leave. He hung his head and sulkingly left, sitting on a bench outside of class. As I joined him, he hurriedly brushed a tear from his face and gazed into the distance. After talking for a while, his tough exterior began to crumble as he stammered, "I hate it here. We're different. I don't even know any of them (the other students). I'm not doing any better here." Under the staunch leadership of committed teachers and a courageous principal, however, this has all changed.

During my years at Muirlands, I watched this staff, led by exceptional teachers, such as Carol Barry, Mary Fipp, and Chris Hargrave marshall support for creating equitable learning. In so doing, they changed the school climate, dissolving the defeating and limiting class system, and building bridges among all students.

Although it has been a long process, the efforts of the staff have paid off. Results of the Abbreviated Stanford Achievement Tests show that all students enrolled in heterogeneously grouped classrooms improved in reading, mathematics and language expression—by an average of six to eight percentile points after one year. Many of the cynics thought that the gifted population's scores would not fare as well. However, according to district data, the gifted students performed as well or better than homogeneously grouped gifted students elsewhere in the district. Another measure of their success is that a higher percentage of minority students have been identified as gifted at Muirlands than at other schools in the district. In an article describing the process of detracking at Muirlands, teachers attribute many of their gains to the kinds of teaching strategies they used, including several Writing to Learn strategies presented in this text and a focus on portfolios. The strategies include: the Cornell Study Method, Big T notes (see 2:80); learning and response logs (see 2:79-87); reciprocal teaching; authentic assessment and portfolios (see chapter 5). (Fipp, Barry, Hargrave, and Countryman 1996)

Design a Variety of Assignments

Building lessons that are multi-intelligenced is a way of making classrooms more equitable. In talking with students who have had repeated failures in school, I often hear comments such as, "I'm not good at school work. I try, but I just can't keep focused. My mind wanders, and I find myself in trouble." Most of the time such students are engaged in paper and pen tasks and rote drill activities, which require them to work alone for longer periods of time Yet, underachievers tend to be kinesthetic/tactile learners. In other words, they need to manipulate and handle materials, be involved in movement, and interact with others. If these students were given an array of assignments that were based on the different intelligences, they would discover that they are much better learners than they ever imagined. Unfortunately, some students never have a chance to make this discovery.

Research shows that programs designed to help underachieving students may, in fact, be locking them into remedial and repetitious worksheet types of activities—activities that do not engage learners and that rely heavily on the linguistic intelligence (ASCD Update 1989, August). Considering the diverse population that public schools serve, remedial education may be one of the most scandalous inequities of schools, for it denies our neediest students the opportunity to become engaged and excited learners.

With a knowledge of the multiple intelligences, teachers can structure classes so that learning is more equitable, giving students an opportunity to unmask their unique combination of intelligences and to develop, more fully, the other intelligences. By experiencing a variety of learning activities, students begin to understand their strengths and weaknesses and gain valuable insights into how they, as individuals, process knowledge. Knowing that their failure is based on a weakness and not on stupidity restores hope, releasing energy for learning.

However, Gardner (1995) warns teachers about "surface" level interpretations of his work. Simply identifying the different intelligences and creating trivial and insignificant assignments will not bring about changes in students. In order for the Multiple Intelligence Theory to have its full impact, teachers must place the various intelligences within the context of their own teaching—thinking deeply about such questions as:

- ◆ What's worth knowing?
- ◆ How will we know that we know?
- ◆ What kinds of assessment will work best?
- ◆ How will we change it to make it better?

Multiple Intelligence Theory is not something that can be plugged into a classroom. It must reflect a teacher's philosophy about how children learn and how learning is assessed. Otherwise, MI Theory becomes just another educational trivial pursuit, where students experience a smorgasbord of activities for the sake of the activities.

THE MULTI-INTELLIGENCES
AND INSTRUCTIONAL EXAMPLES

The following is a brief description of each of the intelligences (Armstrong 1994) and the instructional implications for each:

▶ **Linguistic Intelligence**—This intelligence involves the ability to use words effectively in written or oral communication. A person with this kind of intelligence tends to think in words, using words for a variety of practical functions: to inform, to persuade, to explain, and to remember. In addition, the person understands and enjoys manipulating and playing with language. There is also a keen appreciation for the sounds of language.

Instructional Implication—Offer a variety of linguistically-rich activities, including discussions, direct instruction, reading, journals, learning logs, written assignments for a variety of audiences and purposes, double-entry journals, publishing, choral reading, storytelling, literature circles, poetry readings, panels, debates, Socratic seminars, interviews, readers theater, skits, oral history, television talk shows, speeches, advertisements, word games, documentaries, radio programs, and reciprocal teaching.

▶ **Logical-Mathematical Intelligence**--This intelligence involves the ability to use numbers effectively and to reason well. The logical-mathematical person has the ability to think analytically; to recognize patterns; and to comprehend intricate relationships. Some practical applications of this intelligence include: identifying cause and effect relationships; hypothesizing; classifying and categorizing; drawing inferences; making generalizations; building analogies; solving puzzles; and calculating.

Instructional Implication—Offer a variety of higher-level thinking activities, including Socratic seminars; open-ended problems; independent research projects requiring the testing of a hypothesis; performance-based activities; timelines; brain teasers; formal logic activities; math manipulatives; interpretation of polls and graphs; science and experiments; problem solving and decision-making processes; statistical analysis; developing rationales.

▶ **Spatial Intelligence**—This intelligence involves the ability to visualize and to graphically represent visualizations. Persons with this intelligence have an eye for color, form, line, and shape and their relationship to each other.

Instructional Implication—Offer a variety of visual activities such as graphs, timelines, map work, posters, art work, conceptual mapping, metaphors, analogies, schematics, graphic representation of thematic work, heuristics, diagrams, art work, mosaics, construction projects, symbolic representations, political cartoons, etc.

▶ **Bodily-Kinesthetic Intelligence**—This intelligence involves the ability to express feelings and ideas with body movement. A person with this intelligence exhibits a wide-range of physical attributes such as coordination, balance, strength, flexibility, and speed.

Instructional Implication—Offer a variety of activities involving movement such as role playing, dramatic scenes, hands-on learning experiences, simulations, manipulatives, building projects, dance, field trips, project-based learning, performance-based learning, etc.

▶ **Musical Intelligence**—This intelligence involves the ability to express one's self with music. A person with this intelligence may compose music, interpret or critique music, perform music, or appreciate music. This intelligence reveals an understanding of rhythm, tone, melody, and pitch.

Instructional Implication—Offer a variety of activities involving musical forms such as writing to music;

selecting music to accompany a thematic unit or historical or literary periods; writing raps; creating background music for presentations; increasing memory by using musical associations; energizing; and employing super-learning strategies to enhance learning. (When students appear lifeless, a team of teachers in Louisville have students take a five-minute energizing break by standing in a circle as they play upbeat music. Students take turns leading each other in movements. After a student is finished with a move, a peer's name is called out and that student leads the class in a new movement.)

▶ **Interpersonal Intelligence**—This intelligence manifests a keen understanding of other people's behavior, motivation, and feelings. A person with this kind of intelligence works well with others.

Instructional Implication—Offer a variety of different kinds of groupings in your class, including teams and pairs. Use collaborative and cooperative learning strategies. Give collaborative assignments and assessments some of the time. Others include: think/pair/share strategy, peer evaluations, cross-age tutoring and projects, learning buddies, simulations, creative dramatics, literature circles, interviews, oral history projects, written conversations, and reciprocal teaching.

▶ **Intrapersonal Intelligence**—This intelligence entails the ability to look within and to understand one's self. This kind of person is reflective, self-disciplined, and has self-esteem.

Instructional Implication—Engage in reflective activities such as goal setting, self-regulated learning, learning logs, journals, self assessments, personal responses, expressive writing, reading/writing workshop approaches, independent study, and reflective activities.

Many of the activities from the various intelligences tend to overlap. Consequently, it is not an impossible task to represent the seven intelligences in classroom activities and to give students choices. The extra effort and time are well worth it; for the intelligences help to create a more balanced and equitable classroom.

Thomas Armstrong (1994) suggests that observing students is one of the best ways of identifying their intelligences, *particularly when they are misbehaving.* "The strongly linguistic student will be talking out of turn, the highly spatial student will be doodling and daydreaming, the interpersonal inclined student will be socializing, the bodily-kinesthetic student will be fidgeting." He suggests that, "These intelligence-specific misbehaviors, then, are a sort of cry for help—a diagnostic indicator of how students need to be taught" (28).

Basing our classrooms upon the philosophy that each student comes to us with a unique combination of assets and intelligences rather than deficits enables us to see our students through a new lens—the lens of potentiality. As we look at our students through this lens, our perceptions of how we teach students and how we assess students begin to change, reflecting the different intelligences.

However, creating meaningless, cutesy activities for the sake of art, music, or movement will not enhance achievement. Meaningful multiple intelligence activities cannot be purchased in a generic handbook and implemented like a recipe.

Significant multiple intelligence activities are the result of reflective teachers who take the charge of teaching **all** of their students seriously. Thus, they embed the activities in the content to be taught, and these activities become an integral part of their instruction. Patti Callabrese, a teacher at Stephens Middle School in Long Beach, designed the unit in figure 3.2 in an attempt to weave the different intelligences into a thematic, issue-based unit.

If MI Theory is being implemented in significant ways in a classroom, it will also be present in assessment. The following questions may be helpful in evaluating to what extent MI Theory permeates assessment in a classroom:

◆ Have I included a variety of types of assessment in my classroom? Are all my assessments paper and pencil tasks, or have I included a variety of formats such as art work, dramatic presentations, oral presentations, tapes, videos, etc.?

◆ Does assessment exist separately in my classroom, or is it an integral part of the instruction?

◆ How do I weigh evaluation in my classroom? Are projects, where students have choices from activities representing the different intelligences or where students work in groups, given the same amount of credit as paper-and-pencil tests or written assignments? Am I consistent in my standards, or do different standards for different kinds of work exist in my class? Have I set and announced the evaluation criteria for work involving the different intelligences so that students know how they are being evaluated?

◆ Do my assessments include a variety of sociological formats—some involving individual work, pairings, and group work?

◆ Are students' reflections and critiques of their work used as an integral part of my assessment program?

◆ Do students have opportunities to see and to evaluate each other's work against a standard?

◆ What kinds of work are represented in my students' portfolios? Is there an over-reliance on written products? Do the portfolios represent the breadth and range of multi-intelligenced activities that occur in my classroom?

When MI Theory becomes an integral part of the assessment program, students have more opportunities to become successful learners, for the assessments acknowledge and are built around the varied talents of students.

ROLL OF THUNDER, HEAR MY CRY

INTO–

1. MOSAIC TEAR SCULPTURE – Prejudice in the United States in the South (1933) red, white and blue paper to represent the American flag.

Before beginning this activity, define for the class some specialized vocabulary:

boycott/ Ku Klux Klan/ segregation/
tar and feather/ Great Depression/ sharecropper
night riders/ lynching/ prejudice/ bigot

2. Introduce a map of the area where the story takes place. Point out the distances between where the main characters lived, where they attended school, shopped, went to town, shopped during the boycott. Remind students that transportation for the poor was a horse and buggy. Cars were for the affluent.

3. Introduce the author, Mildred D. Taylor.. Let the students know that his book is the middle of a trilogy about the Logan family.

THROUGH–

4. Read chapters 1-3 in the novel. ISSUE: racial inequality. Discuss the inequities of the schooling, books, lack of bus for the black students, etc.

THINK WRITE—You are Cassie. Write a letter to the editor of the *Strawberry Gazette* clearly stating the inequities of the educational system in your community. You do not think that the children of Great Faith Elementary receive an education equal to that of Jefferson Davis. Include examples from the novel to convince the leaders of the community to take action.

5. Have the students make a storyboard (6 panels), choosing the best/ strongest events—2 per chapter. Students will draw the scenes, and label them in sequential order.

6. Assessment: How to caption drawings; How to use quotation marks.

7. ISSUE: racial segregation. At the time there were separate drinking fountains, restaurants, sections of the city bus. Journal: How is this happening in this country today? In other countries today?

8. Read a short account of the Rosa Parks' story.

Fig. 3.2a. Patti Callabrese uses a variety of the intelligences in this novel unit, making the learning more equitable

9. Journal: Were the Logan children justified in digging the hole that resulted in damage to the school bus? Is it ever justified to purposely ruin other people's property? How else can equal treatment be attained? Bring in an article from the newspaper on a trial that includes racial or social injustice issues. ISSUES: Personal Responsibility; Social Injustice.

10. Keep a journal of your walk/ride to school for five days. What new things have you noticed? ISSUE: Economy.

11. Read chapters 4 and 5. Ask your parents or a relative to tell you a story that happened to them when they were little. It can be humorous, historical, or instructive (a lesson learned). Share your story with the class (oral history). Discuss with the class the importance of oral tradition in preserving family history. ISSUE: Personal Responsibility; Economy; Social Injustice.

12. Go to the library and complete the worksheet: "Mississippi Facts". Point out that some of the locations in the novel are actual places; others are fictional.

13. Draw your favorite scene from the trip to Strawberry. Why did you choose this scene? Make a bulletin board display. ISSUE: open.

14. Read chapters 4 and 5 in the novel. Discuss T.J.'s behavior and Stacey's feelings toward Mr. Morrison with students. Journal topic: Tell about a similar experience in your life when you felt that someone was taking your place in the family. ISSUE: Personal Responsibility.

15. Considering what has been happening between the races in their area, why does Big Ma make Cassie apologize to Lillian Jean again? Journal topic: Was Big Ma right to make Cassie apologize? Defend your opinion. Predict what will happen between the girls later in the story. ISSUE: Social Injustice; Personal Responsibility.

16. Discuss holiday meals. Bring in ambrosia and sweet potatoes to share with the class. Ask what special foods they share at Thanksgiving/Christmas.

17. Read Chapters 6 and 7. Point out the history behind Mr. Morrison's childhood memory. Explain "breeding". Discuss Mr. Jamison's role in the boycott. Why does a prominent white lawyer decide to help. Journal: What could happen to Mr. Jamison as a result of his decision to help the black community? Would you be willing to publicly defend an "underdog"? Show an appropriate segment of "I'll Fly Away". Suggested reading: *To Kill a Mockingbird*. ISSUES: Personal Responsibility; Economy: Racial Prejudice.

Fig. 3.2b. Although this unit is designed for a language arts class, many of the activities can be adapted

18. Discuss historical events from the Emancipation Proclamation in 1863 to the Civil Rights Act of 1968. Remind the students that this story takes place in 1933. How much progress has been made in race relations since then? Bring in a recording of Marian Anderson (not allowed to sing at Constitution Hall in 1939); Martin Luther King's "I Have A Dream" speech. What similar event are happening currently? (i.e. Bosnia, Middle East?) Bring in a newspaper article about a current situation. ISSUE: Social Injustice.

19. Have students complete worksheet "America's Great Economic Depression of the 1930s. Give the students a few days to go shopping. Choose 10 items for price comparison. Discuss their conclusions and findings. ISSUE: Economy.

20. Have students make a storyboard (8 panels) sequencing the last four chapters (4-7) as an assessment.

21. Read Chapters 8 and 9. Write a Biopoem for Cassie or Stacey.

22. Journal: Do you feel that Cassie's plan for revenge on Lillian Jean is a good one? Explain, using details from the novel. In groups, write a skit showing a way Cassie could have dealt with Lillian Jean without using violence. ISSUE: Personal Responsibility.

23 Open head—What was Mr. Avery thinking about the boycott. Draw at least five images and explain on the back what these represent and why you picked them. ISSUE: Economy.

24. Have students complete the "Detecting Gender and Racial Bias" worksheet individually. Discuss in groups. Did everyone have the same answer? Share out, using reporters from each group. ISSUE: Racial Prejudice.

25. Read Ch. 10-12. Discuss revival, mortgage. Have students speculate about the Simms's treatment of T.J. before the revival.

BEYOND–

26. Write down questions that were unanswered at the end of the novel. In groups speculate about these questions. Each group shares out. Class speculates about the answers.

27. Book jacket activity.

28. Assessment—students write short dialogues/conversations that might have taken place in the following situations:

Fig. 3.2c. The multi-intelligences and issues drive this unit

- Cassie tells her mother about the incident in the classroom when Little Man stomped on his book
- Little Man tells Mama about his first day at school
- Stacey and Cassie tell their mother the truth about the school bus incident
- Cassie talks to Big Ma after the apology incident
- Uncle Hammer confronts Mr. Simms
- Lillian Jean tells Jeremy what Cassie did to her
- Papa, Stacey and Mr. Morrison talk about things on the way to Vicksburg
- Cassie asks her father about the origin of the fire
- Cassie and her parents speculate about what will happen to T.J.
- Cassie tells her mother about what happened with Lillian Jean

29. Working in teams, identify four of the most interesting incidents in the novel and create a soundtrack to accompany these incidents.

30. Construct a timeline of the Civil Rights Movement in America.

31. Working in teams, dramatize your favorite scene from the novel.

Fig. 3.2d. These assignments help students synthesize information and to place it in a creative format

A PARADIGM FOR
STRUCTURING SUCCESSFUL CLASSROOMS

Students often fail because many classes are structured for failure without our even realizing it. For years, I thought that I was teaching thoughtfully by following this pattern:

❶ through direct instruction, I would present a highly focused mini-lesson. I spent a lot of time preparing the mini-lesson, making sure that I had visuals, time for interaction, and lots of examples.

❷ then I would model for the students, applying the concepts presented in the mini-lesson. Sometimes, I would model the task, by recording my thoughts on an overhead—a kind of thinking aloud for the class. Other times, we would collaboratively, as a class, do the task.

❸ following this modeling, I expected them to be able to do the task by themselves. Therefore, I made the assignment and counted on them to complete it.

At this point some of my students could do the assignment, but I was always surprised at how many students couldn't. I had always been a firm believer in modeling as a student and as a teacher. Since I always included modeling in my lessons, I couldn't understand why some students still couldn't do the assignment until I read an article on cognitive apprenticeship. Suddenly, the light bulb went on, and I finally saw what was missing in my instruction.

The article, authored by Collins, Brown, and Holum (1991), discussed how to make thinking visible in a classroom by setting up a cognitive apprenticeship. Since then, I have shared their ideas about using the cognitive apprenticeship as an instructional paradigm with hundreds of teachers. After they get over the "stand-offish" title of cognitive apprenticeship and come to understand the principles of it, they are eager to try it in their classrooms. And when they do, they are thrilled with the results.

Our approach to teaching failed because we didn't understand the importance of adding scaffolding and coaching. As we add these two special ingredients to our instruction, students become more successful in understanding difficult concepts. They have been given the extra rehearsal time they need to master them.

According to Collins, Brown, and Hollum, cognitive apprenticeship takes its name from the traditional concept of apprenticeship, involving an expert showing a learner how to master a process and to become proficient at a task. This model of instruction is not appropriate for all instruction, but it is best used when the learning is complex and when the task requires students to combine and apply several different skills to accomplish the task. Examples might include: revising a piece of writing; reading difficult material; solving a two-or three step mathematical problem; or testing a hypothesis.

Often, the skills required to do these more complex tasks are taught in isolation, and students may practice them by individually doing worksheet-type problems or exercises. When it comes time to transfer these skills to authentic problems, students, more than likely, are not able to do them even though they have been taught the skills. As a result, both students and teachers become frustrated. After all, students should be able to apply the skills that we teach to new situations—just as an apprentice in a traditional apprenticeship would. In real life, students and apprentices eventually have to stand on their own expertise.

The cognitive apprenticeship takes the mystery out of the thought processes by allowing students to see the thinking of others and then providing a supportive community in which to practice their own thinking. According to Brown, Collins, and Holum (1991), the cognitive apprenticeship involves the steps of modeling, coaching, scaffolding, articulating, reflecting, elaborating, and fading away placed in this kind of sequence:

STRUCTURING THE CLASSROOM FOR SUCCESS: THE TRANSFER OF EXPERTISE

Modeling—The teacher performs a task, allowing students to observe. During the task, the teacher makes the thinking visible by thinking aloud—letting students hear the internal monologue that occurs when one is solving a difficult task.

Scaffolding—After the teacher models, a student takes on the role of expert while the rest of the class observes. The teacher cues the student, helping to elaborate and refine the thinking and providing support when needed. This adds another layer to the learning before students are asked to do the task independently.

Coaching—The teacher observes and facilitates while students perform the task, providing cues whenever necessary. However, this is often done as a whole class activity so that all students can observe and participate. According to Collins, Brown, and Holum, coaching is evident throughout the entire apprenticeship experience.

Articulating—The teacher asks students to verbalize their knowledge and thinking, giving students the opportunity to see other students' thinking processes which, in turn, builds their own metacognitive skills. Also, as students verbally explain their own learning, they are, actually, rehearsing and refining their learning by trying it out on an audience. Students need to hear these conversations in order to become proficient thinkers and learners. In this process of articulation, Collins, Brown, and Holum explain that students take on the vital roles of being both "producer and critic" (44).

Reflecting—In this structured instructional process, students can compare their performance with others and reflect realistically about what they know and what they don't know. By listening to a variety of other students thinking aloud, they see how others solve problems, and they develop a repertoire of strategies for learning.

Elaborating—The teacher invites students to pose and solve their own problems. By this time, the students feel competent because they have seen a teacher model the task; they have watched other students assume the role of expert and contributed to refining these students' thinking; and, perhaps, even taken on the role of expert themselves, receiving beneficial feedback and support from peers and the teacher coach. They have been part of a learning community that has practiced multiple ways to solve complex and authentic tasks. These experiences give students the expertise to proceed on their own.

Fading away—As students become more proficient in these tasks, the teacher begins to fade away, letting the new "experts" rely on their own expertise. The job of every good teacher is to teach so well that the teacher can fade away, rejoicing in the fact that students have become autonomous learners—willing to trust and engage their own expertise (Collins, Brown, and Holum 1991).

Wanting to try the cognitive apprenticeship method, I decided to use it to teach my students to write summaries. I have always held the firm conviction that, if we teach students to summarize well, then we were giving them a lifelong skill. The advantages of summary writing include:

- ▶ developing vocabulary
- ▶ promoting critical reading and comprehension skills
- ▶ improving learning in general
- ▶ integrating reading and writing
- ▶ causing students to reprocess text by selecting main ideas, rejecting details, substituting synonyms and paraphrasing content material
- ▶ creating meaning by recasting text into their own words and assimilating it with students' prior knowledge

This is a lot of mileage to get out of one strategy, and many of the advantages seemed to fit the skills that my students were lacking. As a teacher, I'm always slightly behind, and I'm always looking for ways to place several skills into one context. When I read the research on summaries, I thought that I had found a gold mine. Thus, I enthusiastically plunged wholeheartedly into summaries. Much to my disappointment, I found that my students didn't share my same excitement: *summaries were very difficult for them to write.* Their summaries were almost verbatim collages of the articles they were reading.

When I used the cognitive apprenticeship process, my students were finally successful. First of all, I gathered a variety of different kinds of writing—editorials, high-interest feature stories, informational writing, essays, texts, and so on. (I wanted students understand that they could use summaries for all kinds of writing.) Then, I applied this process:

DAY ONE

1. As the students entered the room, I handed each a copy of a high-interest feature story taken from our Sunday newspaper and asked them to read it.

2. After they finished reading the article, I explained that we were going to learn how to write summaries, explaining the many advantages of being able to write them. Then I told them that I was going to write a summary, using the following schema:

SUMMARY WRITING SCHEMA

• Key Places—

• Key People—

• Key Events—

*Key words*_____*Synonyms*

*Main Ideas—

---

3. On an overhead projector, I started to fill in the schema, thinking aloud and recording my thoughts. Sometimes, I would ask for their help. When I came to the section on main ideas, I generated several and asked the students if I had missed any, being sure to add their responses. (I tell them that I generally use this schema while I am reading an article, suggesting that they may find it helpful, too.)

4. Then we evaluated the main ideas—placing stars next to the ones that truly represented the main ideas of the text

and scratching out those that didn't. We then looked closer to find the one idea that best captured the article.

5. Using this completed schema, we constructed a summary together, and I recorded our summary on an overhead. After we finished the summary, we revised it, making sure that we had accurately represented the text and that we were satisfied with it.

DAY TWO

1. Students were given another article to read and a copy of the summary schema. Then I divided the students into heterogeneously grouped teams and asked them to create one summary together, using the process that was modeled yesterday and representing the group's best efforts.

2. As the students were working on their summaries, I monitored the groups carefully—only intervening to give a cue when they appeared to be on the way to abandoning the task.

3. I collected the summaries and selected the best summary.

DAY THREE

1. I returned the summaries to each group and placed the best summary on an overhead. A representative from this group became the teacher and talked about what they had done to produce this piece—some of the decisions, problems, and changes they had made. During this relating, I asked probing questions to get the student to elaborate and encouraged the class to ask questions and to make points.

2. Together, as a class, we talked about why this was a good summary and what could have been done to make it even better.

3. The groups were then allowed to revise their summaries, adding their new learning about summary learning. We ended

the class with a discussion about what they had learned about summary writing and how their new summaries differed from their first ones.

DAYS FOUR AND FIVE

1. Another reading was handed out, along with a summary schema sheet. This time, I divided the groups into pairs, asking the pairs to write one summary. The whole process was repeated.

DAY SIX

1. Students were informed that today they would be writing summaries by themselves, but we would practice one more time by having one of them be the teacher and model the process for the class.

2. A volunteer student teacher then wrote a summary on the overhead, with the teacher and other students asking questions and offering suggestions to make it more focused.

3. At the end, the student teacher articulated what was learned about summary writing during the lesson. Other students recorded their learning in a learning log.

4. Students were finally given an article upon which they wrote an individual summary.

Although this seems like a long process, it's well worth the time, for students learn a variety of skills placed in an authentic task—summary writing. By the time students are asked to write a summary of their own, they have experienced the confidence-building steps of modeling, scaffolding, coaching, and articulating their thoughts. They have seen how other students approach the task, and they have had opportunities to revise their work. Therefore, they are guaranteed a measure of success when they are asked to do the process on their own.

In previous attempts to teach summary writing, I had stopped after my initial modeling and then asked them to write a summary. When I added scaffolding—the part where students worked with a team and then in pairs—and coaching, where they heard other students talk about their work, the results were phenomenal. Another fringe benefit was that, for many, the mystery of reading comprehension became unlocked. These students became active and purposeful readers, understanding what they were reading. In fact, many teachers feel that the cognitive apprenticeship approach applied to summary writing is one of the richest strategies shared during the Writing to Learn Summer Institute.

Terri Jo Hagan from Horace Mann Middle in San Diego used the assignment in Fig. 3.3 to apply the cognitive apprenticeship in her classroom.

When a majority of students are failing or not understanding a concept, it is often due to the structure of the classroom. The learning is not structured in order to provide time for scaffolding, coaching, and articulating the learning. These steps work because they allow students time to rehearse their learning before performing alone.

Unfortunately, as I visit classrooms, I see very little scaffolding and coaching being done. Unless, we are willing to look at the structure of the learning in our classrooms, our students, will keep on failing.

On a personal note, I'm haunted by those I didn't reach. I just wish that I had discovered these effective strategies earlier in my career, making me want to recall over three decades of students. If I could just have another chance with them, I would be so much better, and, more importantly, they, too, would be better as a result of my learning. For me, that's the greatest lament: Why did it take me so long?

In urban schools, we are surrounded by a sense of urgency: Every day we are losing kids. Thus, we can never afford the luxury of being complacent or feeling sorry for ourselves. We

```
Write to Learn
March 3, 1993
Terry Jo Hagan
Mann Middle School
```

Materials needed:
- Class set of "When I Think" handout
- 7-10 copies of group
- overhead transparency of "When I Think"
- chalkboard

1. On the chalkboard or on a poster write:

   <u>Underline</u> words, phrases, or lines you like
   Box words you don't know yet
   ? next to words or ideas that don't make sense
   to you

2. Using the overhead projector, model these
   strategies on the first stanza of the poem.

3. On the chalkboard or a poster write:

   Paraphrase things <u>underlined</u>
   Make guesses about what boxed words may mean
   Form questions about things marked with ?

4. On the overhead, model on the right of the big
   T, these strategies.

5. Have the students individually mark and comment
   on the rest of the poem.

6. Place the students in cooperative groups and
   give each group a handout. Explain the
   procedures to them. (FYI: read around, as
   defined by me, means each student offers one
   many responses as turns are taken around the
   circle. The read around stops when every person
   has shared all ideas.)

7. After groups have completed their work, have
   students return to their desks, take out their
   learning logs, and write to this prompt:

   The next class is coming and they've never seen
   this poem. Please explain to another student
   what this poem is about.

Fig. 3.3. This assignment illustrates a modified version of the cognitive apprenticeship as well as an example of a collaborative learning experience

must continually seek better and more effective ways to make our classrooms places of success, where students discover there is a hopeful future for them. It's not enough for us to be catchers of children. We need to be launchers.

TEACHING COMPLEX SKILLS THROUGH DIALOGUE AND PRACTICE (RECIPROCAL TEACHING)

At about the fourth grade level, reading skills begin to decline, for students fail to make the transition from learning to read to reading to learn (NAEP 1989). Thus, they begin to fall behind in almost of all of their subjects since they cannot understand what they are reading. They passively read the words without comprehending.

Reciprocal teaching is an application of the cognitive apprenticeship that is particularly effective in increasing reading comprehension and raising reading scores dramatically. In studies of reciprocal teaching, Palincsar and Brown (1984) found that, after twenty small group sessions, students' reading comprehension increased from 15% to 85% accuracy. When reciprocal teaching was implemented in larger classes, 71% of these students achieved criterion performance as opposed to only 19% of the control students who were involved in individualized skill instruction. Even after an absence of reciprocal instruction for a period of six weeks, students' reading scores declined very little. Furthermore, teachers observed fewer behavior problems in their reciprocal teaching groups than in the control groups.

Palinscsar's and Brown's work in developing the reciprocal teaching process has made us better teachers of reading. In fact, several faculties have committed to having their entire staff trained in the techniques of reciprocal teaching and have agreed to practice these strategies together. Although the assessment data is not available yet, these faculties are convinced that their students on now better readers.

Instead of teaching skills individually, reciprocal teaching combines the active reading skills of summarizing, asking questions, clarifying, and making predictions. These combined skills are taught through a structured dialogue, where the teacher and students alternate in leading the discussion.

Good readers summarize, ask questions, clarify, and make predictions almost automatically—giving it very little thought. However, many of our students don't even have an inkling as to what one does to understand a passage, for they have become passive readers. Therefore, reciprocal teaching attempts to make the thinking of good readers visible through a structured group task. In this task, students see first-hand how meaning is constructed by combining these skills. In turn, students eventually internalize these skills so that they become better comprehenders and more active readers. Over a period of time, students observations', summaries, and questions become much more sophisticated, and they require less teacher intervention or cueing.

When reciprocal teaching is first introduced to teachers, they tend to reject it. For them, most of whom are good readers, the process seems too obvious and drawn out. Also reciprocal teaching is not easy. It takes practice to provide students with effective cues and to know when to intervene and when to disappear. For others, it takes a while to feel comfortable when thinking aloud spontaneously so that it makes sense for students. Nonetheless, with commitment (at least twenty applications) to the strategy and practice, both teachers and students feel more at ease with the process. In fact, after working with reciprocal teaching for a while, most teachers adapt it, changing it so that it meets the needs of what they are attempting to teach better, making the process distinctly theirs.

Reciprocal teaching works better if students are given practice in each of the individual skills of summarizing, predicting, asking questions, and clarifying before putting them in the context of reciprocal teaching. In this way, reciprocal teaching becomes just a next step instead of something dramatically new, and students enter into the dialogue more readily.

Several teachers use the following process to implement reciprocal teaching in their classes:

❶ Setting the Stage—Establish the need for reciprocal teaching through a discussion of how frustrating it is to read something and not remember what it is you've read. Share the information about how reciprocal teaching can raise their reading comprehension dramatically. (Most students become eager at this point because they tend to think that there is no hope for them to become better readers, and they have given up on reading because it is a frustrating experience for them. They also are convinced that they are stupid.)

Explain that they are going to have plenty of opportunities to watch others make meaning and then to practice with a supportive group so that they can all become better comprehenders together. Some teachers begin this discussion with a learning log entry about how they feel when they can't understand something they are supposed to read, and let the discussion come from the students' writing. This entry, then, becomes, the first of a series of log entries as students reflect frequently on the experiences of reciprocal teaching. Assure them that, in time, each of them will have the opportunity to become the teacher and to lead the conversation.

❷ Modeling—During the first few days, the teacher models the reading strategies that are used in understanding text by thinking aloud. While thinking aloud, the teacher records predictions, asks questions, shows confusion, and summarizes on an overhead projector so that students can see the thinking as well as hear it. (This works best for students when the tone is natural and honest and represents a good reader responding to text. Thus, it's probably best not to prepare the response ahead of time but to respond spontaneously so that the modeling is more authentic. The student needs to see the teacher actively struggling with the pieces of a puzzle—dealing with the messiness of solving a problem—and not having a neatly prepared package of answers.)

In modeling, the teacher begins to draw students into the responses and asks them to join in solving the problem of making meaning. The teacher listens carefully to their responses and responds with appropriate cues to help them to elaborate and extend their initial thinking. Adding students' thinking to teacher responses, the teacher demonstrates the richness of their collaborative thinking in making meaning. *In this step, the shift is beginning to take place: from the teacher making meaning to the entire class collaboratively making meaning, in preparation for students leading the dialogue.* The teacher may even ask a student to help record their thinking on an overhead and begins to move away from the front of the class.

❸ **Scaffolding**—Now it's time for the students to take the lead in conducting the dialogue. To build students' confidence, some teachers have the students work in **learning pairs** to practice responding to a text. Then a learning pair comes to the front of the room and leads the dialogue. The teacher's role, at this point, is to cue or to coach students, helping them to extend and refine their thinking. Thus, students become doubly engaged in the material because they are simultaneously involved in the roles of producers and critics since they are continually seeking to refine what they have produced. Finally, an individual student is asked to lead the dialogue. The teacher only interrupts to get students to look more closely at their thinking.

❹ **Practicing and fading**—Students working in small, heterogeneous groups practice the reciprocal teaching process. Within the group, each student takes a turn being the teacher. The teacher monitors the groups, making sure to spend time with each group so that they can receive feedback. At the end of the hour, the class is called together, and there is a processing of the task with students sharing and reviewing how they constructed meaning from the text. As the students become more confident, they take on more responsibility for the conversation, with the teacher contributing less and less.

❺ **Extending**—In their learning logs, students are asked to practice the process as they read assignments on their own.

Teachers use the following chart to help students process their thinking:

Pages	Predict	Clarify	Question	Summarize

In an Integrated Language Arts class, the reciprocal teaching approach is woven into the on-going instruction in this way:

❶ When the class is reading the same novel together, the teacher models the reading strategies involved in reciprocal teaching.

❷ It is extended as students break into literature circles, where in groups they read the same novel and have discussions. Here, the students use the skills of reciprocal teaching to guide their discussions. Different students assume the role of becoming the discussion leader, and the teacher is scheduled into the group to become a discussion observer and coach, giving the team valuable feedback.

❸ As students select individual texts to read, they practice the skills of reciprocal teaching by responding to the texts in their reading logs. Eventually, the students internalize these skills, responding almost automatically.

DEVELOPING ELABORATION SKILLS
FOR EFFECTIVE LEARNING

By providing direct instruction in learning strategies, teachers help students to confidently tackle difficult tasks and enlarge their repertoire of problem-solving skills.

In the past, these learning strategies were often taught in isolation as study skills and not specifically incorporated into subject-matter classes. Thus, students failed to see the practical value of such strategies and relied on trying to memorize materials. Even if they succeeded in memorizing materials, they were unable to retain such information in their long-term memory.

In order to activate long-term memory, students need to find ways to make the information personally relevant, giving them ownership of it. Although there are many effective learning strategies, elaboration strategies are some of the most beneficial ones for students because they link new information to prior information. Hence, the elaboration strategies provide a bridge for new information. When students elaborate, they are actually transforming the information into another form—one that makes it easier for them to remember. Weinstein, Ridly, Dahl, and Weber (1989) reported that elaboration gives students more control of their learning, making them feel less overwhelmed. **To build students' repertoire of elaboration skills**, they suggest having students: create analogies; paraphrase; summarize; transform information by placing it into another format (chart, graph, or diagram); apply the new information; relate it to prior knowledge; compare and contrast; draw conclusions; and teach someone else (18-19). All of these elaboration activities make wonderful entries for learning logs.

Although elaboration can take many forms, there is not one form that ensures students more success than others. Students may select one, or even several, that seem appropriate for the specific task at hand, or they may select the ones that work the best for them. The important point is to make students aware of the variety of options that they have so that they are able to use the elaboration strategies with increasing fluency and flexibility— never feeling trapped by a task.

To encourage this kind of fluency and to help students access their repertoire of elaboration strategies, (Weinstein 1995), feel that students need to be able to answer a variety of questions about the material that they are trying to learn, including:

- What is the main idea of this story or this section of text?

- If I lived during this period, how would I feel about my life?

- How could I use this information in the project I'm working on now?

- How could I represent this in a diagram?

- How could I put this in my own words?

- What might be an example of this?

- How could I teach this to someone in my family?

- Where else have I heard something like this?

- If I were going to interview the author, what would I ask?

- Have I ever been in a situation where I have felt the way the main character feels? (18-19)

Students, working in teams, can practice generating questions for each of the elaboration strategies. As a class, they can decide which questions are the most helpful in getting them to focus on the material. These questions can then become part of an on-going list and be placed in the front of their learning logs as a visual reminder of the elaboration options they have.

CREATING AND ANNOUNCING
EVALUATION CRITERIA

One of the quickest ways to raise achievement is to make sure that students understand how they are going to be evaluated and by giving them multiple opportunities to work with the evaluation criteria. Even if we give an array of challenging assignments and spend hours at home, away from our students, evaluating these assignments, we cannot be sure that our students will learn. How many times, do we, as teachers, feel as if we are beating our head against a wall? In frustration and anger, we often wonder, "Do they even bother to read any of my comments? Do they learn anything from all of this work?"

In all fairness to our students, however, we cannot expect them to somehow mystically tune in on our expectations for an assignment. As students, we've all wasted time and energy trying to figure out what a teacher really wants in an assignment. Not being able to figure out what a teacher wants encourages thoughtless and superficial responses. When students do not know how they are going to be evaluated, they often respond in voiceless, stilted responses, become hostile, or they simply give up.

If an assignment is worth the time and effort that it takes for students to complete and for a teacher to evaluate it, then it certainly merits an accompanying scoring guide or rubric as discussed in Chapter 2.

From the moment an assignment is given, students understand the criteria of evaluation, helping them to focus on the actual assignment. While they are working on the assignment, they can continually refer to the scoring guide, making sure that they are meeting the requirements. Thus, the scoring guide serves as a revision guide to refine their work. The scoring guide becomes a peer group activity, where students can give each other focused feedback by using the guide. During the process of producing the assignment, they have engaging conversations about the criteria for evaluation. Through these conversations, they begin to internalize the criteria for excellence. And when the work is handed back, they can use the scoring guide to understand their strengths and weaknesses and to set goals for improving their future work. Raising scores on state assessments, which involve students performing tasks that are evaluated by state-generated rubrics, can be achieved by using this same method.

When scoring guides or rubrics are used, assessment is linked to instruction, for students have the opportunity to grapple with the evaluation criteria and to change their work accordingly. In so doing, they realize how important it is to be able to move beyond the emotional response to one's work and to judge one's work on the basis of clearly defined standards and criteria. Consequently, they take on the responsibility for their work. What better experience can we give our students? And in this process, they become achievers—probably even lifetime achievers.

PUTTING STUDENTS IN CHARGE OF THEIR LEARNING

Our best attempts fail if we do not let our students do the hard work of learning; we cannot learn for our students. As a teacher and as a parent, I have failed many students and my own children as well. Wanting to be helpful, I intervened when I shouldn't have by solving their problems for them. Unintentionally, I sent them a self-defeating message: You are helpless; rely on me. My actions kept many of them from being achievers, for the job of a parent and teacher is to be able to disappear, knowing that our charges will perform well.

Students grow by confronting themselves as learners, reflecting on their work, and making adjustments in their courses of action. This kind of self-reflection serves them well now and in the future. Imagine a society filled with adults who, instead of hiding from themselves and their actions, are willing to face the daily scrutiny of self-reflection. These kinds of adults emerge from classrooms where:

▶ students are given choices and assume the consequences for their choices.

▶ students are involved in goal setting.

▶ students are taught and practice metacognitive skills—skills that enable then to look at their learning in objective ways by identifying what it is they know and what it is they don't know; devising a plan of action for learning;

and having an internal dialogue that helps them to solve problems. Students become capable because they have learned to think about thought.

- ▶ students are engaged in activities that require self-reflection—learning logs, portfolios, and goal setting.

- ▶ students are knowledgeable of a variety of learning strategies.

- ▶ students are held responsible for revising and evaluating their own work and holding it to a high standard.

- ▶ students are provided with opportunities to give and to receive feedback from peers.

- ▶ students are given chances to document their learning through exhibitions and/or portfolios.

- ▶ students are provided with authentic learning situations where their work is judged by those beyond the classroom walls.

The best thing about these strategies is that they really work with students who have been traditionally labeled as low achievers. In classrooms of achievement, both teachers and students are accountable for learning. If either party denies the responsibility, failure prevails.

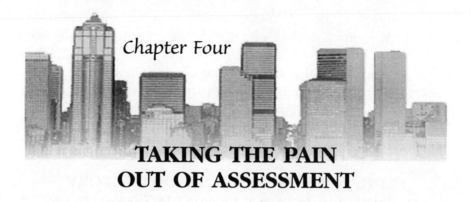

Chapter Four

TAKING THE PAIN
OUT OF ASSESSMENT

"A test?"—The word alone can bring on anxiety attacks—sweaty palms, rapidly beating hearts, and, most of all, complete memory lapses.

For some students, no amount of preparation can ease the trauma of test taking. Paralyzed by their fears, they become convinced that they are stupid and cannot learn.

However, students are not alone in their frustration with tests. Feeling that some of the more traditional and standardized tests do not accurately measure their students' learning, many teachers have embraced the alternative/authentic assessment movement. Using more authentic ways to assess their students' learning makes sense to teachers since they can place assessment into a much broader context. As teachers commit to portfolios, performance-based tasks, exhibitions, and demonstrations, classrooms change dramatically as well as attitudes about assessment.

Authentic assessments match teachers' notions about how students learn. Since this kind of assessment focuses on the process of learning as well as the products of learning, teachers find that they gain keen insights into structuring and restructuring their instruction. When assessments are based on how students learn, they don't exist in isolation at the end of unit, when students anxiously await their sentencing. If assessment is integrated with instruction, students and teachers have many opportunities to look at their learning in a variety of settings and formats, guaranteeing a measure of success for all students.

Thus, it comes as no surprise that the alternative/authentic assessment movement draws heavily upon the field of cognitive psychology. An understanding of these principles helps teachers to broaden the context of their assessments and to design more meaningful assessment tasks.

USING COGNITIVE PSYCHOLOGY THEORY TO IMPROVE INSTRUCTION AND ASSESSMENT

Knowledge is Constructed

How many times have you felt gypped and angry because a test didn't really reflect what you knew? If assessments are structured on the belief that *learning is constructed* rather than memorized, assessments become more inclusive, representing a broader knowledge base.

In this view of learning, the teacher is no longer perceived as having all of the information. Rather, students encounter information, and, in so doing, they construct meaning, placing it into new and personally significant contexts and extending their learning even further. In constructivist classrooms, students have multiple opportunities to grapple with the material to be learned. Thus, the learning is not presented in a "finite" package, ready to be memorized and regurgitated for test purposes. In contrast, learners are invited to:

- ▶ respond to open-ended questions
- ▶ pose questions of their own
- ▶ discuss information openly and freely with peers,
- ▶ make personal connections, seeing where the learning leads
- ▶ link new information with prior information
- ▶ make new connections through critical and divergent thinking
- ▶ elaborate on their initial learning
- ▶ use primary sources, data, and manipulative materials to enhance their learning

Brooks and Brooks (1993), proponents of constructivism, note that in this philosophy of learning, "Assessment and teaching merge in service to the learner" (91). Viewing assessment as a "service to the learner" lessens the waste of valuable instructional time in mind-deadening drill which attempts to prepare students for tests that will have little impact on their learning and their lives.

How many times does instruction come to a screeching halt because teachers feel compelled to prepare students for standardized tests? In New Jersey, I watched a math teacher copy hundreds of pages of sample math test questions. Instruction consisted of students entering the room, picking up the daily allotment of worksheets, and spending the entire class period working through these sheets in isolation with no interaction with peers or the teacher. The teacher's role was reduced to one of record keeping—recording the worksheets his students had, somehow, managed to plow through. After five weeks of this grueling drill, the test day arrived; however, all of this drill was in vain. Instead of instilling confidence, the drill created anxiety. On the dreaded test day, many students elected to stay away, and absenteeism soared. Those students who braved the test scored at the very lowest percentile in the state.

Certainly, these students see their teacher differently than those who are fortunate to have constructivist teachers whose students understand that they are:

> adults who continue to view themselves as learners, who ask questions with which they themselves still grapple, who are willing and able to alter both content and practice in the pursuit of meaning, and who treat students and their endeavors as works in progress, not finished products. (Brooks and Brooks 1993, 9).

Thus, the constructivist classroom is one in which there is a continuous search for meaning, where students ask their own questions, and where students' views are used as points of entry for instruction (Sparks, March 1996, 2). They are not sentenced to an endless parade of worksheets to prepare them for tests.

Assessments, reflecting the constructivist view of learning, are beginning to merge at all levels, including the state level. For instance on more authentic state assessments, the assessments may take more than one class period, involve several activities which build to a final task, and even allow students to have discussions with peers. In these cases, the assessments drive instruction rather than intruding upon it.

Clearly, the following California language arts assessment task served its learners by structuring several open-ended learning experiences into the assessment. (CLAS—Grade 8 Sample Integrated Reading and Writing Assessment Prompt):

SECTION ONE: INDIVIDUAL WORK
(MAKING MEANING)

❶ While reading a short story, students are asked to jot down their thoughts, feelings and questions in the margins and underline any passages that they think are important. (The story has been typed in a double-entry journal format, with the story typed on the left side of the page and room for students' comments on the right.)

❷ When they are finished with the story, students are directed to do a series of activities individually which will help them to construct meaning for the story. These are excellent instructional activities which a good teacher would ordinarily use in the classroom on a daily basis to help students understand a piece of literature:

▶ **writing**—a log entry, giving their first response to the story.

▶ **picking**—something from the story that they think is important and writing about its importance.

▶ **filling**—in a graphic of two empty heads with words, phrases, or even symbols representing a specific character at the beginning of the story and the same character at the end of the story, showing how the character has changed. This is followed by a written description, telling how the character has changed during the story.

▶ **responding**—to selected quotations in a double-entry format.

▶ **extending**—the story by having students create a conversation with the protagonist.

▶ **writing**—a final log entry where they discuss the personal connections they've made with the story and what they think it means.

SECTION TWO: GROUP WORK
(EXTENDING THE MEANING)

In this section of the assessment, students are placed in groups and given a series of tasks to complete, including:

▶ **discussing and taking notes** on the story.

▶ **selecting** symbols for the characters and **explaining** them.

▶ **responding** to a series of hypothetical situations relating to the story and drawing from their own personal experiences.

SECTION THREE: INDIVIDUAL WORK
(APPLYING THE MEANING)

In the last section, two different writing assignments are given, one involving an autobiographical incident and the other a speculative essay.

In this assessment task, reading and writing are not treated as separate entities or as isolated skills. In addition, the assessment is structured so that students have several entry points to engage their learning. This task is specifically designed to seek students' points of view, giving them several chances to reflect upon their thoughts and to redefine their thinking. According to Brooks and Brooks, "Cognitive growth occurs when an individual revisits and reformulates a current perspective" (112).

The constructivist teacher sees students as having the ability to make unique contributions, even having pockets of authority, that will enhance the learning. Therefore, the teacher becomes a guide, inviting students to participate in an unforgettable journey of learning. During this journey, the teacher is flexible enough to allow students to become guides and to direct the learning, often departing from the planned course. Assessment tasks are an integral part of this exciting journey.

Learning Occurs from Social Discourse

Learning theory also supports the importance of group work and social discourse. Although many teachers are committed to cooperative learning instructional tasks, they fail to use social discourse as an assessment tool. When teachers include group work as part of the assessment task, students have time to rehearse and extend their thinking with peers, eliminating many fears associated with taking a test alone. As students present their ideas and listen to the work of others, they begin to reconstruct their knowledge, often elaborating on their original thoughts. Consequently, confidence emerges, and tasks move within their reach.

In our rush to cover material, we often forget the importance of structuring class time so that students can discover the multiple perspectives of the material. By confronting these perspectives, students are forced to sort through and to wrestle with concepts while employing the critical thinking skills of analysis, synthesis, and evaluation.

Part of the strength of the California Assessment Task for Reading and Writing is that it gives students time to discuss their thoughts in groups before they are asked to perform alone. Many teachers have patterned their instruction and some of their assessments after this *collaborative model*:

❶ Begin with an individual task.

❷ Move to a group task which builds on the individual task, thus, giving students an opportunity to redefine and extend their learning.

❸ End with an individual task which requires students to synthesize and extend their learning.

Quite ironically, even though the California Learning Assessment System (CLAS) modeled good instruction for teachers in California and across the nation, it is no longer used. Having become the focus of political opposition, it was discontinued. Unfortunately, this is not unusual. Whenever states or school districts adopt more authentic kinds of assessment, they tend to come under careful scrutiny of the opposition, and are often abandoned prematurely.

Learning Varies Greatly from Learner to Learner

The theory that students vary greatly in their learning styles, intelligences, attention spans, and even their "developmental pacing" has impacted assessment significantly (Herman, Aschbacher, and Winters 1992, 19). When teachers realize that tests can contribute to inequitable learning in their classrooms, they begin to change the format and the setting for the assessment tasks they design. Instead of relying almost exclusively on rigidly timed, paper-and-pencil tasks, teachers begin to consider the following:

❶ tasks and exhibitions involving the multi-intelligences.

❷ varied sociological groupings—individual, paired, groups.

❸ varied time frames—hourly exams and extended periods ranging from a few days to weeks to an entire school year (Herman, Aschbacher, and Winters 1992, 19-20).

Thus, assessments are extended to include a wide-range of classroom activities such as:

▶ producing graphic representations of material

▶ creating dramatic productions—role playing and simulations

▶ participating in debates

▶ transforming knowledge into several different forms

▶ conducting experiments

▶ initiating independent research

▶ interviewing people in the community

▶ participating in an oral history project

▶ solving real world problems

▶ producing authentic work for authentic audiences

While observing an Integrated Language Arts class in Louisville, Kentucky, I joined a group of students who were participating in a literature circle. Having finished reading the play, "A Raisin in the Sun," they decided to do a dramatization of some of the scenes and present them to the class as a culminating activity . In the assignment, students were allowed to choose from a variety of options However, all of the presentations had to include:

▶ a synopsis

▶ insight into the characters

▶ literary devices

▶ issues

▶ quotable quotes

On this particular day, students were checking their scripts to make sure that their scenes reflected the text. One puzzled student voiced some concerns, saying, "Why haven't we mentioned the plant in our script. I don't know why, but the author keeps on talking about that stupid plant." He then turned to me and asked if I knew why. Shrugging my shoulders, I said, "It must be important if the author talks about it a lot." He sat quietly for a moment and then blurted out:

I know. The plant doesn't look so good, but it keeps on living. The plant is like the mother. She has had a rough life, but she also doesn't give up. The last thing she does before moving to the new apartment is to pick up the plant. They're both going to start a new life.

Immediately, he had increased his group's understanding of the play. Not surprisingly, his peers decided to include the episode of the plant in their presentation.

If the teacher had decided to give a traditional test on the play, this new learning would not have been constructed. However, she trusted her students, giving them freedom to present their learning in a unique way. By the way, the student who made this significant observation was a special education student. On a traditional test, he, more than likely, would have shut down completely, not being able to even complete the test. In contrast, this assessment contributed to the student's learning and developed his efficacy. During an IEP conference, the student proudly retold this story, as his mother and teacher listened, to document his ability to learn. The assessment task enabled him to see himself in a new light—a capable learner.

One of the most frustrating aspects of teaching is that not everyone performs at the same pace. There are those students who race through assignments, completing them in record time, and others who just need more time to organize their thoughts. Sensitive teachers adjust instruction to allow for these pacing differences. Strangely enough though, this same consideration is not given to assessments. To make sure that an assessment program is equitable, teachers should not rely exclusively on timed, hourly tests, but rather include a *variety* of time frames— some hourly exams, some extending over two or three days, and still others extending over longer periods of time. Much of the learning is lost if it is always assessed in a short period of time and not given enough time to percolate. Individuals need time to formulate meaningful theories, to develop an appreciation for knowledge, and to cultivate a natural curiosity about the content (Brooks and Brooks, 39).

In Long Beach, California, Barbara Van Oast's science class committed themselves to year-long, community-based, ecology projects as a culminating activity to an ecology unit One of the projects involved students doing a study of where campus trash comes from, resulting in a recycling project. It was so successful that the recycling project was adopted by other schools in the district. This ongoing assessment project forced students to continually look at their learning over a period of time.

Rich delRio, a social studies teacher at Muirlands Middle School, experimented with forms of alternative assessment. Since teachers were required to give final exams at his school, Rich wanted to design a final that was worth his students' and his time—one that would force his students to synthesize all of the learning experiences of their United States history class. In addition, he wanted the final to provide an opportunity for students to discuss the great historical events by having them reflect upon their own historical discoveries. To achieve all of this, he decided to use an extended time frame and different context for his final.

Consequently, he designed a final assessment task entitled "While Cleaning out the Attic," focusing on the reoccurring theme that history is a series of extraordinary events which happen to ordinary people. The assessment task extended over two weeks and involved help from peers to improve the final product (see Fig. 4.1). Thus, the assessment task extended students' learning.

WHILE CLEANING OUT THE ATTIC . . .

I happened to come across a bound packet of dusty old papers in a locked trunk. I wasn't sure exactly what they were but something told me not to throw them out. Later that afternoon I realized that my discovery was a family journal which my ancestors had successfully maintained from colonial times to the year 1900. In it they had written and collected an informal family history of the United States. It contained documents, portraits, maps and the thoughts and feelings of everyday people involved in great events.

I called my friend Alfred Knopf, the publishers, and asked about what I would have to do in order to publish it. He commanded that the materials be organized in the following manner:

1. table of contents/timeline/family
2. 2-3 representative journal entries from each major time period
3. a brief modern explanation of the journal entries/contents
4. maps, portraits, and documents placed in the proper time period.
5. a concluding statement by the historian which reflects on the value of the discovery and the study of American history.

TIME PERIODS

1. Pre-1760 Arrival in Americas, origin of diary, daily life (work, family, language, religion, etc.)

2. 1763-1800 Revolutionary War, the Constitution, famous historical figures and great political ideas.

3. 1800-1850 Westward expansion, transportation, US-Mexican War, Native-Americans, daily life.

4. 1850-1877 Slavery and Abolitionism, the Civil War, Reconstruction, major events, historical figures and ideas.

5. 1865-1900 Age of industry and Immigration, the growth of cities, wealth and poverty, and daily life.

CONNECTIONS

Your journal entries should be connected by a family story. The relationship between characters should always be clear to the reader. Remember items such as birth, marriages, deaths, inheritance, disease, runaways, indentured servitude, slavery, immigration within the U.S., jail, meeting famous people, reading about events in the newspaper all help to make this

Fig. 4.1a. Writing as an alternative assessment in an eighth grade social studies class.

a history with an emphasis on story-line. Your characters should be interesting, but they should be ordinary people who participate in great events. They should come into contact with a wide variety of Americans in different times and places.

TIMELINE

We will complete this assignment in class over the next two weeks. You are required to participate as an editor as well as a writer. On the following days, you will expected to share rough drafts from the time period. You will work in groups to check the accuracy of the material, improve the entries, and discuss the time period. Further revision will occur as homework.

Thursday — 6/3 Colonial Times
Monday – 6/7 Revolution
Wednesday – 6/9 Westward Expansion
Thursday – 6/11 Civil War
Friday – 6/12 Industrialization
Monday – 6/14 Final Drafts due

Your paper will be evaluated on the following criteria:

1. The journal is written in the voice of a person who has lived through the time period. Readers actually feel as if they are re-living these events.

2. There is a strong story-line so that the reader connects the events to each other. None of the events exists in isolation.

3. Each time period has at least two or three journal entries that show an insightful understanding of the time period.

4. Each time period presents accurate historical events which are supported by detail.

5. Maps, portraits, and documents are used to make the story-line more authentic.

Fig. 4.1b. Announced evaluation criteria raise students' performance

Both parents and students responded positively to this exam. During the two-week period, students had a unique opportunity to synthesize their learning by placing it into a new and exciting context. This student's first entry in a historical journal shows her involvement in the learning:

January 15, 1756

Dear Journal,

I've been keeping this journal so that when I return to England, my wife and child will know the events of this war and my part in it. I hope that this journal that I've started will be passed down throughout the generations so that the future children of the family will know their history.

Thank the Lord, earlier this week England and Prussia signed a mutual defense pact. Frederick II had agreed to defend Hanover and we in turn agreed to support him. I met Frederick II once when he came to sign the papers. He seemed a harsh man. Smart, almost old beyond his years. He obviously has been through much.

This war drags on forever. Rations are few, supplies are not spared willingly, yet morale is quite high. Will it be this way in the months of fighting to come? I hope all is well at home and Jen and Max are well. If anything happens to them, so help me I'll...No I won't think of such things. Well, I must get some sleep. Dawn will be here and I need energy for the drills.

Sincerely,

George B. Samuels

In her notes, this young historian explained that the author had written this entry during the Seven Years War and that he eventually returned home to his wife and young son.

As part of the requirement, students also had to complete and include a self-evaluation of the project and an evaluation from a peer. The following is the reader's evaluation of the final Project:

READER'S EVALUATION OF FINAL PROJECT

Directions: Rate on a scale 1 (poor) to 5 (excellent). Provide a justification statement for your rating on each item.

1. Insightful understanding of each time period. _____

2. Accurate historical events supported by detail. _____

3. Is organized from beginning to end. _____

4. Holds reader's interests. _____

5. Is well written. _____

Answer this question in a paragraph.

1. What specific historical information did you learn?

One student commented, "The best thing about this project was the variety of topics able to be written on." Students drew upon this range of topics to exhibit their expertise rather than being limited by a few teacher-selected topics.

Robin Jongerius, a health teacher at Hill Middle School in Long Beach, developed an interesting alternative assessment for her unit on family living. For this assessment, students were allowed to work in groups of three to synthesize all of the information they had learned in this real-world unit. They were asked to use this information to collaboratively write a realistic short story about a fictional infant or adolescent and to give factual details about how the character is growing and developing. Ms. Jongerius designed the following scoring guide to accompany the assignment:

Items To Be Evaluated	Possible Points	Students' Evaluation	Peers' Evaluation	Teacher's Evaluation
The basic elements of growth and development are explained. The eight developmental tasks as defined by Erikson are considered.	25			
The setting and plot of the story is clear.	25			
The story is convincing, effective, and interesting.	25			
Language, mechanics, usage and spelling are used appropriately.	25			
The story is appropriate for the audience intended.	25			
Time in class was used well and the project is turned in on time.	25			
Total Points	**150**			

The students evaluated themselves and each other, using the scoring guide. In addition, they wrote a justification for their scores, identifying areas of strengths and areas that needed more work.

Although many teachers have contributed to my learning, there are a few who have become my authorities—experts in their own right. Carol Barry, a sixth-grade teacher at Muirlands, is one of those. She is a leader in staff development, offering workshops at her school and at the national level and having participated in prestigious national study groups such as the New Standards Project and PACE. With her strong teaching talents and expertise, she successfully led Writing to Learn Projects in Seattle and Jackson, Mississippi. What I love about Carol is that she shares her knowledge, talents, and materials with others—willingly and joyously. She is a teacher's teacher.

During a unit on immigration, Carol's students visited a magistrate, Magistrate Moscowitz, at the courthouse and interviewed him about his views on immigration. As part of the unit, her students also read *Lupita Manana*. Carol helped her students link the real-world information given to them by Magistrate Moscowitz to the novel by designing the alternative assessment in Fig. 4.2.

To make this assignment ever more real-world, Carol had her husband, a lawyer, and his colleagues read her students' responses and gave them feedback. Giving her sixth-graders an authentic audience of professionals created an unforgettable learning experience for them. Perhaps, our students' fear of assessment would be eliminated if we designed assessments such as these—assessments that hurl students into the real world in an engaging way. This "hurling" wasn't fearful for it grew out of the learning experiences of the unit— a perfect example of assessment being embedded in instruction. In addition, Carol structured her assessment so that students could succeed; students understood how to proceed with the task.

Putting the Students in Charge of Learning

Students perform better if they understand their own learning styles, know the criteria for evaluation, see models of other student work, and have a grasp of how their work measures up to set standards. For this to happen, students need time to work with the standards of evaluation so that they can internalize them, developing a critical eye toward their own work. As students look at quality work done by other students, they are better equipped to look at their own work and to address their weaknesses and strengths. Their newly gained insights help them to devise a plan for improvement, putting them in charge of their learning. However, the process is time consuming and requires a strong commitment from both teachers and students, but it is well worth the time. In gauging their work against benchmark models, students understand the attributes of quality work, taking the mystery out of evaluation.

This devoted effort on the part of students and teachers also informs parents of a student's progress. When students can hold informed conversations about the quality of their work, based on rigorous standards, parents sense that there is a keen sense of direction for the learning, and they become staunch supporters of education.

LUPITA MANANA / FINAL EXAM

At the age of 18, Lupita Torres was caught by the INS. She has hired you as her attorney and you will fight against her deportation back to Mexico before Magistrate Moscowitz at the Federal Courthouse.

To win this case you must convince Magistrate Moscowitz of the following:

  1) Lupita is of good character.
  2) Lupita has demonstrated the ability and willingness to work in the United States.
  3) Lupita's future plans demonstrate her desire to become a productive member of society in the United States.

Your writing must contain details from the book which support your statements. For example, to convince the magistrate that Lupita is a person of good moral character, you may tell him that Lupita regularly sends money to her family in Mexico. Your paper should contain a minimum of five paragraphs including an introduction, a body and a conclusion.

Points

____ Your writing addresses each of the three points mentioned above. (5 points)

____ Your writing gives specific details from the book to support Lupita's case. (15 points)

____ Your writing is compelling and efficient. (10 points)

____ Your writing is well organized. (10 points)

____ Your writing contains few grammar, spelling and punctuation errors. (5 points)

Peer Editor_____

Fig. 4.2. This carefully designed asssignment assures students of success

As students begin to assume responsibility for holding their learning to high standards and for improving their work, performance quite naturally increases and self-efficacy emerges. Students see a direct relationship between their efforts and their progress. Thus, an important transition occurs. Students are less likely to be motivated by short-lasting, extrinsic rewards provided by others, but will instead quietly and consistently seek the more satisfying intrinsic rewards of becoming competent learners. Pizza parties and roller skating parties pale in comparison when learners discover their ability to produce quality responses to challenging assignments.

DESIGNING AN ASSESSMENT PROGRAM

The first step in designing an assessment program is to establish clear goals and purposes so that the instruction and assessment can be aligned. Goals and purposes can be identified by taking time to answer these essential questions:

▶ What do I really want my students to know? What is worth knowing?

▶ What kinds of tasks (multi-dimensional) will help them learn this?

▶ How will we know how they are doing?

▶ How can we do it better?

Mary Beth Blegen, 1996 National Teacher of the Year, addressed the importance of such questioning:

We must put our curriculums on the table and ask frightening and challenging questions such as, 'What are the kids learning from that material?' Perhaps even more frightening is what comes after the questions are asked.

Our challenge lies in our ability to assess what we are now doing and to ask ourselves honestly what needs to be changed to make a difference. We need to make real change in all classrooms. We must no longer give lip service to such change. (1996, 1)

This questioning should be the foundation for all that we do in the classroom.

WHAT IS WORTH KNOWING? WHAT DO I REALLY WANT MY STUDENTS TO KNOW?

The question, concerning what students should know and be able to do, seems to have been answered with the adoption of standards by many states and school districts. Since the standards have been written by teachers, administrators, parents, and members of the community, there is wide acceptance that these are things that students should, indeed, know.

However, standards do not completely define or limit what is taught in a classroom. As teachers encounter individual students on a daily basis, additional needs are discovered. The knowledgeable teacher adds concepts that the standards do not cover—filling important gaps. Standards are not meant to dictate the entire learning that occurs in every classroom, nor should they. If this were so, learning would become highly prescribed and assembly-line in nature—eliminating the need for passionate teachers who love their subjects and feel they have much to share with students. If standards completely define the classroom, the danger of stifling students' natural impulse to learn might occur, limiting the opportunity for students to take control of their learning and to discover where the learning leads them. However, standards do make us all keenly aware of the subject matter that needs to be woven into each discipline.

In addition to letting standards identify what is worth knowing, a group of teachers at Muirlands Middle School in San Diego wrote portraits of what students should know by the time they leave each grade level. According to a humanities teacher, the teachers had experienced success with their standards-based, interdisciplinary units, but they felt that their instruction was still somewhat fragmented. They were also fearful that some of their students were missing essential experiences such as being exposed to a variety of genres in reading and writing. These concerns showed that these talented teachers understood intuitively what a strong program should look like; nevertheless, they felt the need to articulate their program in clear terms. Thus, they decided to write descriptive portraits of their instructional programs to guide their instruction and assessment. The language arts teachers have written this description of their program:

LANGUAGE ARTS PORTRAIT
"MUIRLANDS MIDDLE SCHOOL"

❶ The language arts program is literature-based and meaning-centered. It exposes all students to significant literary works. Our literature program at grades 6, 7, and 8 parallels and reflects the thematic units studied in corresponding social studies classes. The year-long theme for grade 6 is "Survival." For grade 7 it is "Change," and for grade 8 it is "Who Are We Americans": Students read and respond to both self-selected and teacher-selected works. They study a variety of literary genres including all types of primary-source documents. At each grade level they study the elements of literature and the elements of style. (Grade 6 novels/novellas include *Marco of the Winter Caves, Walkabout, Pyramids, The House of Dies Drear, The Jataka Tales, Trojan War,* or *The Giver.* The grade 7 list includes *The Bronze Bow, King Arthur and the Knights of the Round Table, Samurai's Tale, A Midsummer Night's Dream, Hamlet,* and a *Tale of Two Cities.* At grade 8, the list includes *The Crucible, When the Legend Dies, The Fall of the House of Usher, Across Five Aprils,* and *To Kill a Mockingbird.*)

❷ The program includes writing to construct and clarify meaning and directs attention to the various stages of the writing process. Students practice a variety of creative and expository writing. Writing is literature-based and process-oriented. Students use writing to extend and reformulate their knowledge, synthesizing new products based on literature. The stages of the writing process are emphasized at all three grade levels. Students write frequently. In pre-writing and during the editing process, students work with rubrics/scoring guides. They talk to each other about their work, act as peer editors, and collaborate on certain pieces. They produce final drafts in which meaning is clear, and the conventions of language are used appropriately. The eight CLAS (California Learning Assessment System) writing formats are taught at all three grade levels, with special emphasis on the following at each grade level:

Sixth—autobiographical incident, first hand biography, evaluation, and short story

Seventh—autobiographical incident, evaluation, short story, and observation

Eighth—problem-solution, observation, report of information, and analysis with speculation about cause or effect

Students at all three grade levels study grammar and language usage. This study is continually reinforced through the peer editing process, emphasizing the practical application of their studies. At the sixth grade level, teachers evaluate grammar usage through students' own writing and provide suitable remediation throughout the year. This is supplemented with specific grammar units that parallel student needs. Emphasis is placed on parts of speech, language mechanics, and punctuation. At the seventh grade level, emphasis is placed on sentence structure, language mechanics, and syntax. Students study parts of speech in depth, providing a solid foundation for more in-depth study at the eighth grade level. At the eighth grade, students build upon the basics. They review parts of speech, language mechanics, subject-predicate, and study subject complements, pronouns, prepositional phrases, and simple, compound, and complex sentences. Students at the 6th, 7th, and 8th grade levels systematically study vocabulary. Some vocabulary is literature-based and some is based on the different levels of the text *Wordly Wise*. Appropriate use of the dictionary is taught at the 6th grade level.

❸ The program includes attention to oral language development and proficiency. Students communicate for a variety of purposes in creative and innovative ways at each grade level. Their reading, writing, and oral communication skills are integrated to help students construct meaning. Scoring guides for oral presentations are used across grade levels throughout the year. Students reflect upon and assess their own performance and the performance of others. Students talk about works they have read; all are given opportunities to participate.

❹ The program includes an assessment component that encompasses the full range of language arts goals and incorporates performance-based approaches to assessment. Students at each grade level regularly work in cooperative groups to discuss and respond to works of literature or to do background research on related topics. These tasks allow for experiences in other content areas such as art, music, science, and history, both through individual work and collaboration. Students produce both short and long-term performance tasks, many of which are presented to real audiences. Students at each grade level, and in various scholastic disciplines, maintain working folders from which they generate individual school-wide portfolios. Each student portfolio will contain student-selected work reflecting each of the following dimensions of learning: effective communication, analytical and critical thinking, global perspective and social responsibility, creativity, citizenship, inquiry and problem solving, and growth and learning. The school-wide portfolio will follow the students from grade 6 to 7 and from grade 7 to 8. This will provide the opportunity for students to review work completed in the previous year and design goals and objectives for the learning year to come. In addition, students can reflect upon their own growth in their school career. This portfolio culture will produce students who are actively involved in their learning.

As teachers met to write these portraits, they came to consensus about learning in their discipline, powerfully binding their classrooms together into a cohesive experience for middle-school students. In addition, they took ownership of the standards and the learning in their classes.

As a teacher, I also felt that my instruction was fragmented. Although I faithfully used the curriculum guide as a way of structuring my classroom, I still worried. Something was missing. I wanted the instruction in my classroom to be more organic, representing my students' needs, and I always struggled with this. Quite by accident, I stumbled upon a strategy that helped me keep this important balance.

During the first week of school, I gave this question to my students: What is worth knowing? I placed the standards from my curriculum guide in one column on the board, saying this is a given of what you are expected to learn this year. In the second column, I placed additional items that I wanted my students to know. In the third column, I asked them to identify what they would want to know if they didn't have to worry about grades. Initially, my students were slow to respond to this question, for they had never been asked. After a few lion-hearted students found their voices, others followed. Soon the board was filled, and an agenda for learning began to emerge.

We, then, looked at the three columns and tried to make connections. Oddly enough, many of the items seemed to fit together quite naturally or could easily be expanded to reflect the students' identified needs. Throughout the year, we used this list to keep us focused and to see if we needed to make additions, reflecting our new discoveries about learning.

WHAT KINDS OF TASKS WILL HELP STUDENTS LEARN THE CONTENT?

As teachers, we cannot afford to fall into a pattern of ineffective instruction. We must continually search for better strategies to increase achievement, even if it means abandoning some of our favorite projects. Too often, we plan in isolation from our students, forgetting what valuable resources they are.

With this in mind, I extended my activity. I had the class brainstorm about ways that they could learn what was listed. Then, I asked them to think about their most successful learning experiences and ones that had been disastrous. Returning to the agenda for learning, the class identified ways to weave the successful strategies into the class. Quite naturally, the next topic for our agenda was assessment. We talked about their feelings concerning assessment and how we could make assessment more valuable in the learning process.

In this type of learning activity, students understand that they are contributing to the structure of the classroom. Meanwhile, the teacher gains valuable insights into the individual learners in a classroom, lessening the time spent on inappropriate strategies.

HOW WILL WE KNOW HOW WE'RE DOING?

Many times, the learning is cut short because teachers have not thought through the assessment portion of an engaging activity. Therefore, the activity loses some of its impact, for students need to know how they are performing throughout the entire instructional activity. Usually, students gain this knowledge too late—at the end of a unit. To really have an impact on achievement and learning, assessment should be expanded so that it is part of the on-going instruction.

An important and natural use of assessment is to *measure the outcomes* of students' learning by looking at the *products* they produce. These products let both the teacher and the students know how well they are meeting the standard, allowing them to monitor their achievements. In some cases, a fill-in-the-blank or multiple-choice, with some modifications, may be the best way to measure students' learning. For instance, having students simply provide *explanations for sections* of these kinds of tests can expand the learning. There are times when it makes sense to use these short-response tests, particularly if factual knowledge or a specific skill, is necessary in order to proceed to more difficult concepts or more complex applications. Nevertheless, these kinds of tests should never be the only kind of assessment.

Students need to experience a variety of assessment formats, including short-response, alternative, and authentic.

In addition to measuring outcomes, assessment is also used to diagnose learning and to inform instruction. Teachers want to be able to identify students' weaknesses and strengths, design appropriate instruction, and give students an understanding of their learning processes. Consequently, they find ways to assess the *process of learning.* In so doing, they unlock many of the mysteries of learning for students and for themselves. When teachers look at both the process and products of learning in their classrooms, they create more balanced assessment programs and enhance their students' learning.

DESIGNING PERFORMANCE-BASED TASKS

Assessment tasks that are authentic, or real world, measure the products of learning more effectively and create an excitement for learning. These tasks take their design from actual work that is encountered in the world beyond the classroom. In moving away from the kinds of assessment that have traditionally separated schools from the real world, teachers are turning to more authentic assessments and performance-based tasks. Often, the terms authentic assessment and performance-based assessment are confused. Meyer (1992), distinguished between these two kinds of assessments:

> Performance assessment refers to the kind of student response to be examined; authentic assessment refers to the context in which that response is performed. In a performance assessment, the student completes or demonstrates the same behavior that the assessor desires to measure. There is a minimal degree, if any, of inference involved. In an authentic assessment, the student not only completes or demonstrates the desired behavior, but also does it in a real-life context (40).

The kinds of tasks which engage even the most reluctant learner are those performance-based tasks that are placed in a real-world context, making the assessment an authentic one. These assessment tasks combine several complex skills and processes and allow students to demonstrate their knowledge by actually performing the task. To guide their responses, students are given the evaluation criteria with the assignment. However, developing performance-based tasks and evaluation criteria can be overwhelming, and teachers often find themselves asking, "How do I even begin?" Several teachers have used the following model in making the transition from more traditional assessment to performance-based assessment:

MODEL FOR PERFORMANCE-BASED TASKS

Start with instructional goals and standards

Identify discipline-based content, processes, and skills

Write a task *(Consider multi-intelligences, real world, interdisciplinary tasks)*

Create a scoring guide or rubric

During an ecology unit, a science teacher may want students to study the long-term effects of pollution on an urban area. To do this, students need to have specific, discipline-based content and skills—ways to identify and measure water and air pollution, knowledge of the scientific method, and how to record and report data. If students are concerned with how pollution affects the population's quality of life, then they also need to learn a whole series of related skills including: preparation of surveys, selecting random samplings, interviewing techniques, and recording and reporting data. In reporting data, they need to become familiar with different kinds of graphs. Once the teacher has specifically identified the instructional goals and standards and placed them into the context of a unit, then performance-based tasks are written, including a culminating task for the unit.

In writing these tasks, the teacher wants to assure that it is equitable for all students—that it is a fair measure task. Therefore, the performance-based task needs to be multi-dimensional, interdisciplinary, and real-world based. It is impossible for a science teacher to include all of the learning in this model ecology unit by devising an hourly test. As a result, the task becomes one that requires students to draw upon a variety of skills to solve a problem that is faced in real life. When students are asked to solve such problems, their sense of efficacy increases, for they have evidence that they can use their learning to solve difficult problems.

Mattie Shoulders, a teacher in Chattanooga, devised the series of performance tasks in Fig. 4.3 for her middle-school science students.

Teachers who want to establish a culture for performance-based assessment make their instruction more realistic and open-ended. To design such lessons, it is helpful to think of the work that is done in the real world by professionals and then to have students complete some of the same tasks. In this kind of assignment, students are asked to assume the role of a professional, and then they are given a related task, resulting in a product or products. For instance, my husband, a professor of government, has his students become legislative assistants for a member of Congress. Their legislator asks them to investigate a specific issue, and they, in turn, must write a two-page report on the issue, giving background information and making a recommendation. Wiggins (1989) defines this kind of authentic assessment:

> Assessments replicate the challenges and standards of performance that typically face writers, business people, scientist, community leaders, designers, or historians. These include writing essays and reports, conducting individual and group research, designing proposals and mock-ups, assembling portfolios, and so on... They enable us to watch a learner pose, tackle, and solve slightly ambiguous problems... to watch a student marshal evidence, arrange arguments, and take purposeful action to address the problems (703).

THE CULMINATING TASK

You have been asked to select and study one or more environmental issues that is occurring in or around the Chattanooga area. Examples of what you might choose to study are:

1. Why is the Asian Clam dying and covering the surface of the Tennessee River? What caused it, and what – if anything – can we do to prevent them from dying?

2. What has been the effect of the Coast Guard and TVA dumping batteries into the Tennessee River? How can this be cleaned up? How can we prevent this from happening again?

3. What is the impact of industrial pollution in Chattanooga Creek on fish and the people who use the creek for recreation and as a food source?

You may think of other issues besides these to study. But, in the end, you will have to pick a particular issue as the focus of your attention.

Your study of pollution and environmental issues in and around Chattanooga must include the following:

1. **An opinion poll** showing what people in the Chattanooga area believe about their town in relation to the topic of pollution and the environment. This poll must be desegregate according to age, gender, race/ethnicity, area of residence, and any other factors you decide are important. You will do this work in your math class.

2. **A detailed 3-D map showing how geography and activity in surrounding area might cause pollution in Chattanooga:** You will study the role geography plays in causing pollution problems in and around Chattanooga, and how activity in communities surrounding Chattanooga might cause pollution problems in our city.

3. **A scientific experiment** conducted in relation to the topic of study you choose, including planning and conducting experiments about pollution and its impact on the Chattanooga area. You can work as part of a group or individually to conduct your experiment. Your experiment will include a hypothesis, research of the topic, collecting and organizing data, and drawing conclusions.

Fig. 4.3a. Performance-based tasks make learning come alive in this science class

You will present the results of your study of pollution, including your opinion poll, your experiment, and your study of geography and action in the surrounding community.

<u>Learning Section 6:</u> PRESENTATION OF YOUR WORK

This culminating activity will present itself in four different forms:

1. **<u>A presentation and display</u>** to a panel of parents and community members who represent appropriate agencies (EPA, news media, TVA, Coast Guard, Vanderbilt University study groups, city council) that are actually involved in correcting and preventing these problems in the Chattanooga area and surrounding counties.

2. **<u>Presentation of formal paper</u>** of research findings to the mayor, city commissioners, and the above agencies.

3. **<u>Write a feature article or editorial</u>** to be published in the newspaper informing the public of our problems, findings, conclusions and recommendations.

4. **<u>In the form of a letter</u>** ask for a response from all the agencies involved, in reference to future actions to be taken to deal with, as well as eliminate, the problems.

5. **<u>The setting and location</u>** will be Lookout Valley School Theater.

6. **<u>The time</u>** is to be announced at a later date.

You will present the results of your study of pollution, including your opinion poll, your experiment, and your study of geography and action in the surrounding community

Social Studies - Mattie C. Shoulders
Science _ Wes Green
Mathematics - Patricia Hanson
Language Arts - Mattie C. Shouders, Wes Green, Patricia Hanson

Fig. 4.3b. Authentic audiences from the community provide an incentive for students to polish their work

Teachers can use the following templates to design more authentic, performance-based assessments:

ROLES FOR PERFORMANCE-BASED ACTIVITIES

City planner, Expert witness, Agency director, Newspaper columnist, Engineer, Historian, Archaeologist, Scientist, Statistician, Curator, Author, Lawyer, Critic, Counselor, Legislator, Elected official, Corporate executive, School Board member, Administrator, etc.

TASKS FOR PERFORMANCE-BASED ACTIVITIES

Disprove, Evaluate, Analyze, Negotiate, Build, Investigate, Create a model, Design, Propose, Compile information, Take a position, Conduct experiments, Advise, Report, Assimilate evidence, Defend, Recommend, Develop a rationale, etc.

PRODUCTS FOR PERFORMANCE-BASED ACTIVITIES

Brochures, Blueprints, Proposals, Scripts, Museum exhibits, Television shows, Ad campaigns, Speeches, Maps, Experiments, Consumer reports, Flow charts, Interviews, Historical documents, Journals, Surveys, Recommendations, Congressional hearings, Newspapers and magazines, Documentaries, Political campaigns, Graphs, etc.

If students are given the opportunity to present their products to real professionals in the field who will critique their work, the assignments take on a new dimension of authenticity, providing unforgettable learning experiences for them.

In experimenting with alternative, performance-based assessment formats, Kim Waldo, a science teacher at Standard Middle School in Long Beach, gave this performance-based task in Fig. 4.4a-c as a culminating assessment for an energy unit.

The Mini Page

As a group of students, you have spent the last nine weeks studying energy. Your job is to take your knowledge about energy and put it into a format that children in second to fifth grades can understand. The format you will use as your guide is the *Long Beach Press Telegram* mini page.

Please assign each member of your group to a job:

Editor: Must have excellent grammar and spelling skills
Illustrator: Draws to express the concept being taught
Publisher: Arranges articles and illustrations on the final draft
Copyist: Copies articles to make neat for publication

Your page should include the following:

1. **Two** articles on energy-related topics you studied during the last nine weeks. *Examples: What is convection? What is a chemical reaction?*

2. Illustrations which show energy in action or how it is used.

3. A simple lab activity students could do at home.

4. A short quiz to test knowledge of energy.

5. Ways to encourage children to look for energy use in their lives. *Example: Send students on a scavenger hunt in their school to find machines that use conduction.*

6. **Two** other ideas that your group must brainstorm to teach children about energy

Each member of your group should do or help on at least two of the activities!!

References: To help in producing your Mini Page, you may use any of the following references:

*First quarter assignments
*Textbooks and related articles
*Mini page

Fig. 4.4a. This creative assessment helped students to synthesize and present their learning in an unusual format

MINI PAGE RUBRIC

A (27-30 points)
Accurate science information, revealing an understanding of key concepts
Has met all writing requirements
Written at an elementary school level
Articles and diagrams capture the readers' interest
Diagrams help explain the concept being taught
Well planned layout of information
Fun for children
Creative—grabs children's attention
Neat
No spelling or grammar errors

B (24-26 points)
Accurate science information, revealing an understanding of key concepts
Has all writing requirements
Well thought through layout of information
Articles and diagrams are written with children in mind
Written at an elementary school level
Diagrams fit with energy being discussed
Neat
No grammar or spelling errors

C (20-23 points)
Scientific information is presented
Has all writing requirements
Information is neatly laid out
Articles are not at elementary school level
Diagrams fit the topic of energy
Diagrams and reading are hard for children to understand
Some spelling and grammar errors

D (15-19 points)
Missing one or more required writing assignments
Diagrams do not fit topic of energy
Page looks rushed and hurried
Information copied from the book
Articles not focused on the topic
Inaccurate scientific information
Spelling and grammar errors

F (14-0 points)
Missing two or more required writing requirements
Diagrams missing or not about energy
Page incomplete
Information copied from the book
Articles not focused on the topic
Inaccurate scientific information
Many spelling and grammar errors

Fig. 4.4b. Announced evaluation criteria help students produce better products

GROUP AND PERSONAL EVALUATION
FOR MINI PAGE

*Answer for each person in your group:

1. Was the person here each day that work was done on the Mini Page?

2. Did the person contribute each day of the assignment? Explain.

3. Did this person complete all work assigned by the group? Explain.

4. Was this person reliable with materials? Explain.

5. Do you feel that the person contributed equally to the production of the Mini Page? Explain.

6. What grade would you give to this person's work? Explain.

*Answer 1-6 for yourself and the following questions:

7. Do you feel that the Mini Page is above, below, or the same quality of work as is usual for you? Explain.

8. What was your main job in the group? Did you complete your job?

9. List your other contributions to the group.

10. Were there any problems in your group that I should be aware of? Please list them.

MINI PAGE PROJECT EVALUATION

1. Did your group complete all parts of the assignment?
2. What makes you most proud about your mini page?
3. What about your mini page could be improved?
4. What is the overall grade you believe your mini page deserves? Give a justification for this grade based on the rubric?
5. IN CONCLUSION, I WOULD JUST LIKE TO SAY:

Fig. 4.4c. This evaluation has students' reflect on the process of learning by evaluating peers' and their own contributions

Mini Pages

QUIZ

1. How does heat energy start?

2. What kind of molecules have lots of heat? why?

3. What is convection?

4. How is sunlight heat?

5. How is energy used in our lives everyday?

HEAT EN

The Mini Pages today gives you
we are learning about today is Heat En
internal motion of the atoms. Heat Ene
Heat energy is transferred by convecti
Heat is transferred from one substance
molecules. Fast moving molecules hav
moving molecules. Heat Energy can b
hands together.

Convection is heat transfer in liq
currents and conduction is a substance
and rapidly than other substances.

EXPERIMENT

Heres something that you kids could do. When your at school or
walking around your neighborhood look for different kinds of Energy.
For example television gives out radiation energy and cars give out
Potential energy and Kinetic energy. When you think of these things
write them down and you will see how much energy you use
everyday.

POTENTIAL

Potential Energy: Energy of shape
What is Potential Energy? Potenti
How does it work? A stretched r
ability, to fly across the room. A woun
potential energy. It has the potential to
around when it unwinds. An archer's t
the potential to send an arrow gliding t
held high above the ground has the po
ground when it falls onto it.

FILL IN THE BLANKS

1. Cars give out _____ Energy and _____ Energy.

2. Television uses _____ Energy.

3. Heat Energy is created when you rub your _____ together.

4. Potential Energy is energy of _____.

5. Kinetic Energy is energy of _____.

6. Heat Energy is internal motion of _____.

Potential	Radiation
Kinetic	Position
Hands	Motion
Atoms	

ANSWER

1. Cars give out Potential Energy and Kinetic Energy.
2. Television uses Radiation Energy.
3. Heat Energy is created when you rub your Hands together.
4. Potential Energy is energy of Position.
5. Kinetic Energy is energy of Motion.
6. Heat Energy is internal motion of Atoms.

```
Q R L V U L A I T N E T O P O T K C
M A S K O V O O C O N V E C T I O N
E D I S R T R F H A W K E G T T S I
W I F R N S E S W E A T E R S O V Y
X A J C T E N E R G Y B Q M W T L O
I T A R V S I M O L E C U L E S L N
Z I V K T F F A L C O N S P U T C E
C O R B W R P S T L O U I S U N A T
G M P E X W L S A N N T N E R S T P
```

RADIATION   CONVECTION
MOLECULES   SWEATERS
POTENTIAL   SUN
ENERGY

y. The Energy
gy is the
lts from friction.
and radiation.
contract of
ergy than slow
bbing four

by convection
heat more easily

red energy.
gy of position.
he potential, or
g also has
of the watch
hed) bow has
A brick being
stake into the

LAB

Introduction: The people here at, "The Mini Page," want you to try a lab. You will have to put a blue sweater, a red sweater, a white sweater, and a black sweater out in the sun. After an hour, go get the sweaters and see which is hotter.

Hypothesis: We at, "The Mini Page," predict the black will be the hottest. Why don't you make a guess before you start too.

Materials: 4 sweaters and of course the sun.

Procedure: 1. Take the sweaters outside.
2. Sit them on a bench, chair, ect.
3. Wait for an hour.
4. Take the sweaters and feel them.
5. Which is hotter?

Data/Observations: Now that you have done the lab, what did you feel? Heres a chart to show you what you felt.

Sweaters	Temperature		
	Hot	Warm	Cold
Blue			
White			
Red			
Black			

Conclusion: What was the hottest sweater? Ours was the black, but yours might have been different. Why do you think the black was the hottest?

It is not unusual for a teacher to design an interesting culminating activity; however, rarely do they follow through by creating scoring guides, rubrics, and other assessments. Thus, the culminating activity is not really a powerful assessment tool. In the above assignment, Ms. Waldo, created a rubric and distributed it when the assignment was given so that students would know how their mini page would be evaluated. From the very beginning, students knew the criteria for evaluation, and the standard they would have to meet in order to produce quality work. In addition, they could use the rubric to guide their revision process. Performance is more likely to soar when students understand the evaluation criteria as outlined in a rubric or scoring guide.

Since the work also involved a collaborative experience, Ms. Waldo devised a group evaluation sheet for students to complete as part of the assessment. And finally, she had students complete a self-evaluation. When students know they are going to be held accountable for their contributions to a group, they take the task much more seriously. Furthermore, in order to become self-regulated learners, students need to scrutinize their own endeavors.

After students finished their mini pages, they walked to an adjacent elementary school and presented them to the students. They were thrilled with the students' enthusiastic endorsements of their mini pages. One student said, "They are so bright; they really understand energy." Ms. Waldo quickly pointed out that their students' success was the result of their thoughtful teaching. Getting rave notices from a real audience made these students willing learners.

When they returned to the school, the students examined the elementary students' quiz scores and the students' feedback on their mini page. Then, they discussed what they would have done differently to improve their product. An example of a student-produced mini page appears Fig. 4.5.

ASSESSING PROCESSES

As exciting as this mini-page assessment and other performance-based assessments are, they, alone, cannot be considered a full and balanced assessment program. It is not enough to look at the products of learning. Teachers can learn a great deal about instruction and about the learning in their classrooms by watching students as they learn, or by looking at the process of their students' learning. They can gather this valuable information through:

- ▶ Essays, which include prompts, evaluation criteria, drafts, and revisions

- ▶ Portfolios/reflections

- ▶ A variety of multi-dimensional projects, including evaluation criteria and process journals

- ▶ Investigations and exhibitions, with students' progress notes

- ▶ Surveys—attitudinal

- ▶ Learning logs/reading response journals

- ▶ Goal setting/monitoring progress

- ▶ Conferencing/conference notes

- ▶ Kid-watching/documented observations/checklists of behaviors

- ▶ Interviews/processing of experiences /think-alouds

In collaborative or cooperative learning activities, the forms in Figs. 4.6 and 4.7 can be helpful in getting students to look at processes.

HOW WELL DID WE DO?

1. How would you rank your team? Place an X by the number which best describes your team's efforts.

Send Help!   Making Progress   Cast of All-Stars

1   2   3   4   5

Give at least two reasons for ranking your team at this level:

2. What were some of the hurdles that slowed your team down?

HURDLE ONE:

HURDLE TWO:

HURDLE THREE:

Which ones can you eliminate? How?

3. What were some of the things that your team did well?
   (Be Specific)

4. Make a list of what each person in your group did.

   Do you need to divide the tasks so that they are more even?

5. What will your team do differently next time to become even more successful and efficient?

Fig. 4.6. Helping students reflect on their groups performance

HOW WELL DID I DO

1. These are the things that I did to help my team: _____

_____

_____

_____

_____

2. My team can always count on me to _____

_____

_____

_____

_____

3. In looking back, I shouldn't have _____

_____

_____

_____

_____

4. My team would have been more productiove if I would have

_____

_____

_____

_____

5. The next time, I'll definitely _____

_____

_____

_____

_____

Fig. 4.7. Self-reflection on group work

When I taught advanced composition classes, I used to have students hand in a self-evaluation sheet along with the finished paper and an early draft. Although the early draft allowed me to see the process of the writing, I found that the self-evaluation sheet often gave me more insights into the writer's process and, at the same time, guided my evaluation of the final product.

In introducing the self-evaluation sheet, I told my students that I was often very frustrated when I evaluated their papers. Sometimes, I found myself wanting to call them and ask a question. In order for us to hold a conversation about their writing, I asked them to complete the self-evaluation sheet in Fig. 4.8 and to mark on their manuscript to guide my responses and evaluation.

By having students complete this self-evaluation:

▶ I received valuable information about the process of learning in producing the piece

▶ It made my evaluation more focused and less time consuming. Instead of wondering where to comment, I immediately commented on the sections that they had marked on their manuscripts, for this was where they would have the most impact. I answered their questions and concerns.

▶ I learned about new things they were trying and encouraged them to be risk-takers. If they had tried something new, and it didn't work, I could help them understand why instead of treating it as an error and marking them down.

▶ Students learned that no paper exists in isolation. Through the experiences gained in writing the paper, they got ideas on how to make the next ones better. Therefore, the assessment became a learning experience—a guide for improving their work.

LOOKING AT MY WRITING

**(Please complete and attach to your paper.
Don't forget to mark on your manuscript. I need your help!)**

1. How much time did you spend on this paper? _____

2. Put a smooth flowing line beside the parts you feel are best.

3. Put an Excedrin headache line (W) under the parts that you had trouble with.

4. Circle new words or "just right" words.

5. Is this a paper that you would like to read aloud to the entire class? ____Why or why not?
_____
_____
_____

6. What did you try to improve on in this paper?
_____
_____
_____

7. Did you experiment with anything?
_____
_____

8. Where did you get your idea? What difficulties did you encounter? Successes?
_____
_____
_____
_____

9. How does this paper compare with others you have written this year?
_____
_____

10. Place an X over punctuation, spelling, usage, or sentence structure where you need my help or clarification.

11. Write any questions that you have about this paper. (I'll try to answer.)

12. Based on your experiences with this paper, what one thing will you do to improve your next piece of writing?

_____

Fig. 4.8. This form asks students to reflect on their writing and to trace their growth as writers, providing focus for evaluation

- ▶ Students had more control over and ownership of the assessment since they were allowed to ask questions and point out things.

- ▶ Assessment became a dialogue, or conversation, between student and teacher and not a deadly monologue. When students received their papers, they felt as if I had responded to their needs. The comments were as important as the grade, enhancing the learning experience. The emphasis changed from "What did I get?" to "What did I do well? What could I have done differently?"

Since students were at the center of this evaluation, it was much more valuable to them. I also found that I looked forward to evaluating papers more, for, in reality, this evaluation process provided me with the luxury of having a conversation with each of my students—far from the maddening crowd and without interruptions.

CREATING A PORTFOLIO
CULTURE IN YOUR CLASSROOM

Portfolios are another way of making authentic assessment a reality in your classroom. Through the portfolio, both process and product are honored as well as the learner's voice. When teacher and students understand the value of portfolios and take ownership of them, the classroom becomes charged with excitement and purpose.

The sixth grader's words captivated me: "You are about to enter the portfolio zone. Hold on to your seats. You'll see for yourself all that I've learned this year." I couldn't wait to see the pieces she had chosen to document her adventure in learning and to read her reflective comments on each. For the next hour, I accompanied her on an incredible journey from an uninvolved learner to an academic all-star. In the process, I realized that her portfolio was a living document of her progress and developing sense of ability (Bimes-Michalak 1994, December, 3).

According to research and a growing number of teachers, the benefits of portfolios are many, including:

▶ linking assessment to instruction.

▶ documenting growth and competence.

▶ monitoring and documenting standards.

▶ giving students the ownership and responsibility for their learning.

▶ making learning more collaborative.

▶ informing instruction.

▶ generating samples of high-quality work.

▶ providing a basis for student/teacher conferences and class conversations about learning.

▶ building students' metacognitive and reflective skills.

▶ helping students to make connections by linking new knowledge to prior knowledge.

▶ communicating assessment information and progress to parents, school officials, and the public.

Despite all of these benefits, many teachers are reluctant to use portfolios. As part of the Writing to Learn staff development program, urban teachers are asked to implement portfolios in their classrooms and to share their experiences and learning with colleagues. At our network meetings, the topic of portfolios always brings a range of emotionally charged responses, from open hostility and abandonment, to the agony of frustration and failure, to enthusiastic endorsement. What makes the difference between a successful and a devastating portfolio experience?

All too frequently, teachers willingly jump, or are coerced, onto the portfolio bandwagon without fully understanding the purposes for keeping portfolios, the portfolio process, or how this process relates to the context of their classrooms. Good portfolios don't just happen; they evolve only after much thought, a great deal of planning, and an unfaltering commitment. There are no generic trip tickets for the portfolio journey. Each teacher must find his or her own path, and this takes commitment which cannot be mandated.

What is a portfolio?

Although volumes have been written about portfolios, a great amount of confusion still exists as to what makes a portfolio a portfolio, and teachers are at vastly different stages in their knowledge of portfolios. For those who are confused, a portfolio is a collection of student's work over a period of time. The collected material represents and documents the breadth and range of the learning experiences in a classroom. Valencia (1990) states that this breadth and range depicts our "… desire to capture and capitalize on the best each student has to offer; it encourages us to use many different ways to evaluate learning" (43).

During the course of the year, students have several opportunities to select items to document their learning and to reflect upon their learning in these selections. In turn, their portfolios are presented as evidence of achievement to an audience, which may be parents, other teachers, peers, outside readers, etc. To create a portfolio culture in a classroom, conversations about portfolios are not limited to specific days set aside for selecting work, but rather portfolios are the fabric that is woven throughout the entire instructional process, providing a clear focus for instruction and on-going assessment.

Paulson, Paulson, and Meyer (1991) provide this definition of portfolio assessment:

> A purposeful collection of student work that exhibits the student's efforts, progress, and achievements in one or more areas. The collection must include student participation in selecting contents, the criteria for selection, the criteria for judging merit, and evidence of student reflection. A portfolio provides a complex and comprehensive view of student performance in context. It is a portfolio when the student is a participant in, rather than the object of assessment . . . It

provides a forum that encourages students to develop the abilities needed to become independent, self-directed learners (60-63).

Why should I consider using portfolios in my classroom?
Portfolios should be a part of every classroom because learning is never completed; it is always evolving, growing, and changing. Unlike most other assessments, portfolios are uniquely responsive to this dynamic process. They allow maturing learners to develop their craft of learning over a period of time and to become actively involved in evaluating their own work. They also serve as a vehicle for individualizing instruction and for making learning a dialogue. Portfolios work because they are authentic, continuous, multi-dimensional, and interactive.

The stages of the portfolio process
In developing portfolios, teachers find it helpful to divide the portfolio process into four stages: *collection, selection, reflection, and presentation*. To have a successful portfolio experience, careful attention must be given to each stage.

The Collection Stage
Over the years, the greatest change in portfolios has occurred in the collection stage. In the beginning, teachers were very vague about what should be included in their portfolios, and their main purpose for using the portfolios was just to get students to love and value their work. Therefore, they would have students simply keep their favorite pieces in a portfolio and reflect on why they had selected them. Although the portfolio experience was a pleasant one, the portfolios really did not represent the breadth and range of the learning experiences in a class. It would have been virtually impossible for an outside reader to get a clear picture of the learning experiences of the students and a portrait of the instruction. Thus, teachers began experiencing some great dissatisfaction, feeling that they were not reaping the full benefits of portfolios.

Carol Barry, a sixth-grade humanities teacher in San Diego, is an example of such a teacher. She has worked with portfolios for five years, and each year her portfolios have changed. In speaking about this change, Carol commented:

My purpose changed. My first attempts focused on simply getting students to love and value their work. Although this is important, I wanted to use portfolios as a kind of assessment, where students would be charged with the more challenging task of documenting their learning.

As a result of this rethinking, Carol identified the essential experiences in her classroom by placing them into these categories: analytical thinking, growth in skills, collaboration, applications, real-world extensions, and creativity. Still Carol worried that this was too prescribed and that students would become so preoccupied with documenting their learning that there would be no place for discovery. Therefore, she continued to monitor her students' responses to portfolios, searching for ways to develop a more balanced portfolio.

At the end of the 1996-1997 school year, Carol had her students rewrite the criteria for the portfolio collection in their own words. She was astonished at how well they could state them, showing their understanding and ownership of the portfolio design.

However, it takes a commitment, time, and effort to get at this level of sophistication with portfolios. I am indebted to talented teachers such as Carol Barry who take on the role of scholar/ teacher and study instruction in their classrooms, contributing greatly to their own and their colleagues' knowledge about teaching and portfolios.

In the beginning, teachers become preoccupied with the overwhelming task of managing portfolios in their classrooms, and they grasp for a *prescribed* portfolio—state-mandated, commercially prepared, or even another teacher's portfolio. One frustrated teacher exclaimed, "Just tell me what should go in my portfolio!" This teacher failed to realize that *the best portfolios are organic;* they grow out of the context of a particular classroom and group of students.

When teachers blindly adopt someone else's portfolio, they probably keep the portfolio process at arm's distance, failing to create a portfolio culture in their classrooms. It's almost impossible for these prescribed portfolios to reflect the instruction of a particular classroom. Since these portfolios do not grow out of the context of the classroom, they don't reflect the changes that occur in the process of learning.

As teachers learn more about their students and reflect upon the essential learning experiences in their classrooms, portfolios change, too, reflecting the increased learning. In fact, as I listen to teachers, who have been successful with portfolios, they always say, "My portfolios are good this year, but next year they'll be better. I've learned so much." Following this proclamation, they are able to hold meaningful discussions about the changes they will make. Just as good teachers change and grow, so do portfolios. In refining their knowledge and understanding of portfolios, they see all sorts of possibilities for them. Rarely, have I seen teachers do portfolios the same from year to year. With evolution, portfolios become increasingly more sophisticated. Recently, I received this note from a teacher in Chattanooga:

> Enclosed is a copy of a student's portfolio. I hope it's okay. It's a start anyway. I'm looking forward to the fall to begin again. I can't wait to make changes! I feel good that it is not a collection folder. We have worked hard on cleaning out papers. I wanted to keep only items that showed the child's progress.

This teacher really doesn't need my approval; she knows her portfolios need to revamped.

As with other assessment measures, the portfolio process begins with some very basic questioning: What is my purpose in having students keep portfolios? Why do I want to do this? Purposes might include: a teaching tool to inform teaching and learning; an assessment tool to document students' learning and their progress toward reaching standards; a research tool to document discoveries about learning. Taking time to identify purpose(s), provides teachers with direction in formulating their portfolios.

Once the purpose is established, the teacher is confronted with more questions: "What will go in the portfolio? What is worth knowing?" Joan Boykoff Baron, in a portfolio discussion at Harvard University, addressed this issue with these poignant words, "If someone looked at my assessments or inside my students' portfolios, would I be comfortable that those tasks represented my values about what I would 'go to the mat for'?" (July 19, 1993).

The following questionnaire helps teachers to define their portfolios:

THINKING ABOUT PORTFOLIOS

1. How do I want to use portfolios in my class?

2. What standards will my students be responsible for meeting this year?

3. What do I want my students to be able to do when they leave my class?

4. What kinds of multi-dimensional activities do I use in my instruction?

5. What are the specific content and process skills my discipline demands?

6. How will my students and I monitor their progress (assessments)?

7. How would my students respond to this question: What have you learned in this class this year?

8. Based on these responses, what kinds of evidence can I collect to demonstrate growth? Will this evidence show students and parents this growth?

9. How will I assess their portfolios?

10. Who will be the audience for the portfolios? What special plans need to be made for this to happen?

As teachers, we get on a content treadmill and teach content without ever thinking about the context of this content. We expect students to make connections when we, ourselves, have made none. However, self-questioning can help us place our teaching into a meaningful context, becoming the heart and soul of good instruction.

This questioning also helps us establish worthwhile portfolios. When teachers fail to spend time planning their portfolios, they are often reduced to collection bins of truly undistinctive work— quizzes, worksheets, etc.—a collection not worth the time and effort of keeping. A colleague once said, "I don't have all of the answers, but, thank heavens, I have lots of questions." Looking at our work with a critical eye keeps us and our portfolios evolving and growing.

When teachers are asked to share their portfolios with colleagues, some become very nervous and defensive. Frequently, I hear the disclaiming remark, "Well, we really do a lot more in my class. The portfolio just doesn't show it." Clearly, these teachers do not feel that their portfolios represent the values that they are willing to "go to the mat for."

Although it is difficult for teachers to accept, disappointing portfolios may also be making a strong statement about the quality of their instruction When quality instruction is lacking, portfolios can never be more than collections of junk— testimonials to ineffective teaching.

During a portfolio planning session, a Long Beach social studies teacher began the frustrating task of identifying the essential learning experiences in his class. After many false starts, he produced this list: being critical readers; having alternative viewpoints of history; understanding the motive force of history— both collective and individual; being able to analyze causes of current problems and to develop solutions; appreciating differences; developing a concern for social justice and a sense of ethics; understanding the importance of working together— community building; and having a conception of responsible citizenship.

However, this was only a first step in defining his portfolios. As he talked with colleagues, he realized that it would be impossible for him to give his students multiple experiences in each of these categories and to include content standards and a range of responses to the work as well. His portfolios would become never-ending tomes. Therefore, he decided to rethink his list by asking, "What really is important for my students to know?" This proved extremely difficult, for he had taken ownership of his criteria already. In watching him struggle through this process, I knew that this teacher would never settle for someone else's prescribed list.

After this vital step, the teacher planned a variety of instructional tasks—assignments and assessments—to accompany his reconsidered table of contents. Thus, a plan for instruction and the criteria for the portfolio were borne out of his strong convictions about what students should know and be able to do in his class and in response to the district's standards.

This teacher's revised portfolio included these items:

PORTFOLIO TABLE OF CONTENTS

- Analytical thinking/Problem solving
- Historical knowledge
- Collaborative work
- Concern for social justice and citizenship
- Growth in content skills and documentation of standards

For this teacher, the next step was to write some descriptors for each of the criteria to assist students in their selections of work and to better inform his instruction. He also needed to think about how the district's standards were reflected in this portfolio and about how the portfolio served as documentation of students' having reached the district's standards.

The following guidelines can be used in the collection stage of portfolios:

❶ Make sure that portfolios contain **longitudinal samples** of students' work. This work should extend over the entire school year, for students need to see how they have grown and changed over the year. Rarely, do they have this opportunity. In addition, the longitudinal sampling of work also validates teachers. At a recent meeting, a teacher confided, " I was really down, thinking that we had achieved very little this year. Then I looked at my students' portfolios. I was astonished at how much learning had occurred. " Thus, portfolios are a good reality check for us, helping us to remain focused and to move beyond our self-doubts.

One word of warning, though; start the year with a portfolio plan. Portfolios do not emerge during the year without one. With a full agenda, portfolios will fall by the wayside—never becoming a reality in your classroom. On the first day of school, let your students know that this is going to be an exciting portfolio year! You may not be satisfied with your plan, but give it a shot anyway. One thing for sure, you'll learn a lot in the process. If you wait for the perfect plan, you'll never begin. Remember: Perfectionists seldom produce anything.

As students begin collecting their longitudinal samples of work, be sure that they place the date on *every item being selected.* As they reflect on their work, it is important for them to know when the piece was produced so that they can see the timeline of their growth.

❷ Include evidence which displays the breadth and depth of the learning experiences in your class and documents the reaching of standards. This includes a rich variety of multi-dimensional activities such as projects, performances, presentations, problem-solving, learning logs, maps, notes, graphs, etc. This may require students to even include videotapes or cassette tapes. (Be sure to not limit the portfolio to written pieces.)

❸ Incorporate a variety of responses to the collected work—peer evaluation, outside readers, narrative, and reflections. (Some teachers set aside a portion of the portfolio for these responses.)

❹ Include growth in learning and accomplishments—both individual and collaborative.

Once teachers have designed their portfolios, the next questions are: How do I physically manage the collection of all the students' work? Where do I store it? To be perfectly honest, in the beginning of the portfolio process, the physical management of portfolios concerns teachers more than the contents. As teachers get a management system under their belts, they then worry about what the portfolio should contain. Consequently, our first meetings on portfolios are dominated by management questions.

For management purposes, each student keeps two folders—a working folder and a portfolio. Teachers store these documents in a variety of ways. Some use plastic crates, designating a crate for each class; some use large boxes; some use individual pizza boxes which students decorate to represent themselves. Most teachers use the crates.

Teachers have various names for the working folder—a garage, the flow-through folder, etc. Regardless of what this folder is called, it contains **all** of the student work. It is used almost daily; it is messy; it is unorganized. In the beginning, many teachers mistakenly think that they have portfolios when they have collected all of their students' work. In fact, they just have the **resource materials** for a portfolio. To be considered a portfolio, there must be student selection, reflection and goal setting, and presentation to an audience. To rephrase an old song, "We've only just begun" when we have the collection folders. They are a means for producing portfolios; they are not an end in themselves.

The Selection Stage
When teachers have figured out the context for standards in their classrooms and the representative work they want their

students to consider in their portfolios, they are ready to provide their students with the portfolio selection criteria. Many teachers make a poster of these criteria, and hang it in the room so that students are always reminded of them. One teacher calls this her "agenda for learning," stating that it keeps her students and her focused on the big picture.

In addition to placing students' work that documents the criteria in portfolios, some teachers have students write their autobiographies for the content area at the beginning of the year, and then, at the end of the year, they write the chapter for the current year. In language arts classes, teachers often have students' do a writer's profile and a reader's profile (see Figs. 4.9 and 4.10) at the beginning of the year and again at the end of the year. These documents are included as part of the portfolio and are used to provide evidence of change over the year.

When teachers first start working with portfolios, they set aside specific days for portfolio selection and organization. Usually, they designate days before the end of each grading period. Students use the day to reflect on their progress during the grading period, assessing their achievements and setting learning goals for the next grading period. As teachers become increasingly more comfortable with the portfolio process, the process becomes more organic. Portfolios become the core of instruction, and they are ever-present in the classroom. Thus, the selection process becomes less formal as students delve into their portfolios at unscheduled times, anxious to record their learning and to reflect upon it.

However, in the beginning, specific portfolio days are designated—days where students look at their working folders and select representative work for each category in the portfolio. This selection process is essential, for it holds students responsible for documenting their learning and for achieving standards. The portfolio's table of contents not only defines the student's selection process, but it also guides instruction. If these are the items that we want students to be able to document, then we must structure instruction so that they have several opportunities to produce such work. Thus, the portfolio keeps everyone focused.

THE WRITER IN ME: A WRITER'S PROFILE

1. List the kinds of writing you do.

2. How frequently do you write on your own when it is not an assignment?

3. When writing for a class, would you rather find your own topic or have the teacher assign one? Why?

4. Do you like to write? Explain your answer.

5. What is the most difficult part of writing for you? The easiest part?

6. Where do you get your ideas for writing?

7. How do you figure out what you're going to say in a piece of writing?

8. What do you think the characteristics of "good" writing are? Is your writing "good" writing? Why or why not?

9. Do you write more than one draft? Why or why not?

10. How do you know when a piece of writing is finished? Do you worry about not being able to finish a piece of writing?

11. What do you do to make a piece of writing better?

12. What does the word revising mean to you?

13. What does the word editing mean to you?

14. Do you ever read your writing aloud to someone after you've finished a draft? Why or why not?

15. Are you will to read your writing to other people? Why or why not?

Can you summarize what you've discovered about yourself as a writer in a few sentences?

Fig. 4.9. In order to become proficient writers, students need to get in touch with the "writer" within themselves

THE READER IN ME:
A READER'S PROFILE

1. List three of your favorite books.

2. What kinds of books do you like to read?

3. What is the hardest part of reading for you? The easiest?

4. How do you go about choosing a book?

5. How often do your read just for yourself and not for an assignment or school?

6. Do you consider yourself a good reader? Why or why not?

7. What are the characteristics of a good book?

8. In class, would you rather read on your own or with a group of students? Why?

9. When you're reading a difficult book or article, what do you do to remember important information?

10. Who is your favorite author?

11. In addition to fictional books, what other kinds of reading do you do?

12. What do good readers do when they read?

Fig. 4.10. Allowing students to come face-to-face with themselves as readers

When students are allowed to select work to document their learning, teachers often become very frustrated. Students do not always select what teachers think they should. Nevertheless, students should be allowed to take charge of the process, or they will not have ownership of their portfolios. To counter this frustration, some teachers have created another category in their guidelines—the teacher's choice for pieces showing growth. Here, teachers select a piece of the student's work, which shows exceptional growth, and writes responses to students, stating why they have made the selection.

At the end of each semester, teachers hold portfolio conferences with their students where the teacher and the student sit together and review the portfolio. This one-on-one time creates a wonderful opportunity for meaningful conversations about learning to occur. The conferences help students to look at their work honestly, to understand their accomplishments, to articulate their growth, and to set goals. While reviewing the portfolio, teachers also offer suggestions for improving the work and help students to develop a critical eye for selecting portfolio pieces that truly represent their accomplishments. In time, students become capable of making more knowledgeable and deliberate choices for their portfolios.

As a follow-up to the conference, students write a letter home describing their achievements, their learning, and their goals for continued work. In addition, the teacher writes a brief narrative of conference observations. Both documents are placed in the portfolios.

The portfolio conferences are invaluable, for they inform instruction and learning, giving both teacher and learner a keen sense of direction. Granted, conducting conferences is time-consuming, but the conference places the learner at the center of the learning and, at the same time, produces a "portfolio culture" in the classroom. Students understand that portfolios are at the core of the learning experience and that their perceptions regarding their learning are of the utmost importance—so important that class time is devoted to the task.

The responsibility for keeping the portfolio should fall completely on the students. Each student is responsible for organizing materials in such a way that they are attractive and easy for an outside reader to read. To achieve this, students may include:

- ▶ a presentation of themselves, including a picture and a short piece about themselves

- ▶ a foreword, or letter to the reader, helping the reader to focus on the contents

- ▶ a table of contents with numbered pages of their selections

- ▶ reflections on the selected pieces, describing their growth in learning

- ▶ responses to their work from peers, the teacher, and outside readers.

The Reflection Stage

Perhaps, the most important stage of the portfolio process is the reflection stage. In this stage, students are required to look at their selected work and to provide a written rationale for the selections. In their reflective pieces, students come face-to-face with their learning by recording: what they've done well; what they need to continue working on; how they've learned; and how they have changed or grown as a learner.

However, this kind of meaningful reflection does not occur automatically. Throughout the year, the class must continually hold conversations about what constitutes good work. Student work is placed on an overhead projector, and the class discusses whether or not the work would be a good portfolio selection to document learning. As students are responding to the work, the teacher asks probing questions to get students to elaborate on their responses and to generate more thoughtful answers. The conversations allow students to hear others reflect or think aloud and they serve as a model for their own reflective responses.

In addition to discussions about good work, conversations are also held on the reflective pieces that students write. Models of good reflective pieces are placed on the overhead and discussed. Students practice writing reflective responses that are specific and meaningful and provide each other with critical feedback. In addition, teachers place their own work on an overhead and reflect aloud about it. When students spend this much class time on analyzing their work and their thoughts, reflecting on their portfolio selection comes naturally, for reflection has become a natural and on-going instructional activity. Hence, their portfolio reflections are richer, revealing their growing ability to look at their work in significant and meaningful ways.

If students have not had this kind of reflective class work, a portfolio response might look like this one, "This is my very best paper because I got 100 on it, and it was very fun. I made a 100 'cuz it was sooo easy." Although the remarks show great pride in one's work, they do not provide the reader with any insight into the student's growth as a learner. For instance, what difficulties did the student have to overcome to produce this work? What specific standards and skills are documented? What successes has the student had? What was the learner's process? When students address these specific issues in their reflective pieces, the reflections provide additional evidence of their achievements and growth.

To begin this reflection process, many teachers start with forms to guide their students' responses. Although some of their forms are included here, **one word of caution: the forms are not an end in themselves.** They are only a point of departure for discussion. The goal is to have students move beyond the forms so that they can articulate their learning clearly—in their own words without prompts. If students never move beyond the forms, their responses are usually rote ones—showing very little thought. In a sense the portfolio response forms become another kind of meaningless worksheet. Another failure of generic reflection sheets is that they fail to address the learning of specific content within a particular assignment, for they tend to overly focus on the process. As we work more with standards and weave standards into our portfolios, I'm sure that we will make our reflections more content-driven. There certainly is a need for this.

```
┌──────────────────────────────────────────────────────────┐
│  PORTFOLIO REFLECTION SHEET                              │
│  FOR INDIVIDUAL, SELECTED ENTRIES                        │
│                                                          │
│  Type of product or assignment (give information about the │
│  assignment to help the reader understand its importance): │
│  _____  │
│  _____  │
│  _____  │
│                                                          │
│  It shows my progress because (talk about the specific skills, or │
│  standards, this assignment reveals; any difficulties you've overcome │
│  in producing it; and what you've learned and done well): │
│  _____  │
│  _____  │
│  _____  │
│  _____  │
│                                                          │
│  Other things that I want you to know about this assignment: │
│                                                          │
└──────────────────────────────────────────────────────────┘
```

If you use the above form, be sure to extend the space for students to make meaningful and full responses. If you leave only a small space, students will limit their responses to short answers. (In the interest of this book, I've shortened the student-response space.)

At the year's end, to bring closure to the portfolio experience, teachers often have students write summative pieces for their portfolios. In these pieces, students summarize their growth over the year. A language arts teacher might use these kinds of questions to guide students' year-end responses:

◆ What does your portfolio say about you as a writer and a reader? What are your strengths?

◆ What continues to be your greatest weakness as a writer? Can you find an example of this in your work? What can you do to correct this weakness?

◆ What growth have you seen in yourself as a writer since September?

◆ What specifically has helped you to grow as a writer? (Peer groups, conferences, self-evaluation, etc.)

◆ Where do you get your ideas for writing?

◆ What continues to be your greatest challenge in writing?

◆ How frequently do you write? Has this increased this year?

◆ What different kinds of writing have you tried this year?

◆ Have you tried anything new in your writing?

◆ Who have been some of your audiences for writing? Who would like to read your writing?

◆ What do you do to make a piece of writing better?

◆ What kinds of reading have you done this year?

◆ What do you like to read? Who are your favorite authors? What authors have influenced your writing? How?

◆ Have you made any discoveries about yourself as a reader and writer?

Using these questions and looking through their documented work and reflections, students write a letter to the reader, telling how they have changed or grown over the year and setting goals for future work. Sometimes, teachers even have students write themselves letters of advice. These pieces are then placed in their portfolios.

The Presentation Stage
With thoughtful planning, the final stage of the portfolio process becomes a celebration of students' accomplishments. When students present their portfolios to an audience beyond the

teacher, a sense of pride emerges. Unfortunately, finding an audience seems to present a challenge for teachers, and they stop short of this celebration stage. As a result, the portfolios are never presented to anyone, and students wonder why they have spent so much time on them.

However, creative teachers have found ways to provide real audiences for the portfolios. One teacher hosts a portfolio reception. The students prepare invitations, using the format of an invitation to an exhibition. Parents and other guests spend the evening sitting with students, participating in portfolio discussions and responding. Light refreshments are served.

At Hill Middle School in Long Beach, California, the school hosts a portfolio day. Parents, members of the community, elected officials, and central office personnel are invited to participate in portfolio presentations. Students flourish from the feedback provided by outside readers, and the guests are always impressed with the students' documented achievements and their ability to articulate their learning.

To involve parents or guardians, another teacher has students make a portfolio date with their parents, or another adult, on a quarterly basis. On the designated date, students take their portfolios home and engage in a portfolio discussion, with the adult responding. One parent enthusiastically responded, "This is the first time that I really understand what my child does in school. I'm so impressed with his accomplishments."

To guide parents' responses, the teacher sends home these questions with the portfolio:

◆ What piece of work did you enjoy most in the portfolio? Why?

◆ Were you surprised by anything? Why?

◆ What does the portfolio tell you about your child or the student?

◆ What are the strengths? The weaknesses?

◆ What do you think the child or student should focus on next?

◆ In what ways has your child or the student changed or grown throughout the year?

◆ Do you have suggestions on how this portfolio can be improved?

◆ Do you have any other comments or advice to give this learner?

Parents, or other outside readers, however, need to realize that they do not have to answer every question on the form; it is just a guide. Also, some parents may not even wish to use it, feeling more comfortable in writing a note or letter to their child. All options should be explained clearly.

During a mid-year parent portfolio session, one parent wrote these comments on a response sheet that asked the parents to read through each item in their children's portfolio and respond to the following questions: Which of the writing pieces is your favorite and why? Has your son or daughter's writing changed since last year? How? Has your son or daughter's attitude toward writing changed since last year? How?

> Choosing just one favorite piece is difficult. I loved the Presidential one because it is filled with his ideas and is clearly written. The Walkabout journal was great, too. I like how Brian took another character's point of view. I enjoyed reading the whole variety of portfolio pieces. Thanks!

> Daniel's writing has changed since last year. He is writing more often and in larger quantity. He is writing more creatively and imaginatively. He is willing to explore ideas and use new terms. Daniel's attitude toward writing has definitely changed this year. He understands the writing process and no longer resists revision and editing. He doesn't have trouble getting started and seems to have clear goals in mind.

Can you imagine the enthusiasm for learning that this kind of specific response from a parent generates in the learner and the teacher? How often do parents and their children have such meaningful discussions concerning learning? How often does a teacher get this kind of feedback from parents?

When students return from the portfolio date with their parents or another adult, they are asked to reflect upon the experience:

◆ How did it feel to present your work to your parents or an outside reader? Were you enthusiastic or hesitant? Why?

◆ Do you think the outside reader understood your achievements? What comments were particularly helpful to you?

◆ Did you get any ideas for improving your work or presenting it differently in the portfolio? Explain.

◆ What was the best thing about the portfolio sharing? The most awkward?

◆ Did anything surprise you?

◆ Did you discover any new questions we should add to the parent/adult response sheet?

◆ Is there anyone else with whom you would like to share your portfolio? How can we make this happen?

As an extra-incentive for the portfolio date, students are released from homework obligations on the evening of the portfolio conference with an outside reader. Some teachers are hesitant to send the portfolios home, fearing that they will never see them again. However, teachers who have tried the outside reading conference have been pleasantly surprised: No portfolios have been lost!

Some other ways of sharing portfolios include:

▶ Inviting members of the school community to drop in on a designated day to read portfolios and to respond. Students, teachers on their prep hours, school personnel such as secretaries, custodians, lunchroom workers, and administrators drop in throughout the day. Refreshments are provided.

▶ Letting older students respond to portfolios. One middle-school teacher in Long Beach pairs up with a senior-high teacher and has the senior-high students respond to her middle-school students portfolios. She has noticed that this important audience makes students work harder on their portfolios.

▶ Using them as a vehicle for discussion at parent conferences and on school-wide parent-conference evenings. Teachers feel that it has given new meaning to these evenings, resulting in significant and meaningful discussions with parents. Instead of teachers explaining what they do in class, the parents simply look at the students' work and ask questions.

SCHOOL-WIDE PORTFOLIOS

Thus far, this portfolio discussion has mainly addressed classroom portfolios, but what happens when a school decides to do school-wide portfolios? How do individual teachers maintain the portfolio culture in their classrooms since the school-wide portfolio may not represent the breadth and depth of the learning experiences in their classrooms? How do the school-wide portfolios change and evolve to represent new learning and the district's commitment to standards?

In many schools, the school-wide portfolio has remained stagnant since its inception, never changing to reflect the new learning of the school. For instance, one school's portfolio has students select what they consider to be their three best pieces of work.

There are no criteria for selection; hence, they do not document a student's learning very well. After reflecting on their selections, students present their portfolios to an outside audience. Although there is definitely a celebration involved in having adults look at students' selected work, these portfolios are not serving the school nor the students as well as they could. However, the school appears to be satisfied with its portfolios, and isn't considering changing them.

A Case Study of an Evolving School-Wide Portfolio

On the other hand, there are schools who are continuously looking at their portfolios and changing them to reflect their new learning and standards. One such school is Muirlands Middle School. It is valuable to look at how their school-wide portfolio has evolved and changed over the years.

Several of their teachers were participants in a national portfolio study at Harvard University. As a result of having successfully implemented portfolios in their own classrooms and from the learning of this national study group, these teachers, spear-headed by the efforts of Carol Barry, decided to create a sixth-grade interdisciplinary portfolio. This was a natural extension of their learning since the sixth grade teams used thematic, interdisciplinary units as the basis for their instruction. (Often school-wide portfolios start this way: beginning with a team's decision to broaden their portfolios to represent the team's efforts.)

Based on this team's success, the team portfolio grew into a school-wide portfolio. Fig. 4.11 shows a table of contents for Muirlands' portfolio, while Fig. 4.12 shows a complimenting criteria-specific reflection sheet which they developed. The criteria-specific inflection sheets have generated more thought-provoking responses from students—much more than the generic ones which were previously used.

Muirlands Middle School
6th Grade Portfolios

1. Demonstrates growth in learning

a. Sets learning goals consistent with stated objectives
b. Locates and uses a variety of sources of information
c. Takes effective and efficient notes
d. Refines, reshapes, or refocuses existing work

2. Demonstrates communication ability.

a. Engages critically and constructively in an oral exchange of ideas
b. Asks and answer questions correctly and concisely
c. Delivers oral presentations using coherent sequence of thought, clarity of presentation, and appropriate nonverbal communication for the purpose of audience
d. Identifies strengths and weaknesses as a communicator

3. Demonstrates analytical skills

a. Observational skills
b. Ability to make reasonable inferences
c. Analyze structure and organization
d. Perceives and makes relationships

4. Demonstrates problem solving skills

a. Defines problem
b. Designs strategy to solve problem
c. Evaluates and articulates problem solving process
d. Collects and analyzes data

5. Demonstrates collaboration

a. Identifies personal interaction behaviors in group process
b. Analyzes behavior of others
c. Assesses group project

6. Applications and extensions

a. Assesses and analyzes local and global issues
b. Articulates understanding of interconnected local and global issues
c. Formulates a response to a local or global issue
d. Responds artistically to contextual information
e. Expresses responses to selected artistic expressions
f. Appreciates the importance of art in expressing human experiences

---

Fig. 4.11. The Muirlands school-wide portfolio describes the criteria for each section

Name _____
Date _____
Selection _____

Muirlands Middle School
6th Grade
Portfolio Selection

<u>Demonstrates Analytical Capabilities</u>

1. Define, in your own words, analytical capability.

_____
_____
_____
_____

2. Why did you choose this piece to show your analytical ability?

_____
_____
_____
_____

3. What are the strengths and weaknesses of your analytical ability? You may wish to comment on your observational skills, your ability to make inferences, your ability to analyze structure or to perceive and make relationships.

_____
_____
_____
_____

4. Describe the strategy you utilized to help you analyze the situation or problem posed in your selection.

_____
_____
_____
_____

Fig. 4.12. Provides students with a frame to make more meaningful responses

Response to their school-wide portfolios was tremendous. Nationally, they received recognition as leaders in the portfolio movement, for they had developed a portfolio that reflected their in-depth and diverse approach to learning—a portfolio that focused on both higher- order and divergent thinking skills and on reading, speaking, and writing. Their portfolio served as a tool for having students look at their learning and their work in significant ways and to comment intelligently, with growing sophistication, about their portfolio selections. For parents, the portfolios demonstrated that their children were experiencing challenging and thoughtful learning experiences. Thus, the portfolio became a vehicle for sharing the context of the learning experiences with parents and others, showing them the inter-relatedness of the learning in all disciplines and making public the expectations for all students. In our Writing to Learn Workshops in other cities, we used Muirlands's portfolio as a benchmark—something we should strive to obtain. They were clearly our heroes, for they provided a high standard for all of us.

However, their school-wide portfolio still continues to evolve and change. Principal Cassandra Countryman powerfully explained the need to keep reflecting on the portfolio:

> When you are a pioneer in the portfolio movement and everyone uses your portfolio as a model, it is easy to become satisfied with your accomplishments and become stagnant. As changes occur at the state and district level, you realize that your portfolio doesn't reflect the new emphasis, particularly on standards.
>
> Although it is tough to let go of the old, you realize that the goals of the state and the district no longer fit in the portfolio. And you move on, integrating what is good from the previous portfolio with a new emphasis on standards and literacy.
>
> In the process, you feel beat up from all of the questioning, but you grow from the experience. Not only is a better portfolio emerging, but it has given us a grand opportunity to look at instruction and to see how we will weave specific subject-matter into our interdisciplinary approach to learning. In fact, all of our staff development this summer will be

based on standards and the portfolio. We are excited because the staff development has been planned and will be presented by our very own teachers.

Thus, the portfolio can serve as a vehicle for staff development, providing an opportunity for teachers to meet and talk about students' work. Muirlands Middle School's current portfolio, a portfolio in which they are attempting to document the dimensions of learning, is illustrated in Fig. 4.13.

It's almost 11 P.M., and I've just finished talking to another teacher friend. Knowing that the book is due, my friends have been calling for the past two days with just one more exciting teaching story to include. Twice, I put the book in the mailing package, breathing a sigh of relief that it was finally finished. And then, twice I ripped the package open, and went back to my computer. They're right, as usual, the stories are too good not to include.

At Newcomb Middle School, the eighth grade portfolios are used to document standards. This year they decided that students would benefit from presenting their portfolios to other teachers as documentation of their learning in middle school. In preparation for this interview, Barbara VanOast taught her students interviewing skills—knowing your purpose, presenting your documentation, looking the interviewer in the eye, and ending the interview. She stressed that presenting their portfolios was like presenting a resume for a job interview, and the teachers to whom they presented would be like future employers.

A portfolio day was set aside and portfolio appointments were made. All 135 students presented their portfolios. Teachers evaluated their portfolios and their portfolio presentations by using a rubric. On evaluations of the process and the day, both students and teachers recorded that this was one of the best learning experiences they have ever had. Even students who had not been successful with their portfolios stated that they would do this again, but next time they would prepare all year long for the event. Many lamented the fact that they had not worked hard enough to really document their achievement. Presenting their portfolios to a real audience added a new

MUIRLANDS MIDDLE SHOOL
DIMENSIONS OF LEARNING

Effective Communication

- communicate through reading, writing, speaking, and listening
- express thoughts and ideas through products and exhibitions
- exhibit appropriate verbal and non-verbal communication for a specific audience

Critical Thinking and Problem Solving

- use observational skills to draw reasonable inferences
- define the problem (questions, analyze, evaluate, and synthesize)
- examine a range of ideas and issues and predict possible outcomes
- perceive, identify, and investigate relationships
- reflect on performances and processes

Global Perspective and Citizenship

- analyze global and social issues from multiple perspectives
- relate present situations to history and make informed predictions about the future
- demonstrate understanding of one's role in a global society
- formulate a response to a societal issue
- collaborate with others to accomplish a common goal
- reflect on issues related to honesty, justice, fairness, equality, self-discipline, and cooperation

Creativity

- express understanding of content through a range of artistic genres
- create an original product
- formulate a response to artistic expression

Growth and Learning

- exhibit abilities to use a variety of sources
- demonstrate work in progress
- analyze, change, and refocus existing work
- engage in self-assessment

Fig. 4.13. An evolving school-wide portfolio

dimension to their learning. These students wanted to take charge of their learning and do a better job.

Some of these same eighth grade students are finalists in a national energy competition. The award will be given in Washington, DC, but the students must raise $11,000 in order to go. One member of the winning team noticed a car dealership on his bus ride home. Thinking this might be a potential contributor to their trip, he left the bus. Entering the dealership, he talked to the receptionist and soon had an appointment with the General Manager. The next day at school, he put together a portfolio of their achievements in science, including information about the contest, representative samples of their work, and pictures of their team engaged in scientific investigations to present to the manager.

This young man, remembering the interviewing techniques that he had learned and armed with his portfolio, impressed the general manager so much that he donated $300 check for the trip. How much more real-world can school get? If we can instill in students this kind of competence and confidence, we have served them well.

In my years of teaching in urban schools, I have found many strategies and practices that are successful, even with difficult populations. However, none of these practices will work if they are blindly copied. All require a great deal of thought and adaptation. Portfolios are no different. They, in themselves, are no panacea. When teachers take the time to define and re-define their own portfolios, within the context of their class and their students, these portfolios become a vehicle for an incredible and unforgettable journey in learning and teaching. When schools take the time and effort to develop school-wide portfolios, they become an excellent tool to document standards and students' achievements and to engage the staff in meaningful conversations about teaching and learning.

Teachers from Reading, PA proudly display their newly designed WTL T-shirts

Chatanooga teachers get charged up for teaching during a WTL Summer Institute

PUTTING IT TOGETHER:
REFORM, STANDARDS, AND OTHER STUFF

Recently, I read about an urban administrators' conference where the speakers were discussing what makes teaching African-Americans, Latinos, and immigrant children such a "wonderful" experience. It was reported that a surprised and frustrated member of the audience immediately jumped to his feet and demanded that the speakers stop ridiculing teachers, complaining that the job was difficult enough. The speakers concluded that the audience expected to hear such words as harrowing, challenging, and disturbing; the term "wonderful" completely threw them off guard, leaving the impression that these urban administrators had lost hope. (Ayers and Ford 1996, xix-xx)

Obviously, that administrator and many of his colleagues were not involved in he reform movement. There is an amazing difference in schools that are involved in reform and those that are not, for I have worked in both. In non-reform schools, rarely do I even have conversations with principals, even though my program may be one of the major staff development efforts in their districts. Sometimes, the principals even forget who I am, despite the frequent letters and attempted contacts. They are just too busy putting out fires to concentrate on instruction. Principals of such schools are terribly isolated. Seeing only the problems of their students and their schools, they tend to lose their vision, mission, and, most of all, their hope.

Ayers and Ford (1996) address how seeing only the deficits of students makes schools places of despair:

Schools tend to focus on the least interesting and simplest of questions. What don't these kids know? What can't they do? School becomes, then, entirely a matter of remediation and repair. Good intentions notwithstanding, feelings of hopelessness and despair define these places for kids and teachers alike (xix-xx).

Although virtually no teacher begins as a fixer, it is easy to move into the role, particularly if the teacher is overcome with hopelessness. I'll never forget walking up the litter-and-glass strewn steps of an urban middle school with a frustrated, new teacher. As we gingerly made our way through the broken glass, she tearfully confided that her degree in education hadn't prepared her for the reality of an urban classroom. Mentioning the array of problems her students brought, she wondered how she could possibly even begin to teach all of them. Unable to contain her emotions any longer, she blurted out, "My students are very much like this glass. I don't think it's even possible to put the jagged and shattered pieces of their lives together again." With only a few months on the job, this defeated teacher was beginning to see her job as a fixer of students. She, literally, had no one with whom to share her teaching frustrations; she had no collegial support.

Sometimes, veteran teachers feel this way, too, but they are not always as honest and open. Thus, they continue to mask their feelings of hopelessness with heart-warming descriptions of their students. Not really believing that their students have assets, however, they continue to give these students a remedial, second-class education.

As shocking as it may seem, many schools pick up the language of reform without ever intending to change. Stanley Pogrow, developer of the HOTS (Higher Order Thinking Skills) Program, calls these educators "Wannabe Reformers." In his article, "Reforming the Wannabe Reformers," he reminds us of how foolish we may sound, "... saying, 'All children can learn,' says nothing about what they can learn, h*ow fast they can* learn, when different types of children are best able to learn certain things and why and so on" (1996, June, 661). Until we can answer these questions with authority and honesty, we will never have distinctive schools known for the distinctive students they produce. We will never have reform.

As much as we want to believe them, words alone will not create reality, and high-sounding phrases will not translate into efficacy. Just saying my students are wonderful will not make them achievers. Unsubstantiated praise is as empty and ridiculous as the self-esteem chants. Real efficacy only occurs when students begin to see the relationship between their efforts and achievement.

In one middle-school, where I worked, over one-third of the students made the school's honor roll. A marquee on the front lawn announced that this was a school of achievement and a gigantic, front hall banner declared—"All children can learn."

Quite ironically, this school's students scored at the very bottom of the district and the state on achievement tests. The faculty found it hard to see the discrepancy, placing the blame on inadequate testing rather than questioning their own instructional and grading practices. Rather than doing the hard work associated with raising achievement, they continued to elegantly and passionately vow that "All children can learn," but they still pursued their malpractice of ineffective instruction, invalid assessment, and inflated grades. Only within the walls of their school could these students possibly be considered excellent. When gauged against the achievement of others beyond the school walls, they fell short of the standards for excellence.

Unfortunately, this school's grading practices are not unusual. A U.S. Department of Education document, concerning different grading practices across schools, reports that the largest discrepancies between grades and achievement occur in high poverty schools. In these schools, the level of academic achievement earning an "A" grade in mathematics and English received a "C," or sometimes even less, at more affluent schools (1994). The practice of rewarding high grades for mediocre, or even inadequate, work has created inequitable learning opportunities. Victimized by grade inflation, these students have inaccurate perceptions of their achievement and their abilities.

Not having a standard to measure themselves against, they do not genuinely understand how well they are, or are not, doing, creating a false sense of well being. In addition, the inflated grades have destroyed the credibility of urban teachers and schools, resulting in the belief that there are two standards--one for urban schools and another set for more affluent schools.

Recently, I ran into this sad reality. As I was singing the praises of an urban senior, whom I thought should be considered for a scholarship at a very competitive liberal arts college, the Director of Admissions said, "Her grades and accomplishments are distinctive. This doesn't always mean anything, but she is from a *good* school." His comment worried me. How many urban schools would have been given this same distinction by him and others? Worse yet, how many seniors would not have even been considered because of the reputations of their schools?

One of the problems is that urban schools have become too comfortable. Those in charge begin to accept and, even seem to expect, student apathy and lack of progress. Unable to break the pattern of failure, they lose hope, thrusting aside their high expectations and resorting to a curriculum of control. The real tragedy is that they have stopped believing in themselves and their students. Ironically, within these schools, there are isolated, talented teachers who know their schools are ineffective and who have ideas on how to make them more effective. However, the task just seems too enormous—beyond their reach. One principal refers to these teachers as "pockets of excellence" in his school, and then he quickly laments that there are not enough to really make a difference with students.

But it doesn't have to be this way. I have worked with urban teachers and administrators who could and would respond to the question about how their students are wonderful in very specific terms, marshaling students' work and achievements as evidence. They would be able to answer the more difficult questions about how students learn based on their own experiences born out of their efforts to reform their schools.

Nevertheless, reforming their schools and making them places of achievement has not been an easy task, nor was the process a quick one. Even after a faculty commits to reform, the transformation requires much work, time, change, risk-taking, commitment, persistence, and courage. Reform has required much more of these faculties than their "talking the talk" of reform; it has commanded them to actually "walk the difficult walk" step-by-step.

The real question is how do we get to this point—to the point where we are the architects and experts who can make our schools places of excellence—places where students, parents, administrators, and teachers begin believing in themselves again? How do we reform ourselves in life-changing ways?

Ever since 1989, several districts have been invited to join a national network of urban middle schools that share the vision of reform. As part of the Edna McConnell Clark Foundation's Program for Student Achievement, these schools must have demonstrated a commitment to reform, making sure that all of their students achieve high levels of academic performance before leaving the eighth grade. In looking at his experiences with the network schools and their reform effort, Hayes Mizell, Director of the Program for Student Achievement, shares these thoughts:

> ... Too many treat reform as a program or a project, a piecemeal effort that can be 'installed' at little expense, personal inconvenience, or political cost. But reform is gritty and demanding work, frustrating because it requires change in attitudes and behaviors that few of us would choose to embrace. Ironically, there are educators who make this choice, and continue to demonstrate, in the face of almost overwhelming odds, that they are willing to change what they think and what they do if that is what it takes to help their students (Lewis 1995, 118).

Reform cannot be purchased in the form of a packaged program. Yet, millions of dollars are wasted each year by school districts looking for a quick and easy answer to make their students achievers. Even ERIC, long respected as a clearinghouse for research, has recently started to present one-day professional development seminars. How could this organization possibly be reading the research on staff development and then package and sell one-day seminars—quick fixes that just don't work?

Genuine reform comes as a result of a school demonstrating a willingness to look at itself honestly and being ready to, literally, turn the school inside-out in order to become more effective. This often means casting aside behaviors and favorite practices that inhibit growth and achievement and the restructuring of the school. As a result of this honest investigation and effort, the school develops a shared mission and vision. This shared vision unites the faculty and serves as a guiding force for reform—hurling the staff into action.

Michael Fullan contends that genuine reform will not take place unless there is this shared vision—a broadening of teacher leadership until it encompasses a *majority* of teachers at the levels of school, district, state, and even the teaching profession itself (1995, 1). It is not enough for a few passionate and excellent teachers or administrators to take on the yoke of reform. In his book, *The Passionate Teacher,* Robert Friedman (1995) addresses the futility of these isolated approaches:

> While individual teachers and their students may pursue passionate teaching ... it may just be too exhausting for most to sustain real change in the face of apathy, exhaustion, or resistance from others within and without the school. Lacking such support, a lot of good ideas atrophy and die (49).

Not only do good ideas atrophy and die, but so do talented people. One of the biggest heartbreaks of reform is when a teacher or administrator who has been a reform leader bails out and asks for a transfer. In one school, an exasperated principal exclaimed, "How will we ever change the school if my best teachers become exhausted and leave?" Over a three-year period, this principal watched five of her most respected teachers— teachers who had initially led the reform effort—leave her school. Unable to change the school's culture, she encountered resistance from many faculty members, who despite their students' failures, saw no need to change. Unfortunately, these faculty members endured and stayed. Therefore, each year the number of teachers who were dedicated reformers lessened, making each new school year a struggle—an uphill battle—to even keep a foothold on their reform efforts. Eventually, this principal, exhausted and frustrated by the lack of progress, asked to be assigned to another school.

In an article entitled, "The Pedagogy of Poverty versus Good Teaching," Martin Haberman (1996) argued that reform is prevented by a blind reliance on an ineffective pedagogy to teach minorities and the poor. Because of low expectations for this population, the learning is usually uncoordinated and thoughtless. Thus, students are sentenced to a series of teacher-directed, repetitive, and uninspired activities. The students, in turn, are expected to comply and not to question or resist. Haberman argued that this ineffective pedagogy continues to thrive in urban schools because groups of adults, whom he calls "constituencies," have a stake in maintaining it. These include: adults who did not do well in school themselves, blaming others for their failure; adults who do not analyze educational problems, believing that "permissiveness is the root of all evil"; adults who fear minorities and the poor, feeling they must be controlled; and adults who are directly responsible for educating these students and who are, virtually, not accountable for doing so (120-130).

Although I have seen many such classrooms, one in particular stands out. During my first visit, the principal greeted me by saying, "Wait till you see this teacher. Students are so well behaved and always on task. There are never any discipline problems." As we entered the room, the teacher sat at his desk in the front of the room, literally, glaring at his students, while the students worked quietly at their desks. The room was eerily quiet. Smiling and giving a nod of approval, the principal left.

As I watched the students, I noticed that they were simply copying a list of 100 words from a ditto sheet to their notebooks. Much to my surprise, not even one student objected to this futile task. Moreover, this ineffective teacher had just received high praise from his principal.

The principal and the teacher in this school did not want to change even though this school had been targeted for reform by the district. Clearly, they did not understand their pedagogical options, valuing control and disciplined response more than effective instruction. The question is: How long can their students endure before they become openly hostile, responding aggressively?

During a Writing to Learn Summer Institute, I used Haberman's article to spur a discussion about hindrances to reform in urban schools. A heated debate ensued. Some were angered by the assumptions that the author made, while others were more introspective and troubled. Their journal entries reflect these differences:

> Mr. Haberman, I am humbled by your remarks. I want so to be the kind of teacher who challenges students, but I am filled with such great self doubts.

> Mr. Haberman, I am angry, for I have been a victim of the pedagogy of poverty most of my life. And now, my students come to me beaten down by this same pedagogy of compliance. They could do so much more, but they just don't know or seem to even care. They would rather be comfortable than challenged.

> When was the last time you were in a middle school devoted to reform? You make a lot of unsubstantiated inferences about urban schools.

Although some rejected his statements about the pedagogy of poverty, they all agreed that the way to move beyond this debilitating pedagogy was to set universally high goals and expectations, identified through a specific set of standards, and to reach these standards through quality and standards-based instruction.

Thus, the teachers, who have been involved in reform efforts for several years, see standards as the guiding force behind creating more effective schools. In their eyes, reform has been hindered because it could not attract the critical mass necessary to make a difference. Because there were no district-wide goals, or articulated standards, skeptics or entire constituencies could opt out, without any consequences—causing a great deal of frustration to those who devoted their energies to bringing about reform in their schools.

Consequently, reform-minded teachers embrace standards, for they feel that their reform efforts will have a keener sense of direction. Since greater accountability is demanded, the buy-in will be much more comprehensive.

Ivor Pritchard (1996) captured these teachers' beliefs in his statement about the purpose of standards-based reform:

> The basic idea of standards-based reform is to create clear, consistent, challenging goals for student learning, and then to make educational practices more coherent by deliberately using those goals to guide both instruction and testing. Common sense suggests that the quality of education is better if teachers are prepared to teach what they're asked to teach in the classroom, if the materials teachers use are designed to enable students to learn what they are supposed to know, and if the tests students are given test them for what they've been asked to learn (2).

According to Pritchard, this coordinated approach to learning breaks down the "obstacles to achievement caused by low expectations" (3).

In a standards-driven system, it is almost impossible for the pedagogy of poverty to survive and thrive. The teacher who had students rotely copy the list of words would be asked to justify such practices according to the standards by a knowing principal.

Ineffective instructional practices are struck down by clearly articulated standards, for distinct messages are sent to each of the stakeholders:

District-level Administrators—The responsibility of seeing that standards are clearly articulated and implemented across the district is yours. To achieve this, you will provide teachers and principals with an array of professional development activities to help raise student achievement; provide appropriate materials for teachers and students; and intervene when schools are not raising students' achievement by increasing the opportunities to learn for faculty and students.

Students—Much time and energy needs to be spent in reaching these standards; learning is a top priority in your life, and it is your responsibility to learn these things. You will spend time in self-evaluation and assessment, identifying your strengths and weaknesses and setting goals for future work in obtaining the standards. In this process of self-evaluation, you will routinely hold your work up against examples of outstanding students' work to guide your own learning. Although you may never reach this level of mastery, these examples will give you concrete ways to improve your work and serve as an inspiration for you to strive longer and harder to produce such work. Thus, you will see that the quality of your work is actually on a continuum, where it moves toward greater proficiency over time.

Parents—The goals of your child's education have been clearly communicated to you; therefore, it is your responsibility to keep informed on progress in reaching these goals, to ensure that your child understands the importance of achieving them, and to support your child in reaching the standards. You will review your child's work frequently, and be asked to respond to it. Holding discussions with your child about work and progress in meeting the standards is extremely crucial. If your child is not progressing, it is your responsibility to investigate the reasons for this lack of progress and to seek solutions. Years of stalled learning cannot be tolerated and accepted.

Teachers—The responsibility of presenting a coordinated approach to learning is clearly yours. You communicate the standards to parents and students. The instruction in your classroom is purposeful and standards-based while assessment tests students' ability to meet the standards through an array of assessment approaches, including performance-based tasks. To make the standards available to all students, a variety of instructional approaches are used, reflecting the different intelligences. For those students at risk of failing, you provide increased opportunities to learn.

Class time is devoted to conversations about standards. Students are given the opportunity to reflect upon their progress, to see other students' work, to evaluate their own work against exemplars, and to set goals. Students and parents are given frequent feedback regarding the students' progress toward standards. Students' work, as well as exemplars, are shared with parents. Students are actively involved in setting goals and monitoring their progress toward reaching them. They take ownership of their learning and contribute to the learning of peers.

You continue to meet with colleagues, looking at your assignments and your students' responses, checking to see if the assignments and the students' work truly meet the standards. These professional conversations improve the quality of instruction and assignments, keep the criteria for evaluation at a high level, inhibit grade inflation, and break down teacher isolation.

Principals—Your job is to make sure that teachers, parents, and students know the standards and the importance of students being able to reach them. As the instructional leader in your school, you ensure that all instruction and assessment are standards-based and that there are opportunities to learn. Thus, much of your time is spent in classrooms, giving teachers meaningful feedback. Teachers respect your knowledge and welcome your assistance in increasing opportunities to learn in their classrooms. To increase these opportunities, you arrange for teachers to be involved in instructional coaching, where they visit other teachers' classes and have informal conversations with each other.

To further improve the quality of standards-based instruction, you schedule faculty meetings, where teachers look at their assignments and their students' responses to these assignments, holding conversations about how to improve the quality of both. Staff development days are spent in ways to help teachers better articulate and coordinate their standards-based instruction. Much time is devoted to conversations about instruction and students' responses to this instruction.

For teachers who are struggling with standards-based instruction, you intervene by providing more directed opportunities to learn.

You collect data to document your school's achievement and communicate the results of this data to teachers, students, and parents. The data is used as a way to look at the learning in your school, serving as a concrete tool to possibly re-focus instruction and assessment.

General public—You will know that there is a level of proficiency which all students should have reached when they complete certain levels of school. This will enable you to have more knowledgeable conversations with school officials, asking them about specific standards and providing them with feedback for refinement and revision of standards.

Thus, through announced standards, varied audiences understand the goals of education, making it almost impossible to shirk the shared responsibility for students' learning. For too long, parents, the general public, administrators, teachers, and students have been able to hide in the fog produced by unclear educational goals. Others sought change without having a guiding focus for this change. Standards provide this focus, answering the often-asked question, "Why are we doing this anyway?" According to Anne Wheelock (1995):

> Schools that focus on 'what all students should know and be able to do' and examine how well students understand and use that knowledge can offer students opportunities to learn that are unavailable in schools that lack this focus. Engaging in standards-based reform does not automatically

guarantee improved student performance, but the strategy of adopting and using standards to guide change can add value to the already positive features of middle school life (41).

The instructional approaches and strategies in this book possess the characteristics commonly associated with standards-based instruction, including:

❶ **Standards are richly illustrated with a wide variety of student work, and students get many opportunities to demonstrate their competencies.** When teachers base their instruction on the multi-intelligences, students have more chances to master the content in a variety of ways. Through the use of alternative/authentic assessment strategies, students are more likely to be able to demonstrate their competencies, making the learning more equitable.

❷ **Focus is on student work, and students reflect on ways to improve their own work**—Rich conversations, centered on students' work, occur frequently in the classroom. Students have the opportunity to hold their own work up against exemplars in order to assess their work and to set goals for improving it. Revision is stressed. Peer assessment and self assessment are part of the on-going work in these classrooms. Students are involved in goal setting throughout the year. Students reflect in such documents as learning logs, reading response journals, and portfolios. They write letters home informing parents of their progress and their goals. They share their work with their parents and receive feedback.

❸ **Students understand the standards, and know what they must do to improve.** The standards have, in effect, provided a learning agenda for the class. These standards are posted on the wall of the classroom. Through classroom conversations and through work with exemplars, students understand the standards and what they must do to improve. They demonstrate this knowledge in reflections, in setting goals, in conferences, in their portfolios, and in writing letters home.

❹ **Assessment is embedded in instruction, becoming a natural part of teaching and learning.** Assessment does not exist in isolation. Since a part of each lesson should involve some kind of assessment, assessment takes on a variety of contexts and formats. Given this array of assessment measures, students are much more likely to exhibit their knowledge and understanding of concepts.

❺ **Students develop a portfolio.** The portfolio serves as a vehicle for students to demonstrate and give documentation of their learning. Both students and teachers determine the type of evidence and how it is to be collected. The work in the portfolio documents standards and the breadth and range of the learning experiences within a class. In developing their portfolios, students learn to look at their work with a critical eye, select work that represents their best efforts, reflect upon it, and set goals for improvement.

❻ **Parents know and understand the standards so that they can help their children to become competent learners.** Teachers inform parents of the standards through letters (written by the teacher and students), conferences, the portfolios, etc. Parents are asked to look at their children's work and to respond to it frequently.

❼ **With the implementation of standards, faculties can focus on meaningful discussions about instruction and assessment, uniting the faculty in a common cause and thrust.**

The standards, emerging from the professional national associations, states, and school districts, also share some common traits. In each of the content areas, standards emphasize learning for understanding, applying higher order thinking skills, mastering content and process skills, and understanding the big ideas of a discipline. It would be hard to argue that these are not things that we would want students to know when they leave our schools.

Nevertheless, as promising as standards may be, the standards will never be reached unless there is a standard for instruction—instruction which leads students to achievement. Newman and Wehlage (1993) propose that "authentic achievement" takes place when students are given assignments where they are asked to produce work which allows them to construct meaning and to interpret knowledge based on disciplined inquiry. In addition, this has value beyond the classroom walls, allowing students to transfer their learning to real-world situations (8).

Often principals asked us to describe what Writing to Learn classrooms looked like. In reality, they were asking us to define the standards of instruction—professional teaching standards. Before encountering the work of Newman and Wehlage, we answered their request by providing them with a list of the most promising practices presented in the WTL Institutes. However, we were never quite satisfied with our list, for it seemed like a grocery list of ideas without much context. Without this context, some teachers picked some of the promising practices on the list and completely neglected others, resulting in an unbalanced curriculum and low-impact instruction.

Frustrated by this, Long Beach's Writing to Learn Leadership Team decided to use Newman's and Wehlage's "Five Standards of Authentic Instruction" (1993) to re-conceptualize the Program, basing the Summer Institutes on our new learning. We ended up adding two more categories to the framework: Writing as a Tool for Learning and The Reflective Teacher. The leadership team felt that this adapted version more accurately represented their classrooms and their work with WTL. As a result of this rethinking, the Institutes had more coherency than ever. Furthermore, the instructional standards allowed us to show that the district's standards were an integral part the WTL instructional approach. We adapted Newman's and Wehlages's model in this way:

INSTRUCTIONAL STANDARDS FOR WRITING TO LEARN: WHAT DO WTL CLASSROOMS LOOK LIKE?

Social Support for Student Achievement—Social support involves high expectations, respect, and inclusion of *all* students in the learning process. The climate supports the staunch belief that all members of the class can learn important knowledge and skills and that mutual respect among all members of the class contributes to achievement by all. Therefore, the teacher structures the classroom so that students work cooperatively and collaboratively on tasks, helping each other to become experts. Students continue to thrive in this tolerant, accepting, demanding, and supportive atmosphere, for they find that they can achieve with effort, persistence, and support. In this community of learners, where all voices are honored, students willingly accept the responsibility for their own learning and the learning of others. Thus, failure is banned, for the community does everything in its power to help themselves and each other to succeed.

Sample activities—A variety of cooperative and collaborative learning experiences, modeling, scaffolding, community building activities, students as teachers, paired activities, peer evaluation, self-evaluation, alternative assessment strategies, class meetings, projects, exhibitions, and conferences, etc.

Depth of Knowledge and Higher Order Thinking Skills— Facts are not presented in isolation, and students are not sentenced to shallow and time-filling tasks. Rather, the instruction is standards-based, thoughtful, and deliberate, involving students in challenging and engaging activities. Students are actively engaged in learning. These activities require students to draw inferences, make implications, analyze, generalize, hypothesize, summarize, problem-solve, synthesize, and evaluate. They tend to be more open-ended, allowing students to discover new meanings and to increase their understanding of content. As a result of the instruction, students are able to make clear distinctions, develop arguments, marshal evidence, construct explanations, defend rationales, critique work, etc. Students demonstrate their knowledge of the standards and make connections to other academic areas in these activities, using the standards as benchmarks for self-evaluation.

Sample activities—Panel discussions, Socratic seminars, debates, town meetings, proposals, role playing, simulations, scripts, documentaries, literature circles, problems of the week, mathematician's chair, author's chair, mini-page assignment, surveys, polls, letters to the editor, Internet, observations, research projects (I Search—student-based inquiry), issue-based instruction, assignments with authentic audiences and purposes, primary/secondary sources, reciprocal teaching, interviews, problem-solving, etc.

<u>Emphasis on the Process of Learning</u>—Specific activities are structured to help students process and monitor their learning and their achievement of the district's standards. Rich conversations occur about the topic, standards, and the process of learning. Conversations and activities focus on the process of learning and on the work in which students are engaged. These conversations are not completely scripted by the teacher. Thus, students are involved in assessing their work, investigating their own and their peers' learning, and setting goals. Much time is spent in working with exemplars so that students understand what they have to do to improve their work. The classroom becomes a place of thought, where students become increasingly adept at reflecting on their work and the work of peers.

Sample activities—Think alouds, revision activities, conferences, peer evaluation, self-evaluation, learning logs, dialectical journals, reading response journals, writers' notebooks, exemplars, goal setting, kid-watching strategies, student and teacher portfolios, etc.

Writing as a Tool for Learning—Writing is used in a variety of ways to increase students' understanding of content material and the district's standards. It is used to:

▶ link prior knowledge to new knowledge, helping students to make personal connections by allowing them to discover what it is they know about a subject.

▶ monitor or process their learning.

▶ extend or reformulate knowledge—placing the learning into a new context or form. (Applebee 1987)

The assignments give students authentic, real-world experiences by using a variety of discourse forms, audiences and purposes, making the students flexible thinkers and writers. The writing assignments should closely reflect the work that professionals do in a particular discipline.

Sample activities—the mosaic, structured freewriting asking questions before reading, story-telling, review strategies, learning log and response journals, analyzing tests, evaluating various assessments, working with exemplars, self-evaluation, peer evaluation, setting goals, think-write assignments, lab reports, statistical analysis, observations, reporting data, editorials, critiques, cause/effect, speculation, proposals, congressional hearings, review strategies, etc.

Connectedness to Real World—The content of the class has value and meaning beyond the instructional context of the classroom. Students' work has impact on their own lives, their community, and the world beyond, certifying their level of achieving the district's standards. Students address real-world, public problems through thematic and issue-based units. They use their personal experiences to make vital connections between their classroom learning and the real world.

Sample activities—Thematic units, issue-based instruction, an array of real-world problems with authentic audiences.

A Well-Balanced Assessment Program—Assessment is embedded in instruction and does not exist in isolation. Assessment should be standards-based and in response to the questions:

- ▶ What is it that I want students to know? What should they be able to do?

- ▶ What activities will help them learn these things?

- ▶ How will we (teachers and students) know how well we are learning? (Wiggins 1989, May, 703-713)

Criteria for assessment must be known, understood, and negotiated between student and teacher before the assessment begins. Both process and products are assessed using a variety of time frames and formats and including standard, alternative, and authentic assessments. Some of the assessments should be authentic and embedded in tasks having genuine purposes and relating to everyday life. Teachers use assessment to guide and to monitor instruction while students use assessment to identify their strengths and weaknesses and to set goals for improving their work. By working with an array of assessments, students take ownership of their learning, and the learning is more equitable. They accept the responsibility for their learning, and, in so doing, share the accountability for learning with their teacher. Students and teachers use the assessments to share their progress with parents and others.

Sample activities—A variety of standard, alternative, and authentic assessments, including:

- ▶ **Process-focused:** oral questioning, observation (kid-watching), interview, process description, think alouds, learning logs, drafts, revisions, reflections, portfolio, conferences, goal setting.

- ▶ **Products:** Portfolio, essays, research papers, log/journal, lab report, story/play, poem, art exhibit, science project, model, video-audio tape, spreadsheet, graphs, collages, etc.

▶ **Performances:** oral presentation, dance/movement, science lab experiments, skits, demonstration of skills, dramatic reading, enactment, debate, musical recital, etc.

▶ **Constructed Responses:** Fill in the blank (word(s), phrase(s)), short answers (sentence(s), paragraph(s)), label a diagram, "show your work," visual representation (web, concept map, flow chart, graph/table, matrix, illustration)

The Reflective Teacher—The teacher takes time to reflect upon teaching, constantly trying to refine the practice. The teacher keeps observational journals of students and a teaching portfolio, using these documents to guide reflections and to inform instruction. The teacher frequently holds conversations with colleagues about assignments and students' work as a means of gaining insight into effective practice. The reflective teacher asks students for feedback regarding instructional practices, and invites students to participate in the planning, implementing, and evaluating of lessons. The structure of the learning shows respect for the voices of students.

Sample activities—kid-watching, teaching as research projects, observational journals, teaching portfolio, student-centered learning experiences

Both teachers and principals responded well to the instructional standards, for they really understood the broader context of the practices and strategies. Teachers have found that one of the best ways of achieving these teaching strategies and keeping content standards at the core of our instruction is through planning thematic and issue-based units. In the beginning, this is frustrating and overwhelming for teachers since it is not easy to place their instruction into the broader context of thematic units. Often, this means abandoning the "learning as usual" in a classroom and starting almost anew. As difficult as it may be, Ruth Mitchell, an educational guru on standards, warns that we cannot fall into the pitfall of matching standards to our current activities. Rather, they must be put into a broader, more meaningful context (Mitchell and Willis, 1996).

As teachers seek to implement standards, two different instructional approaches are emerging. One, along the lines of what Ruth Mitchell describes, is the "boxcar" approach, where learning is more fragmented than ever as teachers move from standard to standard. At the end of a year or semester, the teacher could quite honestly boast that all of the standards were covered. However, the instruction is hopelessly fragmented and students leave more confused than ever, not understanding how to connect any of this knowledge.

At a WTL network meeting, math teachers struggled with this very issue as they shared their portfolios. At one school, the administration had made the decision to have the content standards become the table of contents for all math portfolios. Therefore, the table of contents simply listed the standards—one-by-one. It came as no surprise to open the portfolios and find an array of worksheets, quizzes, and other isolated pieces of work. Furthermore, the reflections were mechanical and rote. One student wrote, "This quiz shows that I understand how to figure areas for different shapes."

As a colleague from another school looked at the math portfolio, she exclaimed, "I wouldn't want pieces of junk like this in my portfolio. This means nothing to students or to the reader, and it certainly wouldn't represent the learning in my classroom. It needs to be more connected." In his quest to document standards, the well-meaning administrator had created another problem: He had isolated the standards from their instructional context. The discussion of the network group, then, turned to how could this portfolio be modified, representing both content and teaching standards.

A more preferable approach to standards' implementation is a concentric circle approach. In this approach, standards are at the core of all instruction; they have their birth in the planning of instructional units and the framework for authentic instruction.

This approach is somewhat like throwing a pebble or stone in water. When a stone is thrown into water, the circles get bigger and bigger, eventually encompassing a whole section of the body of water. In this approach, the standards are placed in the center, and all learning radiates from them—encompassing all that we do in the classroom (see Fig. 5.1)

When teachers take ownership of good instructional practices, making them distinctly theirs, worthwhile and imaginative assignments emerge. Carolyn Latu, a wonderful Chapter One resource teacher, does not teach reading and writing skills in isolation, wanting to increase student's abilities to comprehend, understand, and construct meaning. With this approach to learning being a priority, she thought about how she would weave standards into her instruction while teaching the book, *The Giver*. To address the district's standard regarding essential reading strategies and skills, which helps students to construct meaning, Carolyn gave an assignment that generated the thoughtful response in Fig. 5.2.

In response to another standard addressing the ability to respond to text, Ms. Latu gave these two assignments:

❶ The family unit in *The Giver* share their feelings every evening after their meal. Express your feelings in writing by recording the feelings you experienced yesterday.

Selected student responses show the power of students being able to write in response to literature and to make personal connections through writing:

Yesterday, I felt sad because I found out that my friend has a heart disease and he might have a chance to die. I felt perplexed ...

My painful feeling was when my brother died. No, I would not like to share my feelings to someone. Because when my brother died I was very sad, when I think about it I get sad or start crying. I don't like crying in front of people. I just always keep my feelings to myself. To me it's very painful because I always wanted an older brother.

Fig. 5.1. When standards are at the core of instruction, the outcome is achievement

ASSIGNMENT
STANDARD FIVE: Essential strategies and skills

None of the chapters in *The Giver* have titles. After reading a group of chapters, think about what happened in the chapter, write a one or two sentence summary of the chapters, and then think of a title to fit each group of chapters.

Chapter - Summary - Title

1-2 Talking about family feelings, you have to. "Everyday Life"

3-5 They have a time to die. You have assigned jobs, lives, families. "A Controlled Life"

6-8 Everybody is going to the ceremonies for 1 to 12. "A New Life Ahead"

9-11 Jonas got the most important job in the community. "The Chosen One"

12-13 Jonas met the old man, the Giver. He sees color. The Giver gives Jonas memories. "The Next Step to Life"

14-16 Jonas realized good and painful memories. "The Dark Side"

17-18 Jonas' friends were playing war and he had the memory of it. He told them to stop. "Sad Times"

19-20 The father released the twin, the smaller one. "One out of Two"

21-22 Jonas ran away with Gabe and the Giver. "Told the Truth"

23 Jonas went to Elsewhere and had a difficult time of travel. "A New Life"

Fig. 5.2. This student demonstrates his ability to understand text by placing it into a completely different format

Although in most standards-based instruction, there is usually a scoring guide or rubric to evaluate performance, the above assignment should never be evaluated, for it would kill the purpose of getting students hooked on reading by being able to make personal connections.

After finishing the novel, students completed a report card for the characters in the novel, assigning them grades for achievement and conduct and then providing justifications for their grades. Some students' justifications were vague, for example, "I gave him (Jonas) an A because he is good. He is the best."

In this assignment, a scoring guide would be appropriate, for it is not as personal. Students would benefit from knowing how well they have done—to what degree they have met the standard. In addition, the quality of the students' responses would been greatly improved if a scoring guide or rubric had been provided—one that would have given students more specific guidelines for their written comments on the justifications for the grade; one that would have required students to go back to the text to document their comments.

After a standards-based lesson such as this, it is important to consider, "What happens next?" Instead of building on an activity and extending the learning, we are often in a hurry to move on, missing a teachable moment. For instance, this assignment could be extended by using these assignments to write a persuasive essay, where students develop a thesis statement and provide a rationale for their comments based on the text.

Also, the report card could be the basis for a wonderful collaborative assignment. The students could take their report cards for the characters to small groups. In the groups, they could share their report cards and help each other fill in the following character mind maps, developed by Bill Younglove, a teacher in Long Beach (see Fig. 5.3).

CHARACTER MINDMAP

Directions: Choose three characters from
<u>Bridge to Terabithia</u>. Print their names in the
center circle. Then list one trait for each
character in the trait circles. Finally, print two
pieces of evidence in the boxes, showing that each
character does, indeed, have a trait.

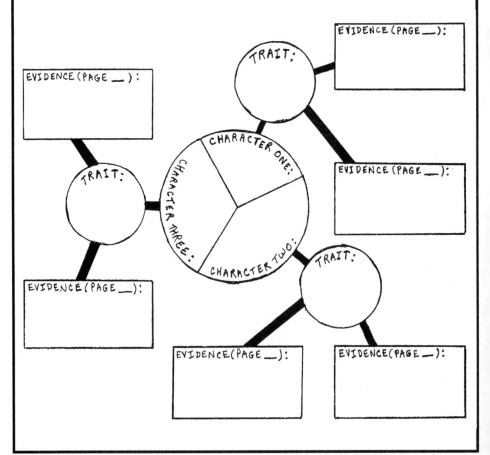

Fig. 5.3. This graphic organizer forces students to return to text to support their observations

After their group work, an individual assignment could be given; the students then could select one of the characters from their mind maps and write an essay analyzing character. What is so exciting about teaching is to think about where the initial learning activity can lead. Almost every good assignment can be extended to increase the learning by including even more standards if we keep an open mind and look for teachable moments.

One of the issues frequently debated in the standards movement is the equality issue: Are special populations capable of obtaining the standards? Should exceptions be made? Jane Ledgerwood, a talented special education teacher, does not want her students to be exempt from the standards, staunchly believing that her students can and will meet the standards. If they are exempt, she is convinced that this will be just another way in which her students are separated from other students, ever widening the gap between them. According to Ms. Ledgerwood, "When instruction is broken down into a series of approachable steps and layers of scaffolding are added to the instruction, special students will achieve." For Jane, the standards are a reachable goal, for she assumes the responsibility of structuring her classroom in ways that will ensure her students' success and achievement. Fig. 5.4 is an example of standards-based instruction in her resource room followed in Fig. 5.5 by one student's response.

Throughout the year, Ms. Ledgerwood's students created word problems to be solved by the class. Her assignment sheet is very specific (see Fig. 5.6), containing several concrete suggestions on how to make their problems better and explaining the criteria for evaluation.

Students understand what they have to do to get a top grade; thus, there is no guess work involved. In peer groups, students use the scoring guide to give each other suggestions for improving their work. During one such evaluation session, one student told another, "Your problem doesn't have a question, and your equation doesn't go with your math problem." With this kind of feedback, students are bound to produce better work.

ADOPT A RECTANGLE PROJECT

Standard: Students will study one-, two-, and three-dimensional figures in a variety of situations to represent, analyze, and solve problems through the use of concrete models.

A. Identify, describe, model, compare, draw, and classify geometric figures.

B. Visualize and represent geometric figures, with special attention to developing spatial sense.

Directions:

1. Name your rectangle. (Example: MATH) Write the name four different ways. What are the vertices?

2. Measure the length and width of it using your choice of units. How accurately did you measure?

3. Draw another picture of your rectangle and draw as many lines of symmetry as you can. Explain what a line of symmetry is.

4. Redraw your rectangle. Draw the diagonals. Name them. Explain what diagonals are.

5. Find the area of each triangle that the rectangle is divided into by diagonals. Show your work.

After you have edited each part of your work with your group and a teacher, rewrite this project using ink and a good piece of paper. You may use felt tip pens or crayons. Please make a cover page with your name, date, course, and period. Include a picture of your rectangle on the cover. Make your project look attractive. Be neat and colorful.

You will receive one point for each of these items:

	Grading
____Rectangle named four ways. ____	
____Label vertices. ____	9-10 — A
____Length and width of rectangle. _____	8 — B
____Lines of symmetry. ____	7 — C
____Diagonals. ____	
____Perimeter. ____	6 — D
____Area. ____	
____Area of triangles. ____	
____Correct spelling, capitalization, and punctuation. _____	
____Neat letters. Attractive presentation. ____	

After you are finished with each item, place a check mark in the blank provided on the right.

Fig. 5.4. This assignment is divided into a series of approachable steps

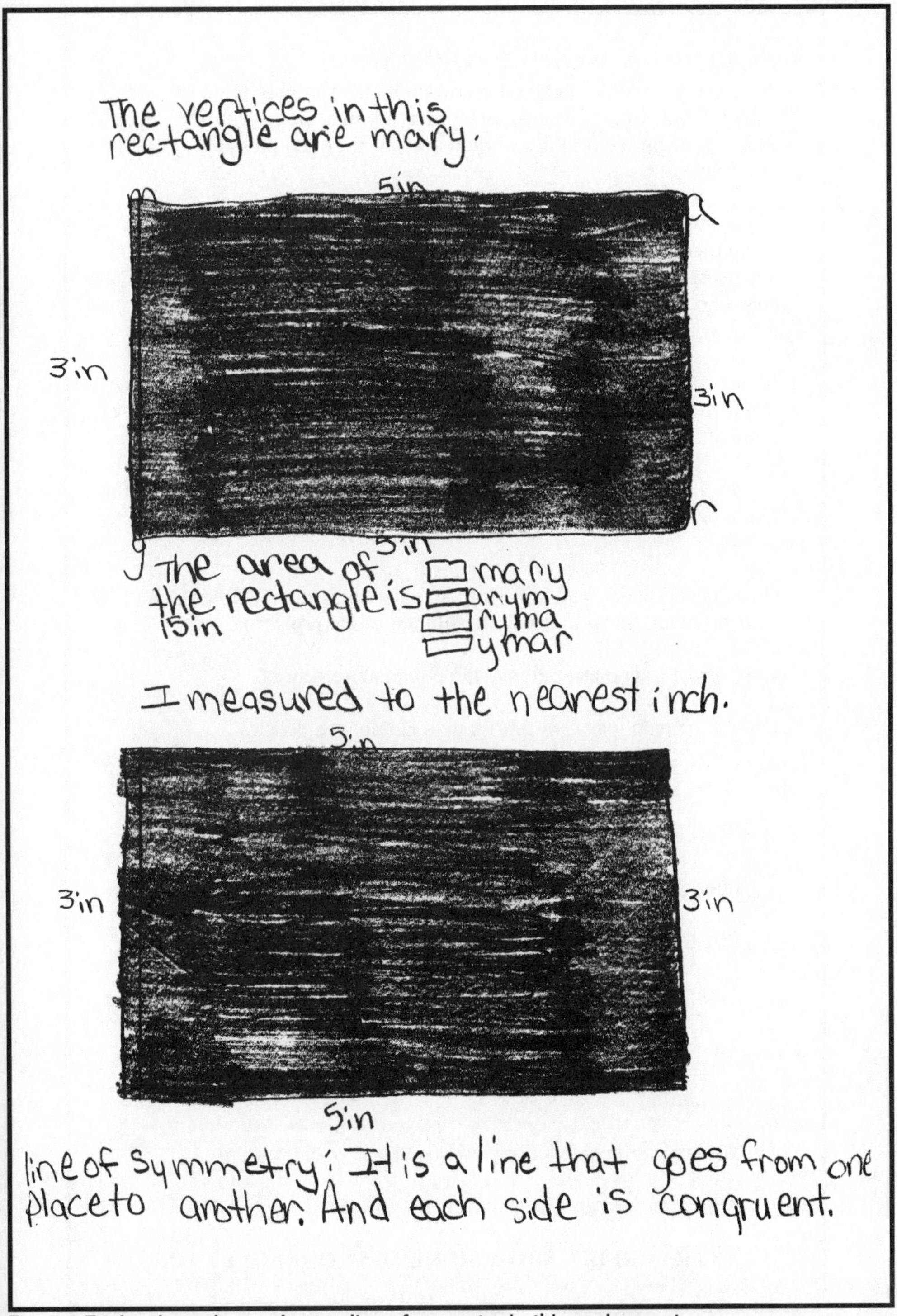
The vertices in this rectangle arie mary.
5in
3in
3in
5in
The area of the rectangle is 15in
mary
arym
ryma
ymar
I measured to the nearest inch.
5in
3in
3in
5in
line of symmetry: It is a line that goes from one place to another. And each side is congruent.

Fig. 5.5 Ericka shows her understanding of geometry in this assignment

CREATING A WORD PROBLEM

You will be creating an original world problem. You may write any type of problem, (coin, work, distance, time, measurement, +, -, x, or .) We will be working your problem in class when you are done, so please keep in mind the following:

1. Make your problem interesting to your classmates. (It won't be hard to make them more interesting than Ms. Ledgerwood's.) Some possibilities are: using humor, exaggerating the facts, relating the problem to an interest common to teenagers, using familiar people in the information or just using your imagination.

2. Illustrate the problem. You may use a drawing, cut a picture out of a magazine, or use any type of illustration you can think of to make the problem more interesting.

3. Try to make the difficulty level comparable to middle school problems. Avoid numbers that will make the problem too frustrating for class members to solve.

4. On a second paper, you will write an equation using variables to go with your problem. Show at least one solution to the problem.

5. Use correct grammar, spelling, and complete sentences.

6. Use ink, crayon, paint, or felt-tip pen. Do not use pencil.

Grading: A—6 or 7; B—5; C—4; D—3

You will receive one point for each of the following:

_____Interesting problem

_____Illustration

_____Appropriate level of difficulty

_____An equation with a variable

_____A solution

_____Correct grammar, spelling, and complete sentences

_____Written in ink, crayon, paint, or felt-tip pen

EXTRA CREDIT: SHOW MORE THAN ONE SOLUTION!

Fig. 5.6. This student-friendly assignment guarantees students a measure of success

In reflecting on the first quarter's work, one student reported that being able to create word problems was the most significant thing she had learned. In response to the question, "How have you changed or grown as a mathematician this quarter?," she replied, "I can read better, and math is easy now." No doubt, this student will be able to meet the district's standards if her teachers continue to have high expectations and to create thoughtful and challenging assignments. With a steady diet of this kind of instruction, these special students will gain confidence in themselves, knowing that they, too, can achieve.

More than ever, I have a great optimism for urban schools. Why? If standards are truly adopted and become the basis of all learning, the dream of all students learning can become a reality. No longer will good instruction be the exception; it will be the expectation for all classrooms. Good teachers will no longer feel isolated, for schools will have a common thrust, and the emphasis rightfully will be placed on instruction and learning. Administrators and teachers will have the responsibility of assuring that schools are, first and above all, places to learn, to grow, and to achieve. Students will understand that they, too, must take the responsibility for their learning and that doing well in school is a key to any future success they may have. And finally, parents will have to become vigilant of their children's progress, letting them know that they are expected to learn and to achieve. Through this organized and cooperative approach to learning, schools will once again be purposeful and respected—distinguished places of learning.

Another way to integrate standards and authentic instruction into the classroom is through thematic and issue-based units. In the appendix, you will find several sample units that Writing to Learn teachers have developed. Although teachers were initially pleased with the units, they are in the process of refining them, for they feel that they can be better—which is a tribute to them. These teachers are reflective teachers, holding the conviction that revision is the key to better teaching. Also, notice that the units are organized in various ways, reflecting the individual differences in teachers. Most teachers like to develop their own format for unit design—one that meets their teaching style and needs. Usually, teachers start with the format that we give, and then change it. A sample template and examples for designing units can be found in the appendix.

For the past eighteen months, colleagues have encouragingly asked, "Have you finished it yet?" Everyone who knows me came to understand the "it" referred to this ever-present-and-never-ending book. In fact, this book has taken on a life of its own. Now that I am finally finishing it, I'm at a loss of words. How should I end? I now understand why primary students simply stop writing and print proudly in large letters THE END. However, I guess I'll avoid this temptation and end with a few last comments.

For too long, urban schools seem to have been paralyzed by the larger problems of society. For too long, we have been playing the futile game of who is to blame—fettering away precious time. We need to move beyond the negatives, realizing that we are in control of our lives and of our schools. We cannot possibly solve all of society's problems, nor can we afford the luxury of letting these problems keep us from our charge to teach. If we wait until all of society's ills are healed, we will have contributed greatly to the problem by condemning generations of students to lives of poverty and failure. We have to stay focused on our students and their achievement, for our students' achievement is our hope—society's hope. William Wordsworth stated, "A child, more than any other gift that God can give declining man, brings hope and forward-looking thoughts." Although children are our greatest hope for a better future, right now we hold their future in our hands.

Our students are ever reminding us of this great truth. Although it was almost two decades ago when I was one of four finalist for the National Teacher of the Year Award, I'll never forget a magical moment created by my students. I walked into my classroom, and all of my students were gathered around a large table. As I looked over their shoulders, I saw a wad of money. Being a humanistic teacher, I shouted, "What in the world is going on here?" Tim Tucker looked up at me and said, "It's our advanced comp. football pool. Do you want in?" I jokingly replied, "I can just see the headlines now: 'Vice squad raids teacher's room.' Put the money away." However, the vice squad never arrived. What did arrive was the biggest bouquet of red roses I've ever seen with the enclosed note, "We're betting on you, teach."

And it's true. We may not always receive bouquets of roses, but we know that our students are betting on us. They want us to help them make sense out of an often chaotic life and to help them cultivate the skills that will contribute to their leading a productive and meaningful life. What better calling than to serve these students? What better compliment than to know that they are counting on us?

After spending the past ten years in talented teachers' classrooms, I can honestly say that I, too, am betting on the teachers in urban schools. I am inspired by their dedication to students, their desire to keep on learning, and their willingness to share with others. What evidence do I have? Even as this book goes to press, teachers are still express mailing, faxing, or calling me with their latest discoveries to include in the book. Even as I type these last words, I hear a Federal Express truck pulling into my driveway. How can I possibly change this manuscript again? Although I hate to close the final chapter on this collaborative endeavor, I really must.

THE END

APPENDIX

Unit Design:
Template and Example Units

Template for Unit Design

THEME

THE BIG QUESTION
(Essential Question)

WHAT DO WE NEED TO KNOW? OTHER QUESTIONS
(STUDENT AND TEACHER GENERATED)

- IDENTIFY STANDARDS (CONTENT AND PROCEDURAL) FOR EACH DISCIPLINE
- DECIDE WHO IS RESPONSIBLE FOR TEACHING WHAT
- CHECK FOR OVERLAP
- IDENTIFY SKILLS TO BE TAUGHT

IN THE END, HOW WILL WE KNOW? WHAT WILL WE DO?
DEVELOP PERFORMANCE–BASED, CULMINATING TASKS, AND SCORING GUIDES

HOW WILL WE GET THERE?
DEVELOP STRATEGIES, BASED ON STANDARDS AND SKILLS

Unit Design Template
Usage Directions

The template is an organizer for planning and designing interdisciplinary, thematic units. The steps include:

❶ Select a theme—Don't confuse themes with topics. Topics, such as chocolate, do not invite genuine inquiry. On the other hand, themes have more breadth, lead to genuine inquiry, court controversy, and are founded in real world problems and tasks. Examples of themes are: Crossing the Border, Making Choices, Facing Adversity, Protecting the Earth, and Coming of Age.

❷ Identify the essential question(s)—Based on the theme that you have selected, what is (are) the question(s) that will guide the inquiry and frame the learning for the unit. These questions will help you to identify the issues. A big question for a unit on Protecting the Earth might be: How is pollution affecting the quality of our lives and future generations? Issues that might arise from this big question are: personal responsibility, the economy, and legislation. For each of these issues, essential or "big" questions can be developed. For instance, essential questions for the issue of personal responsibility might include: What is the individual's responsibility for the collective well being of a society? What sacrifices are individuals willing to make today to ensure a better future for future generations? For legislation: What is the role of government in controlling pollution? How do politics influence this issue?

❸ Identify standards that the unit will address—The standards will guide the learning and keep you on track. With interdisciplinary units, it is easy to get too broad. The standards and the issues will keep the learning focused and purposeful.

❹ Decide who will teach what so that there is no over lap. In your team, assign tasks. Be careful: Don't force fit a theme into a content area and create meaningless activities that only superficially address the content standards and the concepts in your curriculum.

❺ Design culminating activities—The template skips ahead to the culminating, performance-based projects that students will complete at the end of the unit. By defining these immediately, it will help you to design daily tasks that will lead into the culminating ones. Include a scoring guide, or rubric, for each culminating task.

❻ Create a variety of assignments and assessments that will lead into the culminating activity. As you design these tasks, make sure that many intelligences are represented and that you give students choices. In addition, use a variety of assessments that evaluate both the process and the products of learning. Students should have opportunities to evaluate their peers' and their own work.

Notes: Notice that some of the arrows on the template go in both directions. This is an attempt to show the recursive nature of some of the steps. Although this is a template for interdisciplinary units, it will also work for thematic units for a single content area. Just eliminate step four.

Example Unit One
A SCIENCE UNIT

Unit developed by: Barbara VanOast
Grade level: 8
School: Newcomb Academy for Academic Excellence, Long Beach, CA

Teacher notes: Many of the activities in this unit come from the materials developed by the National Energy Education Development (NEED) Project. However, I have placed these activities within the context of a thematic, standards-based unit and extended them.

Thematic Focus of the Unit: Ecology--As the world becomes more technologically advanced; the faster we are polluting our air, water, and land; the faster we are depleting our natural resources.

Issues: Energy Uses/Sources, Renewable and Non-Renewable Resources, Conservation, Sources of Land, Air and Water Pollution

Standards: Physical Science—Changes in energy and the structure of matter affects humans and the environment.

1-a. Energy exists in a number of forms and can be converted from one form to another
1-b. Humans use energy in a number of ways
1-c. Matter changes from one state to another with either the gain or loss of internal energy
1-e. Heat energy can be transferred from one place to another by three processes: conduction, convection, and radiation.

Earth Science—Earth's systems interact and over a long enough time scale, are in balance.

1-a. Earth's natural resources provide sources of energy.
1-b. Conservation of non-renewable resources is everybody's responsibility.

1-c. Human populations have a major impact on earth. As world population grows, some resources become less and less available.

1-d. The earth's supply of renewable resources are replenished by natural processes.

Description of Strategies to Help Students Make Meaning:

1. Linking activities:

a. Energy name game—to make students aware of how much they already know about energy. Students, organized in groups of 10, sit in a circle facing each other, and each makes up a new surname that is energy related. This surname must begin with the same letter as their first name. This energy word could be a source of energy, user of energy, an energy-producing device or a measurement of energy— accept any that relates to energy. For example a name could be, Bob Biomass or Gloria Gasoline. The game begins with one student saying, "My name is . . ." and then the person to the left says the first person's name before stating her own, then the third person repeats the first one's name, the second, and then their own. The game continues around the circle until the last person repeats each name in order, then concludes with his or her own.

b. Energy Mosaics—for students to pool their prior knowledge about uses and sources of energy to make an energy mosaic, in groups of three.

2. Monitoring activities:

a. As students read articles and other sources on energy, have them complete the P.Q.R.S.T. method to improve their comprehension of scientific material:

P— Preview the reading by reading the first and last paragraphs, look at any drawings, charts or photographs, and list your own title for each, then also list any bold print and italicized words in your learning logs.

Q— Make up five questions about what you think you will learn from this reading, predicting what it will be about.

R— Read the entire piece and record the time it took. (The students can start to see how long it takes to read a particular passage so that they may begin learning to organize them time.)

S— Write the summary with the main ideas and key parts of the passage with enough details to give an understanding and to help serve as a review for a test.

T— Take a self test by answering your own five questions without referring to the book.

b. Using a problem-solving model in groups of six, prepare to present on these topics:

1. automobiles and pollution
2. factories and acid rain
3. nuclear power plants and thermal pollution

For each topic:

a. define the problem
b. discover alternative solutions
c. evaluate these alternatives
d. make recommendations for reducing the particular pollution

c. Using another problem-solving model small groups of six prepare short presentations to teach their classmates new vocabulary terms:

1. define the term in understandable language; use synonyms
2. make a visual display of its meaning through a poster or skit
3. teach your audience an easy way to remember the meaning using a rhyme, a rap, or mnemonic you make up.

d. Writing in your learning log—make a list of all the things you know about energy, then list what you want to know, what you wonder about.

e. Give a TV interview on your given energy source, group of four

f. Write an acrostic on your particular energy source using the name of the source

g. Design and make a poster on your energy source including its main uses, where it is found, and if it is an economical source.

h. Partner quizzes: take turns making up questions to ask each other

i. Partner feedback timed: each partner shares what is known about the subject until time is called, then the other begins. This continues back and forth as the time is shortened.

j. Science Bowl—a competitive team game (six students) which tests the knowledge of students and is used as a tool to review before a test, response boards used.

k. Summarize current science newspaper articles on energy and ecology to be written and then presented orally.

1. Problem-solving model—In groups of 4-5, students build a sculpture from recyclable materials they have collected. They need to make it self-standing and give it a title for our "Recyclable Sculpture Museum."

3. Extending and Reformulating Activities:

a. Create a magazine on Ecology and be a reporter who travels to a town which has a problem with the main employer of the town who is planning on expanding the factory. The factory needs to cut down part of a forest in order to make a parking lot for additional employees. Write about the positive and negative impact this expansion could have on the entire ecological community. This impact is told through interviewing five citizens of the town: a conservationist, scientist, mayor, ordinary citizen, and an economist.

b. Establish a white paper recycling program for the entire school to last all year: write articles and announcements for the PTA quarterly and for the daily *Town Crier* for students. These announcements must state the general purpose of recycling and the specific benefits of recycling paper for our planet, our community, and our school.

c. Carry forth a Campus Pollution Project in small groups of six: each group is given a particular geographical area on campus and will work in twos within this area; two cartographers will draw the map of the area including major buildings and streets, making sure to place them directionally correct by using the compass; two surveyors will measure the area using a meter stick, finding the length, width and area; two litter analyzers will find the litter in the area, note its location, count it, separate it and list it as organic or inorganic. They will then make a legend for the map using symbols to indicate what the litter is and where it was located.

Each group will give a presentation to the class stating what they discovered about litter on our campus, stating where it is located, what makes up most of the litter, speculate how it arrived in that area, and make recommendations to rid our campus of litter.

d. Do an individual air pollution lab in the community in seven areas outside our homes. Purpose is to find where the most air pollution in our community is located. Students will use seven petri dishes covered with petroleum jelly and set them out and monitor them for three days, recording daily changes. After bringing them to class, the students will learn a new scientific way to count and calculate thousands of particles which are difficult to see with the naked eye. A bar graph will be made noting the most polluted areas to the least. Also, we will discuss why particular areas are more polluted than others and seek to find solutions to the pollution problems.

4. Culminating Activities

a. Group—Rock Energy Performance—small groups present information on an assigned energy source through song, music, costumes and an original CD cover. (This is a NEED activity.)

b. Individual—Three portfolio entries—Each class makes up its own table of contents for what they want to include in their portfolios. (Example: favorite lab, best work, and new skill.)

Understanding that teaching improves when we are reflective practitioners, many Writing to Learn teachers use the following unit checklist to see if the unit is really a balanced one. Sometimes it is easy to get carried away while creating a unit and to lose focus. The following is Barbara VanOast's checklist for her ecology unit:

POINTS TO PONDER

1. **Content and skills taught through these activities:**

a. **Content/standards**
    Ten sources of energy
    Eight forms of energy
    Transformation of energy
    Methods for conserving energy: personal, homes, and
        community
    Causes of air, land, and water pollution

b. **Skills**
    Scientific method
    Writing a summary
    Increasing reading comprehension—P.Q.R.S.T.
    Data gathering
    Keeping tallies
    Data organization/data tables
    Bar graphs
    Scientific labeling of tables, graphs, drawings,
        photographs
    Metric measurement—liters, meters, and grams
    Identifying lab equipment—graduated cylinder,
        beaker, triple beam balance
    Problem-solving model

2. **Learning activities that are real world and authentic:**

a. establish a white paper recycling program for
    students to actively participate; they gather, decorate
    and deliver boxes to each classroom and office in the
    school (K-8). Pick up and empty these boxes into our
    recycling bin weekly. The money earned from this
    project will be used to purchase bins for other schools
    to recycle next year, since we are the first in the
    district to recycle paper.

b. set up pollution experiments in seven different locations and gather data. Use the data to generate a discussion of what can be done to lessen the pollution.

c. discover what happens to living organisms, such as birds, when there is an oil spill in a waterway, by doing an oil spill simulation lab; encourage creative suggestions and solutions to prevent oil spills and to experiment with substances to absorb the oil and to contain the oil spill.

3. Variety of activities to reflect the different intelligences:

a. linguistics—P.Q.R.S.T., summaries, readings, interpreting data, presentations, portfolio entries, science autobiography

b. logical—data tables, graphs, tallies, organizing labs, measuring, surveying, mapping

c. musical—listen to various songs on ecology and study their lyrics: folk songs, ballads, soft rock and heavy metal; content learned through energy songs and chants (NEED Projects); students are encouraged to create their own songs, chants, and raps about energy and ecology

d. spatial—posters on the sources and forms of energy; posters made on the theme of conservation and recycling; illustrate new vocabulary terms; map making; the energy mosaics

e. bodily kinesthetic—hand and body movements to go with songs and chants; campus pollution survey—students moving about on campus measuring large areas and picking up litter; build small sanitary landfill; collect litter and soil and measure

f. intrapersonal—science autobiography; students divide their life into four phrases and write about the science they encountered in each phase:

phase one—birth to five years, from parent interview
phase two—K-5th grade
phase 3—6th and 7th grade
phase 4—8th grade

Students are to focus on their personal interests and activities to see if there is a continuing thread of interests and skills developing from stage one to stage four—with a science focus; individual learning logs, writing and reading assignments

g. **interpersonal**—small group activities, such as labs on land, air, and water pollution; seven energy experiments, each with a student leader "kids teaching kids"; collaborative tests, both essay and multiple-choice; jig-saw, cooperative learning strategies.

4. **Variety of performance-based activities:** Variety of experiments; transparent energy presentation; rock energy performance; TV Interview; CD cover and group name (videotaped; ecology magazine articles).

5. **Think/write assignment and scoring guide**

Scoring Guide for Factory Expansion Magazine Article

5 points—Opening paragraph—Introduce subject and state the problem

75 points—Middle of paper—5 interviews, representing different points of view; use your new knowledge of energy, ecology, and conservation; make sure to use your new vocabulary terms (Each interview 15 points)

5 points—Closing—State your own opinion of how you think this problem should be solved

5 points—Creativity—Name your magazine, give a title to your article, give names to those you interview, make your paper unique

5 points—Grammar/punctuation—Correct verb tenses; begin sentences with a capital letter; use periods and question marks at the end of sentences or questions; check spelling.

5 points—Proof-read—Make sure your revision is checked at least three times before writing or typing your final copy (self, parent, and friend)

Total—100 points

6. Assess student growth and performance with alternate and authentic assessments:

a. collaborative essay and multiple choice tests (Students from each energy group mixed together)

b. magazine article (think/write assignment) final draft for unit and individual written assessment

c. transparent energy presentation—both individual and group assessment

d. rock energy performance—both individual and group assessment

e. Three portfolio entries—culminating activity:

- favorite lab with reflection questions
- best work with reflection questions
- student's choice with reflection questions

To teach transformation of energy, Ms. VanOast used five experiments developed by the National Energy Education Development Project (NEED), setting up stations around the room. Before setting up the stations, she taught a few leaders, from each class, ahead of time so that these student leaders could supervise the experiments. Thus, "kids were teaching kids." One of the best ways to invite success into any classroom and to increase motivation is to let students become the experts.

Last May, I had an opportunity to interview Ms. VanOast's students. They overwhelmingly said that the ecology unit was their favorite unit for the year, for it had so many hands-on experiments. They particularly enjoyed going out into the community, collecting pollution samples and studying the patterns of pollution. One student said, "It was much more than just reading about the problem of pollution. We could actually see it in our lives." Barbara's students were involved in authentic learning experiences and achievement, for they had constructed meaning and produced products, using "disciplined inquiry. Their work had meaning beyond the classroom (Newman & Wehlage, 1993). In this kind of thoughtful instruction, the standards are embedded; they do not exist as meaningless, unconnected activities. When students are engaged in activities that impact their lives, they have no problem in mastering the standards.

A team of five students—Judy Xiong, Vichanna Heng, Thanh Luong, Genelle Sanders, and Jaimejoy Balanga—decided to keep a scrapbook of their learning in the ecology unit and submit it to the National Energy Education Development (NEED) Project. Much to their surprise, they received a national award in Washington, DC. Their trip was financed by American West Airlines, BP Oil, THUMS of Long Beach, Southern California Edison, Newcomb's Student Council and PTA and a myriad of car washes and bake sales. Thus, it became a community effort and a celebration of learning to send the team to Washington.

These students will surely never forget the learning from this unit of study, for it is grounded in real world and standards-based learning experiences.

A celebration of learning as students receive an award for their work during an energy unit. National Energy Education Development (NEED) Project Award Ceremony *Left to Right:* Vichanna Heng, Barbara VanOast, Genelle Sanders, Judy Xiong, Thanh Luong, Jaimejoy Balanga.

Christi Howarth, a Long Beach humanities teacher, came to the Writing to Learn Summer Institute with an idea for a thematic unit. She tells the story about how she was driving through a Jack-in-the Box Restaurant and listening to a NPR program on the Steinway family. The program focused on their genius and the hardships that they had to overcome as an immigrant family in order to be successful. These comments made her think about her own students, for so many of them were immigrants. She wanted them to see that within each of them there is this same potential waiting to be unleashed. Given time and effort, she knew that this powerful idea could germinate into a meaningful thematic unit. Thus, she came to the Institute excited about having time to develop her new thoughts on immigration.

Ms. Howarth used a different kind of format, organizing the unit around the issues and spending approximately one week on each issue. Seeking to incorporate the depth of knowledge instructional standard and wanting to give her students choices, or the social support for academic achievement standard, she decided to use literature circles as an instructional strategy. In addition, the literature circles definitely addressed many of the district's language arts standards.

Before beginning the literature circles, however, she introduced the theme and issues and modeled responses to literature by having the entire class read *The Crossing* together. Then, students were allowed to choose texts which supported the theme of immigration and to read these texts in groups. Even though the class was reading different texts, the theme and the issues for the unit provided coherency, allowing for the literature groups to share their learning with the entire class.

As a culminating activity, students completed an oral history project, where they interviewed immigrants, telling their stories. The interviews focused on the theme of overcoming hardship and unleashing genius through focusing on the issues of discrimination, survival, perseverance, and self-esteem. After writing their stories, students invited the immigrants to a tea and presented them with their inspiring portraits of immigrant life. Thus, the learning took on authenticity, for the learning had a real audience, giving the assignment value beyond the classroom.

The first week of Ms. Howarth's unit follows, showing how she structured the learning for her class.

Example Unit Two
A HUMANITIES UNIT–(First Week)

Teacher: Chrisi Howarth
Level: Grade 6 .
School: Rogers Academy, Long Beach, California

Theme: Overcoming Hardship: Immigrant Genius
Unleashed

Issues: Survival, discrimination, perseverance, self-esteem

Standards: Listening, participating in discussions,
presenting ideas, strategies and skills,
responding to text, effective writing,
conventions of writing, and reflection upon
writing.

WEEK ONE – INTRODUCTION

DISCRIMINATION

DAY ONE: Divide class into four groups of eight or nine
students. Each group picks an issue/topic: **SURVIVAL,
DISCRIMINATION, PERSEVERANCE, or SELF-ESTEEM**

They brainstorm and write synonyms for each word above,
and provide examples of the topic using personal experiences
or the experiences of those in the world around them. They
designate a leader to share group thinking.

Pass out literature logs and divide into four parts:

Section 1—Survival
Section 2—Discrimination
Section 3—Perseverance
Section 4—Self-esteem

For each of the above issues, the following should be recorded in the log:

• What did our discussion tell you about this issue?
• What does the issue mean?
• What does it mean to you?

Give a brief synopsis of each book on the resource list. Students may sign up for the book they want to read in small groups. These students will be in literature circle groups for the next six weeks. Each period will provide silent reading time, reflective writing time, and discussion time, focusing on the four issues/topics.

DAY TWO: Students receive their books. Teacher does reciprocal teaching with *The Crossing.* Teacher models reflective writing in the log using the same book. Students meet at the end of the period to share reflective writing with each other and the class.

DAY THREE: Introduction of the discrimination topic using "The Cold Within." Students analyze who shows prejudice to whom. Teacher hands out role sheet of immigrant families. Students act out and share how the families have been discriminated against. Remaining students offer solutions to overcoming the immigrants' problems of discrimination.

DAY FOUR: Show Harriet Tubman video and talk about how she and other blacks were discriminated against. Students record on bulletin board how Harriet overcame discrimination. Read excerpt in *Distant Shore* text on Martin Luther King Jr.'s life; students record his attempts to overcome discrimination.

DAY FIVE: Assign students a local immigrant to interview during the next four weeks. They must include all four issues and how they related to the interviewed person's life. They should also include how the immigrant overcame hardship. (Show models of women's oral history projects from previous classes.)

Focus on stereotypes. Students cut out a photograph of a person from a magazine or newspaper who may be easy to stereotype. List five words stereotyping the person. Answer these questions: Who would like your person? Who wouldn't like your person? Students share with the class, and explain how they might overcome the stereotypes and get to know the real individual.

Some of the resources Ms. Howarth used in the unit are:

Grandfather's Journey by Allen Say, 1994
Immigrant Kids by Russell Freeman, 1980
Immigrant Girl: Becky of Eldridge Street by Brett Harvey, 1987
Ellis Island: New Hope in a New Land by William Jacobs, 1990
Journey of the Sparrows by Fran Leeper Buss, 1991
Everyday Heroes by Beth Johnson, 1996
The Tenement Writer: An Immigrant's Story by Joan Sandin, 1981
We Came from Vietnam by Muriel Stanck, 1985
Klara's New World by Jeanette Winter, 1992
Journey to America by Sonia Levitin, 1992
Land of Hope by Joan Lowery, 1992
Immigrants All . . . Americans All, 1989
Ellis Island by Paul Kinney, 1986
Primary Sources for a Multicultural Perspective on American History, Houghton Mifflin Social Studies, 1992

Shirley Kroll, a math teacher in Long Beach, decided to develop the next sample thematic unit on reality math, a unit that she would use throughout the year. She provided the following rationale for her unit:

Reality Math in a Dream World activities present an opportunity to use whole numbers, decimals, and fractions. The activities involve the students in a multitude of mathematical processes. The students are required to determine which process is the most appropriate one to use in a given situation. Often more than one step is required to solve a problem. In their writing, students express their thought processes, fears, and goals about the challenge at hand. By experiencing reality math, my students experience real-life, problem-solving situations and prepare themselves as future consumers.

Example Unit Three
A MATHEMATICS UNIT

Teacher: Shirley Kroll
Level: 6th-8th
School: Will Rogers Middle School, Long Beach, California

Theme: Reality Math in a World of Dreams

Issues: Motivation is the biggest challenge in instruction. The teaching of mathematical principles can be enhanced with the enticement of a future dream. What are the economic factors that influence one's ability to make a major purchase? Will education make a difference in attaining a dream? What considerations would influence your ability to get a loan or credit to finance a major purchase? Are there any strategies which you can employ now to help make your dreams come true?

Standards: Discrete mathematics, numbers, logic and language

Description of Strategies to Help Students Make Meaning:

1. Linking activities:

a. Students are intrigued by the possibility of someday owning their own car. Utilizing brochures from local car dealers and advertisements from the newspapers, have students make a collage of the type of cars, trucks, or vans they would like to own some day.

b. Students are given a sample checkbook, mock paycheck, and a record sheet to help them visualize the reality of a wage earner purchasing a new car. Pay students the minimum wage for attending math class. Raises are awarded for improved behavior, outstanding performance on tests and assignments, and cooperation.

c. Students are given a worksheet on which to record all the important information about the cars of their choice. (The loan is based on a down payment of $500.)

2. Monitoring activities:

1. Students deposit their paychecks weekly, saving enough money to make a down payment on the car of their choice. Finance charges are added, as well as insurance fees. Students are responsible for maintaining their own checkbook records, making deposits on payday and deductions when monthly checks are written to Rogers Bayside Academy Loan Company or insurance company.

2. Reality Math—Students work with partners and a calculator to determine whether the car of their dreams could be purchased on a minimum wage income.

   a. Calculate their first weekly paycheck on the basis of current minimum wage. (Note their shocked expressions.)

   b. Students write in their journals about any of the issues/problems they see in the calculations. Also, they write a response to this question: Will your present wage allow you to realize your dream?

   3. Write, illustrate, and present a skit on the subject of increasing your monthly income. Present classroom strategies of your own and future strategies once you enter the job market. Are there any similarities? Bring in a guest to interview on the subject.

4. Work with a partner to determine how long it will take to purchase the new car. One student fills out the loan papers, and the other is the new car buyer. Switch roles.

3. Extending and reformulating activities:

1. Reality math pursuits continue throughout the year and includes ordinary, daily consumer activities. Each activity involves writing to explain their calculations.

    a. Eating out—restaurant, fast-food, etc. Eating out on a budget or splurging on a meal; calculate the cost of each.

    b. Purchasing groceries—Meal planning project for the student's own family. Present a visual display of the costs. Show all the math involved in the planning, cooking, and presentation of a meal to your family.

    c. Holiday shopping—on a budget or if money were no object (Catalogues with sales tax and shipping charges)

    d. Summer vacation—Plan a dream cruise. (Use brochures from a travel agency.) Calculate air and land charges, discount prices for early reservations, peak season vs. value season, etc.

Units such as reality math bridge the gap between classroom instruction and the real world. I'll never forget my own daughter's surprise when she had to face the reality of monthly rent and car payments. She ended up buying a neighbor's used sedan instead of the sporty car she had envisioned herself driving. Students need to understand that the cost of daily living requires them to make choices and compromises, and the choices they make today will have a lasting effect on their future economic status.

Good teachers figure out how to weave reality-based learning into all they do in the classroom, making the learning an unforgettable and practical experience for their students. Thus, when students leave our classrooms and our schools, they are not overwhelmed by life's problems.

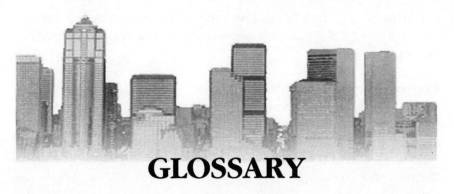

GLOSSARY

Affective—students' emotional responses and feelings toward learning.

Alternative/authentic assessment—assessments that are an alternative to fill-in-the-blank and short-answer response tests. These assessments focus on both the processes and the products of learning and are usually performance-based. Alternative/authentic assessments are embedded in good instruction, taking on a variety of formats, time frames, and sociological groupings.

Attribution theory—reasons that students may give for failing a task, such as luck, ability, difficulty, and effort. (Weiner 1979)

Authentic instruction—instruction which asks students to use disciplined inquiry to construct meaning and to create products, writing, or performances that have value in the real world. (Newman and Wehlage 1993)

Block scheduling—alternative scheduling that structures the school day differently from the usual one-period-per-subject.

Coaching—the role of a teacher in attempting to transfer expertise to students; an intermediate step in helping students become independent learners. This role is in contrast to the teacher as judge.

Content standards—descriptions of what students should know and be able to do at different grade levels in specific content areas. Since students are expected to have mastered the standards before moving on to the next level of schooling, they are sometimes referred to as outcome standards.

Cognition—the process of knowing and learning; development of intellectual skills and procesess such as conception, judgment, perception, etc.

Cognitive apprenticeship—a way of structuring the classroom so that students engage in an intellectual apprenticeship with the teacher, resulting in a transfer of expertise from teacher to students. This process includes a series of steps, or stages, which help the students to become independent learners. (Collins, Brown, and Holum 1991)

Cooperative learning—students working through learning tasks in groups or in pairs. Tasks are structured differently, depending on the purpose of the activity, and specific behaviors are identified. At the end of the activity, time is set aside to process the experience. Students are also asked to evaluate their own and their group's contributions.

Collaborative learning—learning which follows the pattern of: beginning with an individual assignment; moving to a group assignment that builds on the individual assignment and allows students to refine and extend their thinking; and finishing with an individual assignment that extends the learning.

Community of Learners—a class where the teacher and the students are learners and problem solvers together. The learning is more open-ended—students contribute to the design of the instruction; they know their voices are honored; and they have ownership of their learning

Constructivism—a philosophy of learning based on the firm conviction that students are capable of making meaning and that students have much to contribute. Thus, the teacher is more of a guide, helping students to make vital discoveries about themselves as learners and about the material to be learned. The instruction tends to be more open-ended and real world.

Critical thinking—instruction that helps students develop the higher thinking skills and processes, such as analyzing, hypothesizing, synthesizing, evaluating, problem-solving, decision-making, etc.

Culminating activity—an activity at the end of a unit that helps students to synthesize their learning; often used as a kind of alternative assessment.

Curriculum—a description of what and how students will be taught in a specific course; the delivery system for content standards including: outlines, textbooks, supplementary materials such as primary sources, videos, articles, and sometimes sample lesson plans.

Curricular framework—description and sequence of courses that students will encounter during their school experience. Curricular frameworks are done for each content area and should be closely connected to the content standards and the curriculum. The three should comprise a highly coordinated, instructional approach to learning.

Dialectical journal—a journal which allows students to have a conversation with the texts and other written material. Usually, this occurs in the format of a double-entry journal. On the left side, students take notes, and, on the right side, students interpret the text by making personal connections, agreeing, arguing, giving an example, etc. However, there are other forms, depending on the purpose of the assignment.

Direct Instruction—a period where the teacher is providing the information; usually, takes the form of a short lecture or teacher-led discussion.

Divergent thinking—instruction that encourages students to develop creative thinking skills, particularly fluency—the ability to find many solutions to a problem and to take alternative routes.

Editing—the stage of the writing process where the writer checks accuracy in the conventions of language—i.e. grammar, usage, punctuation, spelling.

Educational enabling—the practice where teachers unintentionally rescue students and colleagues, not holding them responsible for their actions or failure to complete a task—creating a "learned helplessness." (Lanfried 1989)

Extrinsic motivation—completing a task for an external reward such as a pizza party, homework vouchers, classroom "bucks," etc.

Freewriting—a writing strategy to help students develop fluency, allowing students to see that they have much to say. Students write freely for a short period of time about anything that comes to their minds. They are not allowed to scratch out or go back and revise during the period since it is strategy to put aside the critical, self-controlling writer. Therefore, the hand must keep moving forward on the page. **Structured freewriting** is when the students are writing on a specific topic.

Intrinsic motivation—completing a task because it contributes to an internal satisfaction and a sense of efficacy.

Kinesthetic/tactile learner—students who learn better from concrete objects or representations which they can touch and move. Example: the use of manipulatives in a math class.

Learning benchmarks—selected and representative pieces of students' work that show mastery of standards at different levels. In holding their own work up against the benchmarks, students are able to gauge their own achievement and progress toward meeting the content standards. Thus, the benchmarks serve as reference points to inform both teachers and students about how well they are doing.

Learning log—an interactive journal where students discover, record, and process their learning by responding to texts and other learning experiences in the class.

Learning/reading styles—different ways in which students process their learning and the reading of materials. Examples: audio, visual, linguistic, kinesthetic/tactic, etc.

Literature circles—a group process, where students read, discuss, and interpret a text or book together. Usually, students assume different roles such as discussion captain, passage finder, questioner, summarizer, and illustrator

Metacognition—thinking about thought. Metacognition involves the skills of: having the ability to have an inner dialogue, or conversation, with one's self; identifying what is known and what is not known; and devising a strategy for solving the problem of learning.

Modeling—the teacher illustrates a process or task before having students complete the task on their own.

Multi-intelligence Theory—Howard Gardner's theory that there are many different kinds of intelligences and abilities which individuals display, including spatial, logical-mathematical, linguistic, musical, bodily-kinesthetic, intrapersonal, and interpersonal. (Howard Gardner 1993)

Opportunity to Learn Standards—these standards describe the kinds of educational experiences and resources the school district provides to help students meet the content and performance standards.

Pacing—varying instructional practices and the length of time spent on each during a class period.

Pedagogy—the study of instruction and teaching

Performance-based assessment tasks—assessments where students are asked to demonstrate or perform the actual skill being assessed.

Performance standards—defined levels which describe *how well* students are meeting the standards. Usually, they are expressed in different levels of proficiency and provide a description of the features of each level. For instance, the state of Kentucky identifies these different levels: novice, apprentice, proficient, and distinguished.

Portfolios—a collection of a student's work and reflections that has been carefully selected by the student to document achievement throughout the year. The portfolio process includes: collection, selection, reflection, and presentation. When portfolios are integrated into instruction, they are a powerful authentic assessment tool capable of providing a learning agenda.

Portfolio culture—when portfolios become an integral part of the instruction and are used continuously as a way to have students look at their work. In using the portfolios this way, students create a learning agenda for themselves, taking ownership of the portfolios. As a result, there are frequent conversations about portfolios, and they are ever-present as an instructional tool to inform the learning and the instruction.

Primary sources—original documents

Reciprocal teaching—a reading strategy to increase comprehension. It combines the skills of predicting, clarifying, questioning, and summarizing into a process, where the teacher and students exchange the role of being teacher.

Remediation—instruction that focuses on drill and skill for underachieving students.

Revision—the part of the writing process where the writer is detached from the writing and asks, "What am I really trying to say and how can I say it better?" This results in *changing* the writing by moving things around, deleting, adding more information, finding just-right words, fixing awkward and convoluted sentences, etc.

Rubric—an analytical guide that describes the features of high, average, and low work and is used as an evaluation or assessment tool. When students are given an assignment or assessment task, they are also given the rubric so that they know how the task will be evaluated. Most rubrics are based on a 1-6 scale, with accompanying descriptions of the work for each number on the scale. Rubrics are used to holistically evaluate large populations of students' writing – ex. NAEP.

Scaffolding—breaking the learning into a series of approachable steps so that students can succeed.

Scoring guide—an assignment-specific evaluation tool or scale. The scoring guide lists the specific items that will be evaluated in the assignment, indicating the number of points each item will receive. The scoring guide accompanies the assignment so that students know how they will be evaluated.

Self-efficacy—understanding and knowing, in very tangible ways, that one's actions can have an impact in the world.

Self-regulated learning—when a student takes control and responsibility for learning—setting goals, planning projects, setting deadlines, monitoring and processing learning, and evaluating and revising work

Teaching standards—instructional standards; provide descriptions of quality instructional practices and educational experiences that will help students meet the content and performance standards. Teaching standards focus on *how* students learn and the instructional implications. Therefore, they serve as a guide to help teachers structure their classrooms for success.

Tracking—the practice of rigidly grouping students according to ability. Thus, the students, within a class, are very homogeneous. Example: Track 1—above average/gifted; track 2—average; track 3—below average.

Voice—the quality in writing that reveals the personality of the writer, making it clear that the writer has a unique way of looking at the world and recording it. When students realize that their writing has a distinctive voice, they want to write, for they start believing in the power of their words.

REFERENCES

Alderman, M. Kay. 1990 (September). Motivation for At-Risk Students. *Educational Leadership.* 27-30.

Applebee, A. 1981. *Writing in the Secondary School: English and the Content Areas.* Urbana: National Council Teachers of English.

Applebee, A. 1984. Writing and Reasoning. *Review of Educational Research. 54* (4): 477-596.

Applebee, A., et al. 1986 (November). *Learning to write in Our Nation's Schools.* Princeton: National Assessment of Educational Progress.

Applebee, A., et al. 1990. *Learning to Write in Our Nation's Schools: Instruction and Achievement in 1988 at Grades 4, 8, and 12.* (Report No. 19-W-02). Princeton: Educational Testing Service, National Assessment of Educational Progress.

Applebee, A. and Langer, J. 1985. Learning to Write: Learning to Think. *Educational Horizons.* 36-38.

Applebee, A. and Langer, J. 1987. *How Writing Shapes Thinking.* Urbana: National Council Teachers of English.

Armstrong, Thomas. 1994. *Multiple Intelligences in the Classroom.* Alexandria: ASCD.

Ashton, P.T. and R. B. Webb. 1986. *Making a Difference: Teachers' Sense of Efficacy and Student Achievement.* New York: Longman.

Atwell, N. 1987. *In the Middle: Writing, Reading, and Learning with Adolescents.* Portsmouth: Heinemann Educational Books, Inc. Reprinted by permission.

Ayers, W., and Ford, P., eds. 1996. *City Kids City Teachers.* New York: The New Press.

Beane, J. A. 1991 (September). Sorting out the Self-Esteem Controversy. *Educational Leadership.* 25-30.

Bereiter, C. and Smart, D. 1982. From Conversation to Composition: The Role of Instruction in a Developmental Process. In *Advances in Instructional Psychology*. Glaser, ed. *Vol. 2*. London: Longman.

Blegen, Mary Beth. 1996. Thoughts on Teaching. Washington, DC: The Council of Chief State School Officers and Scholastic Inc.

Bimes-Michalak, Beverly. 1994 (December). The Portfolio Zone. *Basic Education*. 3-7. Reprinted by permission from the Council for Basic Education.

Bimes-Michalak, Beverly. 1990 (December). Reflecting on Failure. *Basic Education*. 10-12. Reprinted by permission from the Council for Basic Education.

Bimes- Michalak, Beverly. 1992 (October). Unleashing Potential. *Basic Education*. 2-5. Reprinted by permission from the Council for Basic Education.

Britton, J., et al. 1975. *The Development of Writing Abilities (11-18)*. London: Schools Council Publications.

Brooks, G. and Brooks, M. 1994. *In Search for Understanding: The Case for Constructivist Classrooms*. Alexandria, VA: ASCD.

Calkins, L. 1994. The Art of Teaching Writing. Exeter, N.H.: Heinemann Educational Books.

Cole, R. W., ed. 1995. *Educating Everybody's Children: Diverse Teaching Strategies for Diverse Learners*. Alexandria: ASCD.

Collins, A.Brown, J., and Holum, A. 1991 (Winter). Cognitive Apprenticeship: Making Thinking Visible. *American Education*, 6-11; 38-46. Reprinted with permission from the Winter 1991 issue of the AMERICAN EDUCATOR, the quarterly journal of the American Federation of Teachers.

Commission on Chapter One. 1992. *Making Schools Work for Children in Poverty*. Washington, D.C.: American Association for Higher Education.

Cooper, C. 1977. Holistic Evaluation of Writing. In *Evaluating Writing: Describing, Measuring, Judging*. C. Cooper and L. Odell, eds. Urbana: National Council of Teachers of English.

Dweck, C.S. and T. Goetz. 1978. Attributions and Learned Helplessness. In *New Directions in Attribution Research* Vol. II. Hillsdale N.J.: Erebaum.

Elbow, P. 1981. *Writing with Power: Techniques for Mastering the Writing Process*. New York: Oxford University Press.

Emig, J. 1977 (May). Writing as a Mode of Learning. *College Composition and Communication*. 28: 122-128.

Fipp. M. 1994. Transcending the Traditional: Whole Language in the Transitional English Classroom. *Equity and Choice*. 10.3:38-44.

Fipp, M., Barry, C., Hargrave, C. and Countryman, C. 1996 (March). With Equity and Excellence for All. *Middle School Journal*. 15-23. Reprinted by permission from the author.

Florney, V. 1994. *The Patchwork Quilt*. Torrance, CA: Frank Schaffer Publishers.

Flower, L. and Hayes, J. 1980. The Dynamics of Composing: Making Palns and Juggling Constraints. L. Gregg and E. Steinberg, eds. *Cognitive Processes in Writing*. Hillsdale, N.J.: Lawrence Erlbaum.

Fried, R. 1995. *The Passionate Teacher*. Boston: Beacon Press.

Fullan, M. 1995 (November). Broadening the Concept of Teacher Leadership. A paper prepared for the National Staff Development Council: *New Directions*.

Fulwiler, T. and Young, A. 1982. *Language Connections: Writing and Reading across the Curriculum*. Urbana: National Council of Teachers of English.

Gardner, H. 1987. Beyond IQ: Education and Human Development. *Harvard Educational Review*. 57.2:187-193.

Gardner, H. 1993. *Frames of Mind: The Theory of Multiple Intelligences*. New York: Basic Books.

Gillespie, C., Ford, K., Gillespie, R., and Leavell, A. 1996 (March). Portfolio Assessment: Some Questions, Some Answers, Some Recommendations. *Journal of Adolescent and Adult Literacy*. 39.6:480-491.

Graham, A. 1994. Writing to Learn: Placing the Student Center Stage. *Middle School Journal*. 25.4: 7-10. Reprinted by permission.

Graves, D. 1983. *Writing: Teachers and Children at Work*. New Hampshire: Heinemann.

Haberman, Martin. 1996. The Pedagogy of Poverty Versus Good Teaching. In *City Kids City Teachers*. W. Ayers and P. Ford, eds. 118-131. New York: The New Press.

Hawkins, L. 1989 (Winter). Just Because You Cannot Read—Does not Mean You are Dumb. *University of Chicago Magazine*. 21-23. Reprinted by permission.

Herman, J., Aschbacher, P. and Winters, L. 1992. *A Practical Guide to Alternative Assessment*. Alexandria, VA: ASCD.

Hilliard, A. III. 1991 (September). Do We Have the Will to Educate All Children? *Educational Leadership.* 31-36.

Hillocks, G. Jr. 1986. *Research on Written Composition: New Directions for Teaching.* Urbana: ERIC and the National Conference on Research in English.

Jones, M. G. 1994 (March). Performance-based Assessment in Middle School Science. *Educational Leadership.* 35-38.

Knapp, M., Shields, P., and Turnbull, B. 1995 (June). Academic Challenge in High-Poverty Classrooms. *Phi Delta Kappan.* 770-775.

Knapp, M. and Shields, P. 1990 (June). Reconceiving Academic Instruction for the Children of Poverty. *Phi Delta Kappan.* 752-758.

Kopf, Jennifer. 1996, January 31. City Truants find a 2nd Chance. *Intelligencer Journal.* A-1, A-4.

Kotlowitz, A. 1996 (February 8). It Takes a Village to Destroy a Child. *The New York Times,* OP ED.

Kotlowitz, A. 1991. *There Are No Children Here: The Story of Two Boys Growing Up in the Other America.* New York: Doubleday.

Kozol, J. 1995. *Amazing Grace: The Lives of Children and the Conscience of a Nation.* New York: Crown Publishers.

Landfried, S. 1989 (November). "Enabling" Undermines Responsibility in Students. *Educational Leadership.* 79-83.

Lewis, A. 1995. *Believing in Ourselves: Progress and Struggle in Urban School Reform* New York: The Edna McConnell Clark Foundation.

Lowry, L. 1993. *The Giver.* New York: Yearling Books.

Marzano, R. 1992. *A Different Kind of Classroom: Teaching with Dimensions Dimensions of Learning.* Alexandria: ASCD.

McDaniel, T. 1984 (September). A Primer on Motivation: Principles Old and New. *Phi Delta Kapan.* 46-49.

Mitchell, Ruth, Willis, M., and The Chicago Teachers Union Quest Center. 1996. *Learning in Overdrive: Designing Curriculum, Instruction, and Assessment from Standards.*Golden, CO: North American Press.

Moffett, J. 1968. *Teaching the Universe of Discourse.* Boston: Houghton Mifflin.

Murray, D. 1982. *Learning by Teaching.* Montclair: Boynton and Cook. Reprinted by permission from the author.

Newmann, F. and Wehlage, G. 1993 (April). Five Standards of Authentic Instruction. *Educational Leadership*. 8-12.

Newmann, F. and Wehlage, G. 1995. Successful School Restructuring: A Report to the Public and Educators. Madison, WI: Center on Organization and Restructuring Schools.

National Assessment of Educational Progress. 1981. *Reading, Thinking, and Writing*. Denver: Education Commission of the States.

Oakes, J. and Lipton, M. 1992 (February). Detracking Schools: Early Lessons from the Field. *Phi Delta Kappan*, 73: 448-454.

Oldfather, P. and McLaughlin, J. 1993. Gaining and Losing Voice: A Longitudinal Study of Students' Continuing Impulse to Learn across Elementary and Middle Level Contexts. *Research in Middle Level Education*, 17.1: 1-25. Reprinted by permission.

Oliver, E. 1995 (December). The Writing Quality of Seventh, Ninth, and Eleventh Graders, and College Freshmen: Does Rhetorical Specification in Writing Prompts Make a Difference? *Research in the Teaching of English* 29.4: 422-450.

Palincsar. A. and Brown, A. 1984. Reciprocal Teaching of Comprehension Fostering and Monitoring Activities. *Cognition and Instruction*. 1: 117-125.

Palmer, D., LeMahieu, P., and Eresh, J. 1992 (May). Good Measure: Assessment as a Tool for Educational Reform." *Educational Leadership*. 8-13.

Patterson, Chip. 1996 (January 30). A New Alternative School. *Intelligencer Journal*.

Paulson, F. L., Paulson, P., and Meyer, C. 1992 (May). What makes a Portfolio a Portfolio?. *Educational Leadership*. 60-63.

Pogrow, S. 1996 (June). Reforming the Wannabe Reformers: Why Education reforms Almost Always End Up Making Things Worse. *Phi Delta Kappan*. 656-663.

Pritchard, I. 1996 (Summer). Judging Standards in Standards-Based Reform. The Council for Basic Education: *Perspective*. 8.1: 1-20. Reprinted by permission.

Rief, L. 1992. *Seeking Diversity: Language Arts with Adolescents*. Portsmouth: Heinemann.

Scales, P. 1991. *A Portrait of Young Adolescents in the 1990s*. Chapel Hill: The Center for Early Adolescence.

Schunk, D. 1990. Goal Setting and Self-Efficacy During Self-Regulated Learning. *Educational Psychologist*, 25.1: 71-86.

Simmons, W. and Resnick, L. 1993 (February). Assessment as the Catalyst for School Reform. *Educational Leadership*. 11-15.

Sparks, D. 1996 (March). Reformed Teaching Requires Reformed Staff Development. *The Developer*. 2.

Spencer, M. and Dornbush, S. 1990. Challenges in Studying Minority Youth. In *At the Threshold: The Developing Adolescent*. S. Feldman and G. Elliot, eds. 142-43 Cambridge: Harvard University Press.

Tierney, R. and Desai, L. 1991. *Portfolio Assessment in the Reading and Writing Classroom*. Norwood, MA: Christopher Gordon.

United States Department of Education. Office of Educational Research and Improvement. 1994. What Do Student Grades Mean? Differences across Schools. Washington: U. S. Government Printing Office.

Valencia, S. 1990 (January). A Portfolio Approach to Classroom Reading Assessment: The Whys, Whats and Hows. *The Reading Teacher*. 43: 338-340.

Wagner, D. 1995 (October 25). To Read or Not to Read: the Enduring Question of Low Adult Literacy in America." *Education Week*. 1.

Weiner, B. 1979. A Theory of Motivation for Some Classroom Experiences. Journal *of Educational Psychology*. 71: 3-25.

Weinstein, C., Ridley,D., Dahl, T., and Weber, E. 1988 (December) and 1989 (January). Helping Students Develop Strategies for Effective Learning. *Educational Leadership*. 17-19. Copyright 1988 by ASCD. Reprinted by permission.

Wellington, Bud. 1991 (March). The Power of Reflective Practice. *Education Leadership*. 4-5.

Wiggins, G. 1989 (May). A True Test: Toward More Authentic and Equitable Assessment. *Phi Delta Kappan*. 70: 703-713.

Wolf, D. 1989 (April). Portfolio Assessment: Sampling Student Work." *Educational Leadership*. 35-39.

Zinsser, W. 1985. *On Writing Well: An Informal Guide to Writing Non-Fiction*. New York: Harper and Row.

INDEX

Subject Index

A

absenteeism, 49, 171
access knowledge, 68
accountability, 7, 249, 259
achievement, 8-9, 11, 30-31, 42, 97, 117-119, 121-125, 138-139, 144, 165, 168, 191-192, 212, 237, 243-246, 249-250, 252, 255-257, 263, 265, 267, 272, 289-290, 304-305
alternative assessment, 178-179, 182, 184, 256, 303
assessment, 19, 39, 64-65, 125-126, 134, 139-140, 143-145, 159, 167, 169-175, 177-179, 182, 184, 186, 188-190, 192-195, 198-199, 204-205, 208, 210-212, 214-215, 243, 250-254, 256, 259, 288, 301, 303, 305-306
attributes of quality work, 184
audience, 4, 27, 68, 77, 87, 91-92, 110, 112, 152, 184, 204, 212, 216, 220, 228-229, 232-233, 237, 241, 282, 291
authentic assessment, 139, 169-170, 193, 195, 210, 253, 301, 305
autobiographies, 71, 74, 221

B

benchmark, 133, 184, 236
big T notes, 80-81, 139
block scheduling, 6, 301
brochures, 198, 296, 298

C

challenging tasks, 6, 19, 57-58, 118
choices, 19, 43, 74, 91-92, 95, 105, 121-122, 131, 144-145, 167, 224, 277-278, 290, 298
class meeting, 25
classroom log, 53
closure, 49, 57, 88, 227
coaching, 150-151, 156-157, 251, 301
cognitive growth, 174
cognitive psychology, 170
collaborative learning, 22, 27, 57, 158, 256, 263, 302
collection, 41, 212-215, 217, 219-220, 305
community of learners, 4, 20, 22, 36, 57, 59, 135, 256, 302
complex skills, 159, 193
conferencing, 7, 205
constituencies, 247, 249
constructivist classrooms, 170
content standards, 5, 218, 260-261, 278, 285, 301, 303-304
conversations, 4, 8, 11, 19-20, 36, 46, 89, 112, 127, 133, 143, 152, 166, 184, 211-212, 224-226, 239, 241, 251-253, 257, 260, 306

cooperative learning, 4, 19, 79, 120, 143, 174, 205, 287, 302
Cornell study method, 80, 139
creating a portfolio culture, 210
criteria for evaluation, 91, 133, 166, 184, 204, 251, 267
critical thinking skills, 92, 174
culminating activity, 11, 105, 176, 178, 204, 278, 288, 291, 303
curriculum, 77, 112, 121, 123-125, 191, 244, 255, 278, 303

D

deficiencies, 3, 25, 38
demonstrations, 20, 130, 169
depth of knowledge, 256, 290
developmental pacing, 175
dialectical journals, 84, 86, 257
direct instruction, 7, 141, 149, 164, 303
discipline, 32, 71, 187, 190, 216, 247, 255, 258
discourse forms, 95, 103, 133, 258
discussion, 3, 7-8, 23, 29, 63, 66, 82, 86-87, 97, 110, 114, 130-132, 156, 160-161, 163, 216, 226, 229, 232, 248, 261, 286, 293, 303-304
divergent thinking, 68, 124, 170, 236, 303
documenting growth and competence, 211
double-entry journal, 84-86, 172, 303

E

ecology, 178, 194-195, 282-284, 286-287, 289
editing, 18, 116, 188-189, 230, 303
educational enabling, 44, 303
efficacy, 15-16, 30, 57, 177, 195, 243, 304
elaboration, 164-165
energy, 7, 16, 91, 118, 140, 166, 181, 198, 204, 239, 250, 279-280, 282, 284-290
essential questions, 186, 277
evaluation, 4, 19, 25, 48, 91, 97, 110, 112-115, 133-135, 145, 165-167, 174, 180, 182, 184, 189, 194, 200-201, 204-205, 208-210, 220, 250-251, 256-258, 267, 306
exemplars, 251, 253, 257-258
exhibitions, 8, 168-169, 175, 205, 256
extend or reformulate knowledge, 258
extrinsic rewards, 16, 59, 186

F

failure, 28-30, 44, 57, 68, 140, 149, 168, 211, 226, 244, 247, 256, 272, 303
feedback, 4-5, 8-9, 48-49, 51, 58, 79, 112-113, 131-132, 135, 152, 162-163, 166, 168, 184, 204, 226, 229, 231, 251-253, 260, 267, 282
framework for writing, 65